Does God Love You No Matter What?

Bouncing Back

Wayne Rice and Mark Oestreicher

Riding Those Mood Swings

Rich Van Pelt and Helen Musick

Just Look at You!

Darrell Pearson and Stan Campbell

NEXGEN®

Building the New Generation of Believers

An Imprint of Cook Communications Ministries
Colorado Springs, Colorado

Does God Love You No Matter What?

© 2003 Cook Communications Ministries

Published by Cook Communications Ministries
4050 Lee Vance View
Colorado Springs, CO 80918
www.cookministries.com

Editorial Manager: Doug Schmidt
Product Developer: Karen Pickering
Series Creator: John Duckworth
Series Editor: Randy Southern
Cover Design: Granite Design
Interior Design: Becky Hawley Design, Inc.

Unit 1: Bouncing Back
© 2003 Cook Communications Ministries
Editor: Randy Southern
Writers: Wayne Rice and Mark Oestreicher
Option Writers: Stan Campbell, John Duckworth,
Sue Reck, and Randy Southern
Inside Illustrator: Joe Weissmann

Unit 2: Riding Those Mood Swings
© 2003 Cook Communications Ministries
Editor: Randy Southern
Writers: Rich Van Pelt and Helen Musick
Option Writers: Sharon Stultz, Nelson E. Copeland, Jr., and
Ellen Larson
Inside Illustrator: John Hayes

Unit 3: Just Look at You!
© 2003 Cook Communications Ministries
Editor: Randy Southern
Writers: Darrell Pearson and Stan Campbell
Option Writers: Stan Campbell, Nelson E. Copeland, Jr.,
and Sue Reck
Inside Illustrator: John Hayes

Printed in the U.S.A.

Contents

Unit Three: Just Look at You!

How to Customize Your Curriculum

We know your time is valuable. That's why we've made **Custom Curriculum** as easy as possible. Follow the three steps outlined below to create custom lessons that will meet the needs of *your* group. Let's get started!

 Read the basic lesson plan.

Every session in this book has four to six steps designed to meet five goals. It's important to understand these five goals as you choose the options for your group.

Getting Together

The goal for Getting Together is to break the ice. It may involve a fun way to introduce the lesson.

Getting Thirsty

The goal for Getting Thirsty is to earn students' interest before you dive into the Bible. Why should students care about your topic? Why should they care what the Bible has to say about it? This will motivate your students to dig deeper.

Getting the Word

The goal for Getting the Word is to find out what God has to say about the topic they care about. By exploring and discussing carefully-selected passages, you'll help students find out how God's Word applies to their lives.

Getting the Point

The goal for Getting the Point is to make the leap from ideals and principles to real-world situations students are likely to face. It may involve practicing biblical principles with case studies or roleplays.

Getting Personal

The goal for Getting Personal is to help each group member respond to the lesson with a specific action. What should group members do as a result of this session? This step will help each person find a specific "next step" response that works for him or her.

Consider your options.

Every **Custom Curriculum** session gives you 14 different types of options. How do you choose? First, take a look at the list of option categories below. Then spend some time thinking and praying about your group. How do your students learn best? What kind of goals have you set for your group? Put a check mark by the options that you're most interested in.

 Extra Action—for groups that like physical challenges and learn better when they're moving, interacting, and experiencing the lesson.

 Media—to spice up your meeting with video, music, or other popular media.

 Heard It All Before—for fresh approaches that get past the defenses of students who are jaded by years in church.

 Little Bible Background—to use when most of your students are strangers to the Bible or haven't yet made a Christian commitment.

 Extra Fun—for longer, more "festive" youth meetings where additional emphasis is put on having fun.

 Fellowship and Worship—for building deeper relationships or enabling students to praise God together.

 Mostly Girls—to address girls' concerns and to substitute activities girls might prefer.

 Mostly Guys—to address guys' concerns and to substitute activities guys might prefer.

 Small Group—for adapting activities that might be tough with groups of fewer than eight students.

 Large Group—to alter steps for groups of more than 20 students.

 Urban—for fitting sessions to urban facilities and multiethnic (especially African-American) concerns.

 Short Meeting Time—tips for condensing the meeting. The standard meeting is designed to last 45 to 60 minutes. These include options to cut, replace, or trim time off the standard steps.

 Combined Junior High/High School—to use when you're mixing age levels but an activity or case study would be too "young" or "old" for part of the group.

 Sixth Grade—appearing only in junior high/middle school volumes, this option helps you change steps that sixth graders might find hard to understand or relate to.

 Extra Challenge—appearing only in high school volumes, this option lets you crank up the voltage for students who are ready for more Scripture or more demanding personal application.

Customize your curriculum!

Here's a simple three-step plan to customize each session for your group:

1. Choose your options.

As you read the basic session plan, you'll see icons in the margin. Each icon represents a different type of option. When you see an icon, it means that type of option is offered for that step. The five pages of options are found after the Repro Resource student pages for each session. Turn to the option page noted by the icon and you'll see that option explained.

Let's say you have a small group, mostly guys who get bored if they don't keep moving. You'll want to keep an eye out for three kinds of options: Small Group, Mostly Guys, and Extra Action. As you read the basic session, you might spot icons that tell you there are Small Group options for Step 1 and Step 3—maybe a different way to play a game so that you don't need big teams, and a way to cover several Bible passages when just a few kids are looking them up. Then you see icons telling you that there are Mostly Guys options for Step 2 and Step 4—perhaps a substitute activity that doesn't require too much self-disclosure, and a case study guys will relate to. Finally you see icons indicating Extra Action options for Step 2 and Step 3—maybe an active way to get kids' opinions instead of handing out a survey, and a way to act out some verses instead of just looking them up.

2. Use the checklist.

Once you've picked your options, keep track of them with the simple checklist at the end of the option section (just before the start of the next session plan). This little form gives you a place to write down the materials you'll need too—since they depend on the options you've chosen.

3. Get your stuff together.

Gather your materials; photocopy any Repro Resources (reproducible student sheets) you've decided to use. And... you're ready!

Unit One: Bouncing Back

If at First You Don't Succeed . . .

by Wayne Rice

You hold in your hand a great curriculum for junior highers. What makes it great is not so much the quality of the writing, the creativity of the ideas, or even the way it's organized. What's great is the relevance of the topic. *Bouncing Back* is about failure or "messing up"—and that's something every junior higher can relate to. After all, junior highers mess up a *lot*.

In fact, failure is something of a defining characteristic of early adolescence. If a junior higher messes up, it's a good sign he or she is normal. Psychologists who study 11 to 14 year olds usually describe early adolescence as a "transitional" stage of life. What they mean is junior highers are in the process of leaving behind their childhood and becoming adults. They do this primarily by the trial-and-error method, with emphasis on the "error" part. Junior highers are trying on all kinds of personalities, beliefs, and behaviors in order to establish an identity of their own and to find their new place in the world. It's not an easy task, and most kids find the road to adulthood to be a rough one—full of potholes, detours, and an occasional head-on collision.

Do you remember what it was like to be a junior higher? I sure do. I remember vividly the embarrassments and frustrations of trying to make friends, trying to be accepted by other kids, trying to look cool, trying to become independent of my parents, trying to deal with my emerging sexual feelings, trying to be a good Christian. I tried hard at all of these things, but usually did or said the wrong thing, hurt somebody, and only made things worse. Almost always I ended up feeling guilty, discouraged, and a bit foolish.

Then I would go to church or Sunday school and feel even worse. I would hear stories about people who always did the right thing and who lived the Successful Christian Life. Good Christians don't sin, I was led to believe, or at least not much. If they did sin, they were very minor sins, more like little mistakes that were forgiven instantly or hardly worth forgiving at all. I wondered what was wrong with me. My sins were big sins, not little ones, and I just knew that I could never have a relationship with God like all of these other people. Maybe someday I could, when I became an adult, but not now. It was just too hard while you were still a kid. So I pretty much gave up on trying to live the Successful Christian Life.

You may have some kids in your junior high group who feel that way right now. They may be on the verge of throwing in the towel. According to researchers, dropping out of church peaks during the junior high years. You may also have kids who have been so devastated by their failures, or the failures of others, that they have become angry, depressed, or even suicidal.

If you have kids who are struggling with failure, *Bouncing Back* will provide some real encouragement for them. As you spend the next few weeks dealing with the topic of failure, you can help your group members understand some of the following concepts.

God Doesn't Expect Immediate Perfection out of You and neither Do I

Failure is OK. In fact, it is expected. The Bible says that we are all sinners (Rom. 3:23), which is another way of saying that people mess up a lot more than they think they do. Some people (especially religious people) like to think that they never mess up, which is why God continues to remind us that we do. That's also why God sent His perfect Son to die for us and to save us from all of our failures. Thanks to Jesus, we don't have to pay the penalty for all the times we messed up. Instead, when we get to heaven, we will be perfect in the eyes of God even though we have all been a bunch of failures. That's what grace is all about.

You can demonstrate the grace of God in your group by the way you relate to your junior highers. Let them know that you like them even though they mess up. Junior highers can't be expected to act like adults. They are junior highers. Over the years, I have had very few serious discipline problems with junior highers simply because I allowed them to be themselves. Sure, there were kids who talked when they weren't supposed to, who made disgusting noises in the middle of meetings, who passed notes in class, who made insulting remarks to each other, and so on. But I didn't punish kids for being kids. Instead, I tried to understand, to help them learn from mistakes, and to affirm their behavior when it was positive. If you catch kids in the act of doing good rather than always catching them doing something bad, kids will be encouraged toward good behavior. I'm not saying you shouldn't have rules and shouldn't try to maintain order in the classroom or in the church. But rules need to be enforced with grace and understanding that reflects the love of God.

Failure Isn't Fatal

Failure doesn't have to have the last word. Failure can be your teacher rather than your executioner. Failures can become stepping-stones to success. You can learn from your failures.

In this regard, junior highers can be taught the meaning of commitment. Commitment has a lot more to do with failure than it does with success. If you are committed to something, then you hang in there and keep going even when things aren't going too well. Historians tell us that the inventor Thomas Edison made over nine hundred light bulbs that didn't work before he finally made one that actually did. In other words, he *failed* nine hundred times! Although he must have been discouraged at times, he stayed with it simply because he was committed to inventing a light bulb. He didn't give up.

The Christian life is a lot like that. You don't get it right the first time or even the second. Every time Edison made a light bulb that didn't work, he learned one more way not to make a light bulb. It was actually a positive experience. Failure became his teacher. Maybe what we need to do is to help our junior highers learn from their mistakes, rather than to be defeated by them. Our emphasis should be on commitment—hanging in there. Spiritual growth takes time.

In Ben Patterson's book *Waiting*, he tells of a young man who was appointed president of a bank at the tender age of 32. The promotion was far beyond his wildest dreams and very frightening, so he went to the venerable old chairman of the board to ask for advice on how to be a good bank president.

"What is the most important thing for me to do as a new president?" he asked the older man.

"Make right decisions" was the gentleman's terse answer.

The young man thought about that for a moment and said, "Thank you very much; that is very helpful. But can you be a bit more specific? How do I make right decisions?"

The wise old man answered, "Experience!"

Exasperated, the young president said, "But, sir, that is why I'm here. I don't have the experience I need to make right decisions. How do I get experience?"

"Wrong decisions," came the old man's reply.

Junior highers need to know that spiritual growth and maturity doesn't come easily. It usually comes by making mistakes and failing over and over again. The key to success is not how many times you fail, but what happens when you fail. If you learn from your mistakes and keep going, you are living the Successful Christian Life.

If You Fail a Lot, You're in Good Company

At the funeral of one great man in American history, the eulogy included these words: *"Here lies the most perfect ruler of men the world has ever seen."* Of whom was this said?

When he was 22, he lost his job as a store clerk. He applied for law school, but was turned down because his education wasn't good enough.

At 23, he went into debt to become a partner in a small store which failed. Three years later, his partner died, leaving him with the debt that took him years to repay.

At 28, after falling in love with a young lady and courting her for four years, he asked her to marry him. She said no.

He embarked upon a political career, and at age 37, on his third try, he was finally elected to Congress. Two years later, he ran again and was defeated. He suffered a nervous breakdown.

At 41, he ran for the position of county land officer and lost.

At age 45, he ran for the Senate and lost.

Two years later, he sought the nomination for Vice President of the United States and was defeated.

At 49, he ran for the Senate again—and lost again.

But at age 51, against all odds, he was elected President of the United States. He never finished his second term, however, because he was assassinated.

By now, you know who I'm describing—the most inspirational and highly regarded president in American history, Abraham Lincoln.

It is probable that if you took the names of history's most respected people—those whom we all regard as heroes—you would have some names that belong in the Failure Hall of Fame. What made Abraham Lincoln great is that he did not allow failure to destroy him.

Scripture is rich with examples of people like this, who failed miserably yet achieved great things for God. Abraham, the founder of Israel who was called "the friend of God," was once a worshiper of idols. Joseph had an ego problem, ended up in prison, and became prime minister of Egypt. Moses was a murderer, but later was the one whom God used to free the Israelites from slavery. Jephthah was an illegitimate child who joined a gang of thugs before God chose him to be his representative. Rahab was a prostitute who was later used in such a mighty way that God listed her in His hall of fame in Hebrews 11. Jonah and John Mark were missionaries who quit—but God used them anyway. Peter denied Christ three times and cursed Him, only to become a great spokesman for the early church. Paul was such a scoundrel that it took a long time before the other disciples would believe that he was truly a Christian. The files of heaven are filled with stories of great people who were once great failures.

As you spend the next few weeks with your group members, share some of your own story with them. Let your junior highers know that you are no stranger to failure. Let them know that if they fail, they are on the right track. It means they are alive. There are some who might say that Jesus Christ failed because He was executed after only three short years of ministry. But we know better, don't we?

Let your junior highers know that they can look forward to a time when their failures will become victories, or as Robert Schuller has put it, their "scars will be turned into stars." That's the good news of the Gospel. Junior highers need to know that failure is normal, and that when they do mess up, they can rest assured that God loves them still. They need to know that when they make mistakes, they can learn from them. And they need to know that when they sin, they can receive forgiveness and a fresh start. No matter how great their failures, they need to know that God is greater yet.

Wayne Rice is cofounder of Youth Specialties and author of several books including Junior High Ministry *and* Enjoy Your Middle Schooler. *He also conducts seminars for parents called "Understanding Your Teenager."*

Ever Had One of Those Days?

The images on these two pages are designed to help you promote this course within your church and community. Feel free to photocopy anything here and adapt it to fit your publicity needs. The stuff on this page could be used as a flier that you send or hand out to kids—or as a bulletin insert. The stuff on the next page could be used to add visual interest to newsletters, calendars, bulletin boards, or other promotions. Be creative and have fun!

Does the thought of embarrassing yourself in front of others send shivers up your spine?
Have you ever wondered how you could ever recover from a certain mistake or failure? Join the club! And join us for a new series called *Bouncing Back*. You may be surprised at what you learn about success, failure, and embarrassment.

Who:

When:

Where:

Questions? Call:

Unit One: Bouncing Back

Ever feel like a failure?

It'll knock you out!

Pass it on.

MISTAKE MANAGEMENT, INC.

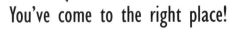

You've come to the right place!

SESSION

1

How Embarrassing!

YOUR GOALS FOR THIS SESSION:
C h o o s e   o n e   o r   m o r e

☐ To help kids recognize that everyone faces embarrassing situations.

☐ To help kids understand how to react when they're embarrassed.

☐ To help kids learn from the examples of biblical characters on how to handle embarrassment.

☐ Other:_____
_____

Your Bible Base:

Numbers 22:21-33
Matthew 14:1-12
John 3:1-3

How Much Would You Pay?

EXTRA
ACTION

SMALL
GROUP

LARGE
GROUP

FELLOWSHIP &
WORSHIP

EXTRA
FUN

MEDIA

SHORT MEETING
TIME

SIXTH
GRADE

(Needed: Cut-apart copies of Repro Resource 1, chalkboard and chalk or newsprint and marker)

Have kids form small groups. Instruct the members of each group to share a really embarrassing situation that happened to them or someone they know.

After a few minutes, ask the members of each group to decide which of the situations they've shared is the most embarrassing. Then instruct them to put together a short skit acting out that situation. Give the groups about four minutes to prepare the skits; then have each one perform its embarrassing situation for everyone else.

After each group has performed, come up with a title for that situation and write it on the board. Leave space on the right side of the board for a column that you'll use later.

After all of the groups have finished their presentations, use your best judgment to give each group a rating based on how embarrassing its situation was (especially in comparison to the other situations). This rating should be in the form of a "price tag"—the more embarrassing the situation, the higher the price tag. Prices should vary from $10 to about $70. Make sure the combined amounts of the groups' price tags total much more than $100.

Then hand out $98 of "Embarrassment Bucks" (Repro Resource 1) to each group member. Say: **Let's pretend that every one of the situations that were acted out is going to happen to you in the next 24 hours. You need to decide which ones you would most want to avoid by paying the "embarrassment price." You don't have enough money to avoid them all, so you'll need to choose which are the most important for you to avoid.**

Give group members a few minutes to figure out which situations they'd pay to avoid and which ones they'd end up accepting. Have several group members share their plans and their reasoning. Let your kids keep their "embarrassment bucks" as a fun reminder of this session.

Embarrass-moments

(Needed: Copies of Repro Resource 2, pencils)

Hand out copies of "Embarrass-moments" (Repro Resource 2) and pencils. Read each situation aloud to your group members. Then give them a minute to write what they'd do in that situation. Ask several volunteers to share and explain their responses before you move on to the next situation.

After you've gone through all three situations, say: **Embarrassing situations are part of life—they're unavoidable.** This would be a great place to share an embarrassing story of your own to show your group members that embarrassing situations happen to everyone.

After sharing your story, say: **The problem a lot of people have—especially junior highers—is that the way they react in the midst of an embarrassing moment often makes the situation worse. Let's look at some people in the Bible who didn't handle embarrassment well. Maybe we can learn from their mistakes.**

Embarrassment in the Bible

(Needed: Bibles, chalkboard and chalk or newsprint and marker)

Have group members turn to John 3:1-3 and read the story of Nicodemus coming to talk to Jesus.

Then ask: **What group was Nicodemus a part of?** (The Jewish ruling council.)

What did most of the Jewish leaders think of Jesus? (They didn't like Him; they were afraid of Him.)

Does it sound like Nicodemus believed that Jesus really came from God? (Yes.) **Why do you think Nicodemus chose to come to Jesus at night?** (Perhaps so that no one would see him.)

OPTIONS

HEARD IT ALL BEFORE

LITTLE BIBLE BACKGROUND

MOSTLY GIRLS

MOSTLY GUYS

SHORT MEETING TIME

URBAN

JR. HIGH / HIGH SCHOOL COMBINED

Explain: **Nicodemus had a fear of embarrassment. Apparently, he thought that if his ruling council buddies saw him talking to Jesus, they'd give him a hard time and make fun of him.**

Write the following on the board: "Fear of embarrassment might mean we care too much about what other people think of us." Then say: **Obviously, you can't live your life completely free from caring what other people think of you. But if you let other people's potential opinions control you, then you might make bad choices.**

Have group members read Matthew 14:1-12. This is a great story, but many of your kids probably won't know the background to understand what's going on. So after you read the passage, retell the story, filling in some information.

Herod was the king. John the Baptist was a prophet who talked about Jesus' coming and baptized Jesus at the beginning of Jesus' ministry. Herod had taken his brother's wife, and John the Baptist had the guts to speak publicly against Herod for doing this. Herod wanted to kill John, but was afraid of how the people would react. At Herod's birthday party, his new stepdaughter (Herodias's daughter) danced for the guests. Herod, in a flashy move to impress his guests, told her that he'd give her anything she wanted. Her mom had already coached her in what she should say if the situation arose—she asked for John's head on a platter. Herod knew he'd be embarrassed in front of his guests if he didn't follow through on his offer to the girl, so he had John beheaded.

Write the following on the board: "Fear of embarrassment causes bad decisions." Then ask: **Can you think of an example in your world of a time when a junior higher might make a bad decision out of fear of embarrassment?** (Drinking beer because kids might laugh at you if you don't; lying to avoid embarrassment; getting in a fight just so people won't think you're a wimp.)

Have kids read Numbers 22:21-33. Then ask: **How would you react if your donkey suddenly talked to you?** This question doesn't really have anything to do with the point of this session, but you have to address the obvious oddity in this story!

Who was with Balaam? (His two servants.)

How were the servants traveling? (On foot, alongside Balaam.)

Why did the donkey move off the path three times? (To save Balaam's life.)

Why do you think Balaam beat his donkey three times? (Some might suggest it was to discipline the donkey, but a beating wouldn't be necessary for this. Balaam was probably embarrassed in front of his servants because it looked like he didn't know how to control his donkey.)

Write the following on the board: "Our reactions to embarrassing situations might make the situation worse." Then ask: **Can you think of any examples in the junior high world in which this would be true?** (Yelling or hitting can make you look like a baby and cause you to lose friends. Trying to blame someone else can make you look like someone who won't take responsibility for his or her actions.)

What's the best way to react when you get embarrassed? (Some possibilities might include ignoring the situation or laughing at yourself.)

Advice Column

(Needed: Copies of Repro Resource 3, pencils)

Say: **Let's practice a little how best to react in embarrassing situations by giving advice to the three Bible characters we just looked at: Nicodemus, Herod, and Balaam.**

Hand out copies of "Dear Advice-meister" (Repro Resource 3). Your kids should still have pencils from Step 2. Have group members work in pairs to write advice-column answers to each letter. After a few minutes, have several volunteers share their responses.

Close the session in prayer, asking God for courage and strength for your group members to react well to embarrassing situations.

EMBARRASSMENT BUCK$

NOTES

EMBARRASS-MOMENTS

Embarrass-moment 1

You're a little sleepy today in school due to staying up late last night preparing two presentations for different classes. When your teacher calls on you to come give your presentation, she wakes you up from a momentary cat nap. You stumble to the front of the room and start rambling through a science topic you weren't very excited about in the first place: "The reproductive systems of whales." The teacher stops you after a minute and asks what your topic has to do with the Civil War. Everyone starts laughing as you realize you're making your science presentation in history class. What would you do?

Embarrass-moment 2

You're at a party with some popular kids you don't know very well, but would like to. Being a little nervous, you eat a few more nachos with bean dip than your stomach is happy to receive. You make a break for the bathroom just in time. Coming out of the bathroom, you feel a whole lot better, but you realize the bathroom really stinks now. You close the door and hope no one goes in there for a while. But ten seconds later, the prettiest, most popular girl in school opens the door to the bathroom and shouts, "Oh, gross! I think something died in here! Who was in here?" Everyone stares at you. What would you do?

Embarrass-moment 3

You're really thirsty and beg your math teacher to let you go get a drink of water. He's been frustrated with kids using that as an excuse to leave class for long periods of time. He says you can go if you're back within two minutes; if you're not, you'll get a detention. You run to the drinking fountain, but something's wrong with it. When you push the button, it splashes you in the crotch of your pants, making it look like you "had an accident." You have less than one minute to get back to math class. What would you do?

Dear Advice-meister

Dear Advice-meister:
My name is Nicodemus, but I prefer to be called Nick. This Jesus — I'm pretty sure He really comes from God. Unfortunately, all of my pals think He's a wacko. I know they'd never let me hear the end of it if they knew I went to see Him. What should I do?

Sincerely,
Nick-at-Nite

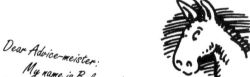

Dear Advice-meister:
My name is Balaam. (Don't rub it in — I know it's a dorky name.) My problem sounds dumb — it's my donkey. She keeps wandering off the road and making me look like I don't know what I'm doing right in front of my servants. What should I do?

Sincerely,
Donkey Problems

Dear Advice-meister:
I'm sure you know me — I'm Herod, the King. Here's my problem: I'm sitting at my own birthday bash, having a great time. My cute little step-daughter comes in and does this beautiful dance for me and my guests. My guests totally love her, so I'm thinking, Here's my chance to impress them. I offer her anything she wants! (Kinda stupid, huh?) I thought she'd ask for her own telephone line or for a few CDs. But no, she asks for the head of this prophet named John. I'm afraid to kill the guy, but I know my guests will think I'm a total wimp if I back down on my promise. What do I do?

Sincerely,
Herod

STEP 1

Bring in a "Stretch Armstrong" doll (available where toys are sold). The arms and legs of this figure are designed to be stretched to great lengths; they then return to their original shape. Have kids form two teams. At your signal, each team should pull an arm as far as it can. At a second signal from you, teams should let the arms go. The winning team is the one whose arm "bounces back" more quickly. (In case of a tie, let teams try again with the legs.) Use this activity as a way to introduce the topic of "bouncing back" from embarrassment. If you can't find a Stretch Armstrong doll, bring in two or more basketballs in various stages of deflation. Have kids form teams for a basketball dribbling relay race. Teams with the most deflated basketballs will no doubt complain about their disadvantage; if you like, give everyone a prize after the contest. Use this activity to introduce the idea that our ability to "bounce back" from embarrassment is affected by the resources inside us.

STEP 4

You'll need a large padded exercise mat and several banana peels for this activity. First, choose something that all of your kids know by heart (the Pledge of Allegiance, lyrics to a TV theme song, etc.). Explain that the object of this contest is to recite the words in the calmest voice possible, without pausing— while slipping on a banana peel, falling down, and getting up. Place a banana peel on the mat. Let your first contestant give it a try; then applaud him or her. Bring out a new banana peel, if necessary, and repeat the process with the next contestant. Award a prize to the person who shows the most grace under fire. Use this activity as a reminder that one good way to deal with our embarrassments is to ignore them and just keep going.

STEP 1

To begin the session, have kids tell three stories instead of one. Two should be made up (or accounts of things that happened to other people). One should be a true story of an embarrassing thing that actually happened to the person. After each person tells three stories, the other group members should vote for the story they believe is true about the person. Keep score to see who has the most correct guesses. Make a note of all the stories, real and imagined, for the "price tag" activity that follows. With each person providing three stories instead of one, you should have plenty of embarrassing situations to choose from.

STEP 4

Instead of having kids write out their advice, designate your group members to be a "panel of experts." Line up chairs as if your kids were appearing on "Oprah"; then read one situation at a time from Repro Resource 3. Let kids respond at will. Some kids may respond to every situation. But if you see that some people are not responding at all, you may need to ask specifically what advice they would recommend in one of the situations. Since group members don't have to write down everything they want to say, you should be able to cover more territory. If this is true, create some potentially embarrassing situations of your own and let your panel of experts offer advice about them after they discuss the biblical scenarios listed on Repro Resource 3.

STEP 1

Rather than using the Repro Resource 1 activity, try a different approach. Have kids form small groups. Instruct each group to come up with the most embarrassing situation possible for a junior high kid. Encourage group members to be creative and humorous (but not offensive or disgusting) in their scenarios. After a few minutes, have each group share its scenario. If possible, ask a few adults from your church to serve as a panel of judges for this activity. If that's not possible, you should judge the activity yourself to determine which was the most embarrassing situation. Award prizes to the winning group. Afterward, ask volunteers to share some of the most embarrassing situations they or people they know have faced. Then move on to Step 2.

STEP 2

Have kids form three groups. Assign each group one of the situations on Repro Resource 2. After reading its assigned situation, each group should come up with (a) the worst possible response or thing to do in that situation, and (b) the best possible response or thing to do in that situation. After a few minutes, have each group share what it came up with. Allow other group members to comment on the suggestions.

HEARD IT ALL BEFORE

STEP 3

Kids may think of Bible characters like Nicodemus, Herod, and Balaam as unreal, older people whose feelings of embarrassment couldn't possibly match their own. Help kids see the humanness of the Bible characters you study; to make it easier, you may want to choose one or more of the following to replace the characters in the session plan: (1) A young follower of Jesus fled at Jesus' arrest, losing his clothes in the process (Mark 14:51-52). Some suggest that this was John Mark, writer of the Gospel of Mark, who later made another mistake—deserting Paul and Barnabas on a missionary trip (Acts 13:13). (2) Mary, the young mother of Jesus, had reason to be embarrassed when she became pregnant while unmarried (Luke 1:26-38). Yet she trusted God enough to sing a song glorifying Him (Luke 1:46-55). (3) Young David must have looked silly trying to wear Saul's armor (1 Sam. 17:38-39a), but instead of being embarrassed he took it off and kept going toward his goal (1 Sam. 17:39b-50).

STEP 4

Jaded kids may question the point of giving advice to three dead people who didn't even ask for it. Instead, discuss how kids could have reacted most constructively to the real-life embarrassing situations they shared in Step 1. Should they have cared less about what others thought? Could they have taken time out to plan their responses more carefully? What steps can they take to react more thoughtfully and less emotionally the next time they're embarrassed? What do they need to trust God for (friends, acceptance, confidence, etc.) in order to fear embarrassment less?

LITTLE BIBLE BACKGROUND

STEP 3

Of the three Bible stories covered in this step, the session provides background material for one of them. But if your group members don't know a lot about Scripture, you'll probably want to be prepared to summarize the stories of Nicodemus and Balaam as well as the death of John the Baptist. You should be sure to point out that because Nicodemus risked embarrassment to go see Jesus, we have the most quoted verse of the Bible. Explain that John 3:16 is part of Jesus' response to the questions Nicodemus was asking Him during this secret visit. Also let kids know that Nicodemus eventually responded to Jesus' love and concern. He was one of the two who took care of Jesus' body after His crucifixion (John 19:38-42). Also be prepared for any questions concerning Balaam's story. (See Num. 22.) If kids don't show enough interest to ask about this odd story, you should try to generate some curiosity on their parts. Be ready to provide kids with references for reading on their own during the coming week (if anyone is interested).

STEP 4

Rather than repeating the stories just covered in Step 3, you might want to write "Dear Advice-meister" letters from *other* biblical characters who suffered embarrassment. For example, you could use similarly updated language to describe Peter's embarrassment at not staying on top of the water in his stroll with Jesus (Matt. 14:22-33), the disciples' inability to remove an evil spirit from a young boy (Mark 9:14-29), and Eutychus falling asleep during a sermon and plunging off a windowsill (Acts 20:7-12). As young people see that there are all sorts of good stories tucked away in the pages of Scripture, they may be more willing to begin to search for them on their own.

FELLOWSHIP & WORSHIP

STEP 1

Before the session, prepare several pairs of name tags. On one name tag in each pair, write an embarrassing situation that someone may face. On the other name tag in the pair, write a positive response that another person might give to that embarrassing situation. (For example, on one tag you might write "You just stopped at Taco Bell and now have major burrito breath"; on another tag you might write "I just got these new breath mints. Would you like one?") Make sure you have at least one name tag for everyone in your group. As kids arrive, give each one a name tag. Allow kids a few minutes to find the right partner. When everyone is paired up, ask: **How many of you have ever been in an embarrassing situation? How did the people around you respond to your embarrassing situation?** Get a couple of responses. **How would you have felt if someone had offered you a kind word during your embarrassing situation?** After you get a few responses, explain that we all face embarrassing situations. In this session, you're going to take a look at how to deal with them.

STEP 4

Hand out paper and pencils. Ask your kids to write a letter to God, telling Him of something they're really embarrassed about. It could be something they've done or something about them or their family. Emphasize to your group members that no one else will read what they write. When everyone has finished his or her letter, encourage kids to spend some time in prayer, asking God for His help with—and if needed, His forgiveness for—the situation. Assure kids that nothing is too big or too small for God to care about.

STEP 2

Change the situations on Repro Resource 2 as follows:

• *Embarrass-moment 2*—You're at a party with some popular kids you don't know very well, but would like to. You're eating some cheese pizza when the cutest guy in school comes over and starts talking to you. You chat for a while, then he moves on. Ready to faint, you head to the bathroom and discover a big string of cheese hanging from your chin. What would you do?

• *Embarrass-moment 3*—It's time for the end-of-the-year awards assembly. You're getting a few awards—perfect attendance, honor roll, a volleyball letter—so you know that you'll be making a few trips to the stage. On the first one, however, you trip and fall flat on your face. The entire auditorium rocks with laughter. What would you do?

STEP 3

After you've written the three results of fear of embarrassment on the board, ask: **What can we do to handle these fears?** As a group, come up with some practical ideas for overcoming the fear of embarrassment—specifically as it relates to caring too much about what other people think, making bad decisions, and reacting in ways that make the situation worse.

STEP 3

When you get to the Bible story about Herod and the daughter of Herodias, stop long enough to ask your guys: **What's the silliest or most embarrassing thing you've ever done because there was a good-looking girl involved?** If your guys aren't willing to share stories about themselves, they'll probably be quick to do so about each other. The stories are likely to be funny and embarrassing, but try to show kids from the story of John the Baptist that sometimes guys do extremely wrong things out of misplaced loyalties or the desire to impress others (usually females). While your guys aren't likely to put someone else to death, they might reject or embarrass others to the point where those people "wished they were dead." Challenge your guys from this point on to be true to themselves and their beliefs, rather than sacrificing self-esteem for a little temporary attention from a member of the opposite sex.

STEP 4

Skip the exercise on Repro Resource 3. Instead, use the time to try to initiate a little male bonding among your guys. They've already shared some embarrassing moments from the past, and they've seen what the fear of embarrassment can do if they aren't careful. Challenge them to rise above "normal" junior high behavior and stand up for each other during embarrassing or uncomfortable situations that may arise in the future. Many guys seem to thrive on putting other people down just to seem a little higher themselves. If your group members can learn to overcome this tendency, they may be quite surprised to see what a difference it will make in their lives during junior high and high school.

STEP 1

Rather than having kids form groups to act out embarrassing moments from the past, have each person write one down, being as specific as possible. Group members should not see what others are writing. Collect kids' stories as they finish; read one at a time. (Be sure to include a tale of your own!) As you read each one, let kids guess who wrote the story. At that time, also determine the "price tag" as instructed in the session.

STEP 2

After kids complete Repro Resource 2, have them select a topic such as "Embarrassing Moments in Television Sitcoms," "Embarrassing Moments in History," or so forth. Instruct each person to write a scenario similar to the ones on Repro Resource 2, but from a real or fictional character that others should be able to identify from a few clues. Provide an obvious example to give kids an idea of what you're looking for. Here's one from "Embarrassing Moments in English Literature": **Boy, do I feel stupid. We had such a good plan, or so we thought. We were young and in love, but our parents couldn't get along so they didn't want us to see each other. We were going to run away. With a little help, I took a potion that made me appear to be dead so that everyone would leave me alone. I was going to come to and join my man. But he found me and thought I was really dead, so he killed himself. I came out of my coma-like state, and there he was with a knife through his heart. Boy, was I embarrassed! Who am I? What would you do in my place?** English students should identify Juliet. But anything goes when your kids write scenarios of their own. They can create embarrassing situations for Bart Simpson, Batman, Queen Elizabeth, or anyone else they choose.

STEP 1

Show a few goofs from a "sports bloopers" videotape (like *Football Follies, Super-Duper Baseball Bloopers, Baseball's Funniest Bloopers,* or *Greatest Sports Follies;* check your video rental store for availability). Be sure to prescreen the segments you plan to show. After playing them for the group, ask: **How would you feel if you'd made those mistakes? What do you think happened to the mistake-makers? What embarrassing moments from your own life are you glad people can't watch on video? When you see that even sports stars make errors, does it make you feel better about your own goofs? Why or why not?**

STEP 4

Play and discuss one or more contemporary Christian songs that encourage kids to bounce back from failure and embarrassment and to trust God with their futures. Possibilities include "Tomorrow" (Amy Grant), "The Sky's the Limit" (Leon Patillo), "Every Step of the Way" (Billy Sprague or Kathy Troccoli), "Following the King" (White Heart), "Believing for the Best in You" (Michael and Stormie Omartian), and "Right Where You Are" (Kenny Marks). After each song you play, ask: **If you listened to this song after making an embarrassing mistake, do you think it might help you feel better? Why or why not? What is the message of this song for someone who makes mistakes? What reasons does the song give for being hopeful about your future?**

STEP 1

Replace Step 1 with a shorter opener. Send one group member (the seeker) out of the room. The rest of the group members will then try to "hide in plain sight"—to stay perfectly still and blend in with their surroundings so well that they seem to disappear. When everyone's found a place, let the seeker in. The last person to be noticed and tagged by the seeker wins. Ask: **Have you ever been so embarrassed that you wished you could disappear or sort of melt into the floor? If so, when?** To save more time, skip Step 1 entirely and start with Repro Resource 2 in Step 2.

STEP 3

Instead of reading and discussing three Bible stories, study just the story of Moses, who resisted talking to Pharaoh for fear of making an embarrassing mistake (Exod. 3:10-14; 4:1-5, 10-16). Discuss God's reaction—reassurance, offers to help, a reminder of His power, anger at Moses' continuing resistance, giving Moses a helper to go with him, and more promises of step-by-step guidance. Ask: **How do you think God feels about our fear of embarrassment? Why? What help does He offer us?** In Step 4, skip Repro Resource 3. Instead, return to the situations on Repro Resource 2. Ask: **What's the worst that could happen as a result of this situation? How could God help a person survive that?**

STEP 2

Add the following situation to Repro Resource 2:

• *Embarrass-moment 4*—You're walking down the street with some friends when you notice someone with long beautiful hair and a shapely body walking in front of you. You start talking about how beautiful she is and how much you'd like to go out with her. However, when the person turns the corner, you discover that it's a man. Your friends start laughing at you and threatening to tell other kids at school about the kind of person you'd like to go out with. What would you do?

STEP 3

Ask volunteers to share some examples of embarrassing situations that escalated and even got out of hand because a person didn't know how to respond to embarrassment. For example, perhaps a person who was embarrassed at school sought revenge against one of the people who laughed at him. Or perhaps someone chose to live a lie rather than owning up to an embarrassing situation. After a few volunteers have shared, move on to the Bible study to see how Bible characters responded to embarrassing situations.

STEP 2

For your high schoolers, add the following scenarios to Repro Resource 2:

• *Embarrass-moment 4*—You've just gotten your driver's license and are driving to school for the first time. As you pull into the lot, you lean over for just a second to turn up the radio, and take the steering wheel with you. The car jumps the curb and you wipe out a stop sign. Everyone in the parking lot is watching. What would you do?

• *Embarrass-moment 5*—You're picking up your date—it's the first time you've gone out—and she's not quite ready. You play it cool and talk with her parents for a few minutes. Everything seems to be going well. Then you notice that your fly is unzipped. What would you do?

STEP 3

Before you get into the Bible study to see how biblical characters dealt with embarrassing situations, ask a few of your high schoolers to share some embarrassing situations that they experienced in junior high and explain how they dealt with them. If they see now that they could have handled the situations differently, encourage them to explain why a different response would have been better.

STEP 1

Don't ask your sixth graders to share or act out embarrassing situations. Instead, before the session, you should create a list of embarrassing situations that sixth graders might face. Your list might include things like finding out in the middle of the school day that your pants are ripped, forgetting your lines in the school play, being the only person in your class to flunk a test, getting so upset on the playground that you cry in front of your friends, and other similar incidents. Assign each embarrassing situation a "price tag," based on how embarrassing the situation is—the more embarrassing the situation, the higher the price. Hand out the "embarrassment bucks" from Repro Resource 1. Then continue Step 1 as written in the session.

STEP 2

Add the following situation to Repro Resource 2:

• *Embarrass-moment 4*—You're hosting your very first slumber party at your house. Everything is going great until your little sister announces loudly that you still sleep with a stuffed animal. Some of your friends start snickering and ask you if it's true. It is. What would you do?

DATE USED:

Approx. Time

STEP 1: *How Much Would You Pay?* _____
❑ Extra Action
❑ Small Group
❑ Large Group
❑ Fellowship & Worship
❑ Extra Fun
❑ Media
❑ Short Meeting Time
❑ Sixth Grade
Things needed:

STEP 2: *Embarrass-moments* _____
❑ Large Group
❑ Mostly Girls
❑ Extra Fun
❑ Urban
❑ Combined Junior High/High School
❑ Sixth Grade
Things needed:

STEP 3: *Embarrassment in the Bible* _____
❑ Heard It All Before
❑ Little Bible Background
❑ Mostly Girls
❑ Mostly Guys
❑ Short Meeting Time
❑ Urban
❑ Combined Junior High/High School
Things needed:

STEP 4: *Advice Column* _____
❑ Extra Action
❑ Small Group
❑ Heard It All Before
❑ Little Bible Background
❑ Fellowship & Worship
❑ Mostly Guys
❑ Media
Things needed:

Try, Try Again?

Choose one or more

☐ To help kids recognize the difference between moral mistakes (sin) and other mistakes.

☐ To help kids learn four important questions to ask about mistakes.

☐ To help kids apply the four questions to a pretend situation and to a real situation.

☐ Other:_____

_____

Your Bible Base:

Genesis 4:3-8
Luke 22:54-62

STEP 1

No Mistakes Allowed

(Needed: Prizes [optional])

Have kids form two teams. Explain that the teams will be competing in a game in which no mistakes are allowed. You will ask each team a question. If the team answers the question correctly, it gets a point. The team with the most points at the end of the game is the winner. Emphasize that the team's first answer is the only one you'll accept. Players may not change their minds after giving an answer. Also emphasize that the teams must listen very carefully because no questions will be repeated.

Use the following questions for the game (or come up with some of your own):

Question #1
Rabbit, duck, penguin, elephant, zebra, porpoise, groundhog, antelope, minnow, water bug, and dog. How many of the creatures I just named spend most of their time in or on water? (Five.)

Question #2
Carl had six sisters—Elvira, Judy, Pam, Tracy, Patricia, and Penelope—and six brothers—Tom, Kurt, Franklin, Anton, Paul, and Peter. He also had a dog and a cat. Name three of Carl's sisters.

Question #3
I had the weirdest dream last night. In it, four monkeys rode across the bright orange horizon on horses named Buck, Chip, Frank, and Felix, while a flock of buzzards hovered overhead. The sheriff, a parakeet named Tex, walked up to me and chirped, "Howdy, pardner!" What was the second horse's name? (Chip.)

Question #4
Bacon, bed, butter, BMW, belt, box, bell, bean, bubble, bike, and broom. Name all of the items I just mentioned that you can eat. (Bacon, butter, and bean.)

Question #5
The rock group Fuzzy Bike Seat opened their concert with their hit song "That's My Lemonade." But then they played a bunch of songs that no one had heard before: "The Cost of Crying," "Your Face Is Killing Me," "Riding Shamu,"

"The Paw That Broke the Camel's Snack," and "Barney's Nightmare." What was the third song of the concert?
("Your Face Is Killing Me.")

Question #6
Circle, square, triangle, oval, pentagon, and semicircle. What's the total number of straight lines of these shapes?
(Thirteen.)

Question #7
Freda's half sister Karen said that Philip's cousin Sam called Trent to tell him that Sonia said that Maria likes him. Who's Philip's cousin? (Sam.)

Question #8
Shirt, wig, socks, underwear, bracelet, tie, sandals, slacks, necklace, hat, belt, and dress. Name the four items on the list that start with the letter "S." (Shirts, socks, sandals, and slacks.)

Question #9
I just read the book *Pets That Kill*. It was very scary. The first chapter was called "The Mouse That Munched." It was gross. The second chapter was "Cats That Carve." It was terrifying. These were followed by "Chainsaw Chimps," "Parrots That Poison," "Turtles and Trash Bags," "Dynamite Doggies," and "Hungry Hamsters." What was the second chapter? ("Cats That Carve.")

Question #10
Ping-Pong, in-line skating, pinball, cross-country skiing, surfing, softball, bowling, hang gliding, skateboarding, running, and swimming. Name the activities that involve a ball.
(Ping-Pong, pinball, softball, and bowling.)

Award a bag of candy or some other prize to the winning team. Use the idea of making no mistakes to introduce the topic of failure.

Here Comes the Judge

(Needed: Copies of Repro Resource 4, pencils)

Say: **We're now going to visit "The People's Junior High Court." The junior highers you're going to read about are almost real. The mistakes they've made are totally real. It will be your job as judge to sentence them for their mistakes. The sentence may be as easy or as stiff as you think is appropriate. You may even choose to let the offenders go free.**

Hand out copies of "The Penalty Fits the Crime" (Repro Resource 4) and pencils. Give your group members a few minutes to read the situations and write their suggested sentences.

After a few minutes, have several group members read their sentences for each scenario.

Afterward, ask: **Do you ever make mistakes? If so, how often?**

What kinds of mistakes are most common for junior highers? Why do you suppose that is?

What's the best way to deal with a mistake after you've made it? Why?

STEP 3

The Big Four

(Needed: Bibles, chalkboard and chalk or newsprint and markers)

Say: **As you can see from the four cases on Repro Resource 4, mistakes can be really serious or they can be really minor. Some mistakes may make you feel dumb, but aren't really wrong. Other mistakes are wrong, and we know it. These mistakes are sin. We're going to learn four simple questions to ask ourselves after a mistake that will help us sort out how we need to respond.**

The first question is "Was it my fault?" Write this question on the board. **Asking this question isn't as easy as it seems because many people often try to put the blame on someone else for their own mistakes. So asking this question requires you to be very honest with yourself. If you really can't figure out if the mistake was your fault or not, pray to God, asking Him to point out whether it was your fault or not.**

If the answer to "Was it my fault?" is yes, then you've already completed the important response by admitting your mistake. Write "Admit your mistake" under the first question on the board.

Cover up what you've written on the board so far. Ask: **What's the first question you should ask yourself after you make a mistake?** ("Was it my fault?")

If the answer is yes, what should you do about it? (Admit your mistake.)

Explain: **The second question is probably the most important one.** Write "Was it sin?" on the board.

Then ask: **What is sin?** Get several responses. If no one mentions it, suggest that sin is anything that goes against what God wants.

Say: **Everyone makes a lot of mistakes. Many of those mistakes are sin and many of them aren't. Let's see if we can tell the difference.**

Read each of the following sentences. Have kids yell out "Yup!" if they think the mistake is a sin and "Nope!" if they think it's not a sin.

O P T I O N S

EXTRA ACTION

HEARD IT ALL BEFORE

LITTLE BIBLE BACKGROUND

MOSTLY GIRLS

MOSTLY GUYS

SHORT MEETING TIME

JR. HIGH / HIGH SCHOOL COMBINED

- **I just killed someone.** (Yup!)
- **I accidentally erased my dad's work report from the computer while trying to log-on to my space game.** (Nope!)
- **I forgot to do my homework.** (Nope!—assuming it was an honest mistake,)
- **I told my friend that she's fat.** (Yup!)
- **I copied one little answer from my fat friend's test.** (Yup!)

Point to the "Was it sin?" question on the board. Ask: **If the answer to this question is yes, what should our response be?** Get several responses. Then write "Ask forgiveness" under the second question on the board.

Cover up everything you've written on the board so far. Ask: **What's the first question you should ask yourself after you make a mistake? If the answer is yes, what should you do about it?**

What's the second question you should ask yourself? If the answer is yes, what should you do about it?

Then explain: **The third question is probably the hardest one. It's also the one a lot of people skip. The question is "Was anyone hurt?"** Write this question on the board.

Then say: **Our mistakes often hurt other people—sometimes physically, but usually emotionally. If someone's been hurt, the best response is to deal with it.** Write "Deal with it" under the third question on the board.

Ask group members to suggest a few examples of how to deal with mistakes that hurt others. (For example, if someone lies to his or her parents, he or she should go back and tell them the truth. Or if someone calls his or her friend a name, he or she should apologize.)

Cover up everything you've written on the board so far. Review all three questions and responses.

Then explain: **The final question is very important. It's the question that decides whether the mistake was completely bad or whether something good can come out of it. The question is "What can I learn from this?"** Write this question on the board.

Say: **Even the worst mistakes can have some positive results if we learn from them and change our actions to avoid making similar mistakes in the future.**

Take a few minutes to look at two Bible characters—one who didn't learn from his mistake and one who did.

Have group members read Genesis 4:3-8. Then ask: **When God pointed out Cain's mistake in how he gave his offering, how did Cain react?** Some of your group members may reply that Cain went out and killed Abel, but that's jumping the gun. First, Cain got angry. In other words, he wouldn't admit his mistake.

Explain that this was just the beginning of a pretty miserable life for Cain. He never learned to own up to his mistakes. Note that in Genesis 4:9, after God asks Cain about Abel, Cain answers, "Am I my brother's keeper?" He obviously didn't admit his mistake in killing Abel either.

Then have group members turn to Luke 22:54-62. Before reading the passage, ask if anyone knows who Peter was. (He was one of Jesus' disciples.) Have someone read aloud the passage, in which Peter three times denies knowing Jesus.

Ask: **What was Peter's response when he realized his mistake?** (He wept, indicating that he knew he was wrong.) **How was Peter's response different than Cain's?** Get several responses.

Before moving on to the next step, review the four questions on the board one more time.

Practice Makes Perfect

(Needed: Copies of Repro Resource 5, pencils)

Say: **Let's practice using these four questions on a pretend mistake.**

Hand out copies of "Mistake Management" (Repro Resource 5). Your kids should still have pencils from Step 2. Read the "fake mistake" at the top of the sheet; then give group members about two minutes to answer the four questions below. After a couple of minutes, ask several volunteers to share their responses.

Then ask your kids to think of a mistake they've made in the last month or so and write it in the "My Mistake" section on the sheet. When they're finished, have them answer the four questions that follow. Encourage group members to be honest in their responses. Emphasize that no one else will see their sheets.

When everyone is finished, ask for volunteers to share their responses. Do not force anyone to share who doesn't want to.

Close the session in prayer, asking God for courage for your group members to confront their mistakes honestly and deal with the results.

THE PENALTY FITS THE Crime

You're the judge for cases involving the following junior high mistakes.
What should the penalty be for each one?

MISTAKE #1

Keith's friend James always pinches Keith on the back side of his arm. It hurts a lot and really ticks Keith off. One day, Keith couldn't stand it anymore. After James pinched him, Keith spun around, swore at James, and punched him in the stomach really hard. What should the penalty be?

MISTAKE #2

Teresa's softball team really needs to win some games if they are ever going to make the playoffs. During last week's game, all Teresa had to do to secure a victory for her team was catch the fly ball that came her way. Unfortunately, she dropped the ball, and the other team scored two runs, winning the game. What should the penalty be?

MISTAKE #3

Mike is feeling really guilty. He lied to his parents by telling them he was spending the night at Phil's house. He really went to Alex's house—even though his parents don't allow him to hang out with Alex. Mike and Alex spent the whole night out with some other guys, egging houses and spray painting walls. What should the penalty be?

MISTAKE #4

Cal's chore is to take the trash cans out to the curb every Tuesday night for the Wednesday morning pick-up. He forgot last week, so the cans are totally full. On Wednesday morning, he walks out the front door to go to school and sees the garbage truck driving past his house. He's forgotten again. What should the penalty be?

NOTES

MISTAKE MANAGEMENT

FAKE MISTAKE

Yesterday you passed along some gossip about one of your friends that wasn't true. Now your friend's pretty bummed at you.

1. Was it my fault?

2. Was it sin?
Action needed:

3. Was anyone hurt?
Action needed:

4. What can I learn from this?

MY MISTAKE:

1. Was it my fault?

2. Was it sin?
Action needed:

3. Was anyone hurt?
Action needed:

4. What can I learn from this?

NOTES

STEP 1

Have kids form two teams—a "Cops" team and a "Robbers" team. Give each Robber either "stolen money" (a play dollar bill on which you've marked an "S") or "owned money" (a play dollar bill marked with an "O"). Instruct the person to conceal the money on his or her person. At your signal, Cops should chase Robbers from one end of your meeting place to the other. Each Cop who tags a Robber should bring him or her to you. However, only Cops who catch Robbers who happen to have "stolen money" win a prize. Robbers who have been "unjustly" caught with "owned money" win a prize. Everyone else loses. Use this contest to introduce the importance of telling the difference between actions that "break the law" and those that don't. The "real Robbers" (those who had stolen money) are like sins; the "fake robbers" (those with owned money) are like mere mistakes.

STEP 3

When you get to the "Yup" and "Nope" statements, designate a corner of your meeting place as "jail." Each time you "confess" to one of the mistakes, kids should drag you in or out of jail according to whether they think you sinned or not. If kids disagree with each other and try to pull you both ways, ask them to explain before they tear you in half.

STEP 2

When you get ready to do Repro Resource 4, let your group members decide the penalties for each offense by acting as one of the characters in the scenario. For example, the first scenario would include Keith and James for sure, but remaining group members could assume the roles of friends of both characters, perhaps a teacher who witnessed the punching incident, and anyone else you can think of to plug in to the situation. The second scenario could include Teresa, her friends, and people on the team who are angry at her. In each case, let the participants discuss what the penalty should be. In most cases, they won't reach a consensus, but let them see if they can arrive at a compromise that will satisfy everyone involved.

STEP 4

Step 3 is a bit lengthy, so save a little time in Step 4 by having members of your small group work together rather than individually on the "fake mistake" on Repro Resource 5. Let kids talk through the four questions rather than writing down their responses. (They may take notes on their sheets as they talk.) You might also want to personalize the offense described by using names of people in your group. When you get to the personal application of the four questions, you'll want to have kids work individually. Members of a small group can cover a lot of ground effectively by working together; you should allow them to do so whenever it is expedient.

STEP 1

Begin the session with a series of activities or games at which all of your kids are bound to fail. You might want to set up several different stations in your meeting area, each one with an almost-impossible task for kids to complete (although the tasks shouldn't seem impossible to your kids). For instance, you might have kids try to stack 15 dominoes on top of each other vertically. Or you might have kids try to balance a large stack of coins on their elbow and then catch them in their hand. After everyone has had an opportunity to try at least two or three tasks, ask: **How do you feel about failing at these tasks? Why? Are there any other kinds of failure that bother you more? If so, what are they?**

STEP 2

For added fun, you might ask a volunteer to play the role of the defendant in each case. As a group, kids should come up with a penalty for each case—a penalty that the defendant (your volunteer) can perform in the meeting area. For instance, for Mistake #4, Cal's penalty may be to pick up all of the trash in your meeting area—after the rest of the group has had a few minutes to spread some litter around.

STEP 3

Kids who have discussed moral issues at school may question whether all of the "Yup" and "Nope" statements fall easily into the "sin" and "not sin" categories. For example, if killing is always a sin, what about military service and capital punishment? Is it a sin to tell your friend she's fat if her weight endangers her health? Acknowledge that it may not always be easy to answer the "Was it sin?" question. Point out, however, that instead of avoiding the question, we should get other Christians (pastors, teachers, parents, etc.) to help us sort right from wrong when we aren't sure.

STEP 4

Kids who are "old hands" at filling out response sheets like Repro Resource 5 may do so without much thought and without the slightest intention to follow through. You can't force them to take the exercise seriously, but you can offer an incentive (a small prize, for example) for each person who completes the "Action Needed" sections and includes a realistic estimate of how much time would be needed to complete the actions.

STEP 3

Have kids form two groups. Let each group look up and discuss one of the Bible passages. Give the groups time to dig as deeply as they can. If possible, try to position an adult leader in each group to ask prompting questions for group members to consider. If your group members don't know the Bible well, it is sometimes better for them to cover one passage thoroughly rather than multiple passages quickly. The group interaction will also challenge them to take responsibility for discovering biblical truth on their own. They can soak up a lot of what you have to say, but they need to interact with Scripture on their own. Give kids the opportunity to do so whenever you can.

STEP 4

Make sure that the people in your group know what you mean when you ask if an offense was "sin." Don't assume that they have an accurate definition of the word. At one extreme, some people might equate anything bad (intentional or not) with being sinful. They need to see that bad things happen to people that have nothing to do with sin. At the other extreme is the possibility of assuming that "sin" relates only to the most heinous acts that one can imagine. A white lie or "innocent" gossip is not considered sinful by some people. People at both extremes need to have a more accurate understanding of what sin is.

STEP 1

Set up a table with creative materials—modeling clay, paper, pencils, colored markers, and so on. Have kids form pairs. Explain that you want each pair to create something using the materials on the table. However, before you tell them what you want them to create, pretend that you've forgotten something in your office. As you leave, say: **I want the projects completed—and done right—by the time I get back.** Leave the room, giving no further instructions. When you get back, explain to your kids that they were supposed to make a scale model of a nuclear reactor. Express your disappointment at the fact that they didn't do the project "right." Then, coming back to reality, talk with your group about what just happened. Ask: **Have you ever been in a situation in which someone told you that you'd made a terrible mistake when you had no idea that you were doing it? If so, how did that feel?** Allow time for responses. Then say: **God has given us guidelines to help us avoid a whole bunch of mistakes—mistakes that are actually sin. Sometimes, though, mistakes are just mistakes. Today we're going to take a look at how we can tell the difference and how we can respond in either situation.**

STEP 4

Have kids refer to what they wrote for "My Mistake" on Repro Resource 5. Then explain that you're going to have a short, impromptu worship service in which kids can bring that mistake to God and ask for forgiveness (if it was a sin), for healing, and for the courage to deal with it. Play some quiet, instrumental music. Encourage kids to pray silently, bringing their mistakes to God. After a short time, pray for all of your group members, that they would be able to deal with their mistakes in a God-honoring fashion.

STEP 2

Make the following changes to Repro Resource 4:

• *Mistake #1*—Jenny typically speaks her mind. Today she told Kristi that Kristi's hair looked just terrible. Kristi turned and left in tears. What should the penalty be?

• *Mistake #3*—Pam is feeling really guilty. She lied to her parents by telling them that she was spending the night at Katie's house. She really went to Jennifer's, although her parents don't want her hanging out with Jennifer. They spent the whole night running around with some high school guys that Jennifer knows. What should the penalty be?

• *Mistake #4*—Chris's chore is to keep up with the dishwasher, making sure it's run when full and that clean dishes are put away. But she just hasn't had time lately. Another Monday morning has rolled around with no clean dishes for breakfast. What should the penalty be?

STEP 3

For a biblical example of a woman who made a mistake—a very large one—turn to Genesis 3:1-20. Ask for volunteers to read this passage aloud. Then ask: **How did Eve respond when God confronted her with her mistake?** (She totally passed the buck.) **What was the result of her action?** (The ultimate result was that sin entered the world. Also, she and Adam were banished from the garden and their perfect lives became very un-perfect.)

STEP 2

Many junior high guys are already experts at dodging responsibility for anything that goes wrong. So before you have your guys establish proper penalties for the offenses on Repro Resource 4, give them an opportunity to demonstrate just how good they are. Read the situations once; then let volunteers act out the roles of the people who made the mistakes. (You'll need to rewrite Mistake #2 with a male character instead of Teresa.) As you go through the situations, ask your volunteers to give excuses for *why* they messed up. In most cases, a good excuse giver can make it seem like someone else is completely at fault for his own mistakes. If your guys are good at this, you'll need to spend some time convincing them to be honest with themselves as they answer the first question in Step 3.

STEP 3

Sometimes young people—especially guys—seem to think that Cain got an unfair evaluation from God. After all, he presented an offering just like Abel did. Guys seem to relate to the feeling of being "shafted" even though they're trying to do their best. If this issue comes up in your group, give Cain his "day in court." Assign one person to be Cain, another to be his attorney, and a third person to be Abel's lawyer who is prosecuting for murder. Conduct the trial. Attorneys should present all of the evidence they can find and make their arguments as strong as they can. You should serve as judge so that you can keep all of the facts straight. If no one else mentions it, bring up the fact that Cain is cited in the New Testament for his evil actions, and not the insufficiency of his offering (1 John 3:12).

STEP 1

After teams compete to answer the questions provided for them, give them some time to write questions of their own with which they can challenge the other team. Some teams may have more fun writing questions than they do answering them. You need to listen closely to each question, however, to determine whether it's written clearly enough to be answered. Continue the scoring by awarding a point to each question asked that the other team cannot answer. But since so much effort is going into this part of the competition, you might want to award *three* points for each question the other team does answer correctly.

STEP 4

You opened the session with questions. You covered four major questions that kids should remember. Now conclude the session with a few more questions, just for fun. Find a copy of *The Kids' Book of Questions* by Gregory Stock (Workman Publishing). It contains 260 opinion questions for young people to consider and answer. For example, here are three to pique your kids' interest:

• "Would you rather be a rich and famous movie star or a great doctor who saves a lot of people but is not wealthy or well known?"

• "Would you be willing to never again get any gifts and surprises if instead you could just ask for anything you wanted and have your parents buy it for you?"

• "If you could live someone else's life for a week—just to see what it would be like—would you want to? If so, who would you pick and why?"

STEP 1

Set up a Sega, Nintendo, or interactive CD game in your meeting place. Line kids up, explaining that each person gets 15 seconds to play, taking up where the last person left off. Continue until everyone's gotten to play at least once. Then ask: **What kinds of mistakes is it possible to make in this game? Is this game very "forgiving" when you make a mistake? How did you feel about mistakes others made before you? When you make mistakes trying something like this, does it make you want to give up, try again, or what?**

STEP 4

Instead of using the "fake mistake" from Repro Resource 5, show one of the following video segments (after prescreening it yourself). Have kids apply the Repro Resource 5 questions to the mistake(s) made.

• *Home Alone.* Show early scenes in which Kevin (Macaulay Culkin) is put down by other kids, and then forgotten when his family flies to Paris.

• *Of Mice and Men.* Play the scene in which the mentally slow Lenny (John Malkovich), who has been warned about being careful with a puppy, discovers that he has accidentally killed it.

• *Back to the Future Part II.* Show the scene in which time-traveling Marty McFly (Michael J. Fox), who has been told not to interfere in history, buys a sports almanac that will enable him to win bets on past sporting events.

• *American Graffiti.* Play a scene in which Steve (Ron Howard) and Laurie (Cindy Williams) hurt each other's feelings as they argue about their college plans; or show a scene in which the nerdy Terry (Charles Martin Smith) finds himself drinking and pretending to be someone he isn't.

STEP 1

Instead of using the quiz, begin your meeting by making as many mistakes as you can in a minute or so. For example, say **Good morning** if you're meeting in the evening; call a group member by the wrong name; thank another for something that someone else did; give the wrong date for an upcoming event (be sure to correct it later); etc. When kids notice your mistakes, deny that you've made any. Have a volunteer (with whom you've arranged this beforehand) persist in pointing out your errors; then you get angry, walk over to the person, and pretend to strangle him or her to death. Then regain your composure, claim that you don't make mistakes, and move on to Step 2. Before getting into serious discussion, thank your volunteer. Then ask: **How do you feel about people who make mistakes? How do you feel about people who won't admit their mistakes? Why?**

STEP 3

Instead of studying the stories of Cain and Peter, read and discuss Proverbs 6:1-5. Explain that the mistake referred to here was taking responsibility for somebody else's debt—which at the time could end in slavery. Ask: **According to these verses, what should you do if you've made a mistake?** (Humble yourself; undo right away what you've done.) **Why be humble?** (If you won't admit you've made a mistake, you can't learn from it or undo it.) **Why hurry?** (Some mistakes have dangerous results; the longer you wait, the easier it is to pretend things will work out by themselves.) In Step 4, skip the top half of Repro Resource 5 and just have kids work on the "My Mistake" section.

STEP 1

Play a couple of segments from a sports "bloopers" video compilation. If possible, try to find a segment that shows a very popular athlete (perhaps Michael Jordan or Deion Sanders) making a mistake. Afterward, ask: **How do you think _____ felt about making that mistake? How do you think he** (or **she**) **reacted? Why do you think he** (or **she**) **reacted in that way? What can we learn from _____'s attitude toward making a mistake?**

STEP 2

Add the following scenario to Repro Resource 4:

• *Mistake #5*—Ramon knows that his best friend was involved in vandalizing a school classroom over the weekend. On Monday, the principal asks Ramon if he knows anything about the vandalism. Ramon says no, lying to protect his friend. What should the penalty be?

STEP 2

Make the following changes to Repro Resource 4:

• *Mistake #3*—Mike lied to his parents by telling them that he spent the night at Phil's house. He actually went to Alex's house, where there was a huge party— several kegs, lots of people, and no parents. Mike drank so much that he got sick. What should the penalty be?

• *Mistake #4*—Cal's chore is to keep the car, which he uses quite a bit, filled with gas and clean. He hasn't washed it for two weeks, and the gas tank is almost on empty. He figures that he'll take care of it on Saturday. However, on Friday morning, Cal's mom tells him that she and her prayer group are going to visit several nursing homes, and that she's taking the car. What should Cal's penalty be?

STEP 3

Point out that another thing we need to learn about mistakes—besides how to deal with ones that we make—is how to deal with mistakes other people make that affect us. Spend a few minutes talking about how we typically respond when someone's mistake affects us (we get angry), and what we could do to change or respond differently, using Christ as our model. Jesus typically confronted people with their mistakes—usually gently, but sometimes with anger (with the money changers in the temple, for example). He always responded with love, and He always forgave.

STEP 1

Have kids form two teams. Let the teams take turns giving each other challenges, trying to "stump" the other team. For example, a team might challenge its opponents to make ten straight shots— using a paper wad and a trash can—with-out a miss in under two minutes. If a team cannot meet the challenge issued by the other team, the challenging team gets a chance to meet the challenge. If the challenging team can meet its own challenge after its opponents have failed, it gets a point. The team with the most points at the end of the game is the winner. Of course, there will be some failure as teams try to meet their challenges, so this activity can serve as an introduction to the topic of the session.

STEP 2

Read the description of Abraham Lincoln found on page 11 of this book (in Wayne Rice's article "If at First You Don't Succeed . . ."). See if your group members can guess who you're talking about. Afterward, ask: **What's the worst failure you've ever experienced?** Be prepared to share your own worst failure with the group. Then ask: **What can we learn from Abraham Lincoln about dealing with failure?**

DATE USED:

Approx. Time

STEP 1: *No Mistakes Allowed* _____
- ❏ Extra Action
- ❏ Large Group
- ❏ Fellowship & Worship
- ❏ Extra Fun
- ❏ Media
- ❏ Short Meeting Time
- ❏ Urban
- ❏ Sixth Grade
- Things needed:

STEP 2: *Here Comes the Judge* _____
- ❏ Small Group
- ❏ Large Group
- ❏ Mostly Girls
- ❏ Mostly Guys
- ❏ Urban
- ❏ Combined Junior High/High School
- ❏ Sixth Grade
- Things needed:

STEP 3: *The Big Four* _____
- ❏ Extra Action
- ❏ Heard It All Before
- ❏ Little Bible Background
- ❏ Mostly Girls
- ❏ Mostly Guys
- ❏ Short Meeting Time
- ❏ Combined Junior High/High School
- Things needed:

STEP 4: *Practice Makes Perfect* _____
- ❏ Small Group
- ❏ Heard It All Before
- ❏ Little Bible Background
- ❏ Fellowship & Worship
- ❏ Extra Fun
- ❏ Media
- Things needed:

SESSION 3

Friendly Fire

YOUR GOALS FOR THIS SESSION:
Choose one or more

☐ To help kids recognize that pride is the source of almost all quarrels.

☐ To help kids understand that sometimes we need to give up our "rights" in order to fix friendship fights.

☐ To help kids choose one "right" to give up for friendship.

☐ Other:_____

Your Bible Base:

Genesis 13:1-12
Proverbs 13:10

Sumo Pillow Fight

(Needed: Masking tape, two pillows, prizes [optional])

Before the session, use masking tape to make a circle approximately four feet in diameter in the middle of your floor. As group members arrive, divide them into two teams. Explain that the teams will be competing in sumo pillow fights. Have each team choose a contestant for the first battle. Give each contestant a pillow. Explain that the object of the game is to push your opponent out of the circle. However, the contestants may only touch each other with the pillows. Both contestants must grasp their pillows with both hands during the entire battle. The first contestant to step on or over the line is out. The winner of each round scores one point for his or her team. Continue the game until everyone has had the opportunity to do battle at least twice. Afterward, you may want to award small prizes to the winning team.

Use the sumo pillow fight activity to introduce the topic of "battling" with friends. Ask: **How often would you say you get into minor arguments with your friends?** Get several responses.

How often would you say you get into major fights with your friends? Again get several responses.

Friction Fuel

(Needed: Copies of Repro Resource 6, pencils)

Hand out copies of "Friction Fuel" (Repro Resource 6) and pencils. Explain that the sheet contains a list of several items that might cause conflict between friends. Two of the items have been left blank for group members to fill in their own suggestions. After group members have come up with a couple of additional ideas, have them rank the items from 1 to 18 according to how likely they are to cause a fight between friends (with "1" being "most likely to cause a fight" and "18" being "least likely to cause a fight"). Give kids a few minutes to complete the sheet. When everyone is finished, ask several volunteers to share and explain their rankings. If you have time, you might want to periodically ask for real-life examples of when one of the items on the sheet caused a conflict between a group member and his or her friend. Be prepared to share a couple of examples yourself.

After you've gone through the sheet and several volunteers have shared their responses, ask: **So what's the number one cause for fights between friends?**

After you've gotten several responses, say: **Let's take a look at what the Bible says is one of the major causes of conflicts and quarrels.**

The Problem of Pride

(Needed: Bibles)

Have group members read Proverbs 13:10. Then ask: **According to this verse, what is one of the roots of quarreling?** (Pride.)

What is pride? Group members will probably offer several definitions and may focus on the idea of being proud of something. If no

one mentions it, suggest that pride is false confidence that you're right or that your way is the best (or only) way.

Then ask: **How might pride cause conflict between friends?** (Fighting usually results from two people wanting their own way.)

Explain that you're going to be looking at the biblical story of Abram to get an idea of how to handle conflict between friends. Have group members turn in their Bibles to Genesis 13:1-12. Ask a couple of volunteers to read the passage aloud. In this passage, Abram and Lot and their herdsmen are quarreling because they have too many people and animals living on the same piece of land. Abram, the uncle of Lot, had the right to choose whatever land he wanted. He could have sent Lot packing. Instead, he gives up his right and allows Lot to choose the land that he wants.

After reading the passage, ask: **What was causing the conflict between Abram and Lot?** (There wasn't enough land to allow both of their herds to graze.)

As Lot's uncle, living in a culture in which older relatives had tons of authority, what could Abram have done in this situation? (He could have decided what land he wanted and told Lot to get lost.)

What did Abram do instead? (He allowed Lot to choose first which land he wanted.)

What is a right? (No, we're not talking about the opposite of a wrong! A right is something you deserve.)

What are some rights we have in this country? (The right of free speech, the right to worship as we desire, etc.)

What are some rights we might expect in a friendship? This may be a hard question for your group members to answer. If so, get them started with suggestions like the right to be listened to and the right to expect honesty.

Then ask: **If pride is one of the major causes of conflict between friends, what can we learn from Abram's example about solving quarrels?** (Sometimes it may be necessary to give up some of your rights in order to solve or avoid a conflict.)

How hard is it to give up your rights? (For many people, it's really, really, really hard.) If no one mentions it, point out that Jesus gave up His heavenly rights in order to become a human being and die for us.

Ephesians 4:26   Matt 5: 21, 22
James 1:19
Proverbs 29:11

How do you deal with anger?

The Bill of Rights

(Needed: Copies of Repro Resource 7, pencils)

Hand out copies of "The Friendship Bill of Rights" (Repro Resource 7). Your group members should still have their small wooden destructive devices (better known as pencils) from Step 2. Let kids work in small groups to list as many "friendship rights" as they can think of. After a few minutes, ask each group to share its answers. As each group shares, instruct the other group members to pay attention, adding any rights to their sheets that their group didn't come up with.

After all of the groups have shared, ask: **Which of the rights on your sheet would be easy for you to give up? Why?** Get several responses.

Then ask: **Which of the rights on your sheet would be hard for you to give up? Why?** Again get several responses.

Ask several group members to choose one friendship right listed on their sheet and explain how giving up that right might solve or prevent a conflict between friends. Encourage kids to use real-life examples when possible. You should be prepared to share at least one example yourself.

As you wrap up the session, ask group members to circle one friendship right on Repro Resource 7 that would be very difficult for them to give up. Explain that circling that right indicates a desire to try to give up that right in order to avoid or solve a conflict with a friend.

After a few minutes, close the session in prayer, thanking God for the gift of friendships and asking Him to give your group members the strength and courage to give up certain friendship rights for the sake of maintaining peace with friends.

FRICTION FUEL

Number the following items from 1 to 18 according to how likely they are to cause a fight between friends (1 = "most likely to cause a fight between friends"; 18 = "least likely to cause a fight between friends"). You'll need to fill in two of the blanks with ideas of your own.

___ RULES

___ Borrowing stuff

___ *Spending too much time together*

___ **Money**

___ Deciding which video to rent

___ **Other friends**

___ **Boyfriend/girlfriend**

___ **Lies**

___ *Clothes*

___ **Put downs**

___ *Busy schedules*

___ Deciding how to spend your time

___ **ANNOYING HABITS**

___ Bossiness

___ **Not talking**

___ Other _____

___ Gossip

___ Other _____

NOTES

The Friendship Bill of Rights

With my close friends, I have the right to expect the following:

1.

2.

3.

4.

5.

6.

7.

8.

9.

10.

11.

12.

NOTES

EXTRA ACTION

STEP 2

Have kids form small groups. Give each group a copy of Repro Resource 6, a pair of scissors, a strong refrigerator magnet, and a steel surface (folding chair, coffee can, etc.). Have the groups cut the 18 items from the sheet. Each group should experiment to see how many of the items can be placed between the magnet and the metal before the magnet no longer sticks to the metal. Each group should then put that number of slips, choosing only the "top friendship breakers," between the magnet and the metal. Go from group to group, finding out which items kids chose. Afterward, discuss how these friendship-breakers can cause friends to lose their "attraction." Ask: **How many things can come between friends before the friends no longer stick together?**

STEP 4

Establish a "trading post" at the front or back of your meeting place. Have each person come to the trading post and "give up" one or more rights (which he or she has torn from Repro Resource 7) in exchange for a "friend-ship"—a small plastic toy boat. Let kids take their boats home as a reminder that not insisting on having one's way can help keep a friendship afloat.

SMALL GROUP

STEP 1

Before the session, arrange to have a few kids fake a serious argument with each other. Toward the end of the sumo pillow fight, one person might accuse another of cheating. That person might then accuse the first person of lying. A friend or two might then take up for each of the feuding parties. The fight should culminate with one of the "sides" deciding, "We just can't stay for a meeting with a cheater like him. We're walking home!" The other side might then determine, "We're sorry. We're just in no mood to meet. We've got to leave too." See how the remaining group members react. In addition to the emotional turmoil that is caused, kids should quickly see that unsettled conflict can seriously damage "group dynamics." After a couple of minutes, your actors should return. As you continue the session, kids should have in mind the especially destructive potential of conflicts among members of a small group.

STEP 4

Have kids work together to compile "The Friendship Bill of Rights." As they come up with ideas, write a master list on the board. After you've compiled the list, have kids prioritize the rights as a group. You won't be able to be precise about the preferred order, but it doesn't matter. If everyone agrees that one thing is very important, put it at the top of the list. If kids agree that something isn't important, stick it at the end. When kids disagree, put those things in the middle. Type up the master list and make copies of it to hand out at your next meeting. At that time, review what you discussed during this session and ask group members to post their list of "rights" in places where they will see them frequently.

LARGE GROUP

STEP 1

With a large group, you might want to expand the sumo pillow fights. You'll need to bring in two mattresses. Divide kids into teams of four, making sure that each team has a mix of large and small kids. Tape off a large area in your room to serve as a "battleground." Bring two teams into the battleground at a time. Assign each team a mattress. Explain that team members must stand behind their mattress, holding on to its edges. The object of the game is to push (using only the mattress) your opponents out of the battleground area. The team that pushes its opponents out of the battleground area wins the match and advances to the next round. Continue until only one team remains. Afterward, use the activity to introduce the topic of "battling" with friends.

STEP 2

Have kids form teams. Instruct each team to come up with a scenario in which famous friends get into a fight. For instance, one team might come up with a scenario in which Fred Flintstone and Barney Rubble get into an argument about who's the better driver (Fred: "My feet are bigger, so I can stop the car faster"). Another team might come up with a scenario in which the Lone Ranger and Tonto get into a fight about their horses (Tonto: "Just once, *I'd* like to say 'Hi ho, Silver, away!'"). After a few minutes, have each team describe or (even better) act out its scenario. Then move on to the Repro Resource 6 activity.

STEP 3

If kids associate the story of Abram and Lot with their flannelgraph days, you may find it hard to get them to consider it anew. Instead, study these passages on the causes of quarrels: 2 Timothy 2:23-24 (stupid arguments; resentment); James 4:1-3 (wanting what we can't have; not asking God for what we want); I Corinthians 3:1-3 (being spiritual babies; jealousy). You might also look at these passages on ways to "bounce back" from quarrels: Proverbs 15:1, 18 (give gentle answers; be patient); Proverbs 26:20 (don't gossip about problems you're having with a friend); Ephesians 4:26-27, 29-32 (start working on your problem quickly instead of letting it grow; say things that build each other up; be kind, compassionate, forgiving).

STEP 4

With today's emphasis on the rights of children, some kids may have been taught at school and elsewhere that they should be careful to guard their rights, and not give them up. Avoid giving the impression that people really have no rights, or that kids should give up all of their rights for the sake of keeping friendships intact. For example, kids should not let "friends" abuse them physically, use them sexually, pressure them into doing wrong, or endanger them. Point out that true friends wouldn't do these things anyway. The main right we should be willing to give up is the "right" to always have our own way.

STEP 3

The Abram and Lot story is a good example of yielding one's rights for the good of a relationship. But if your kids don't know much about the Bible, it may be better to focus on the general principle of yielding rights rather than on one specific instance. An excellent reference that will apply to many different personal struggles is Jesus' Sermon on the Mount (Matt. 5–7). During the session, focus specifically on Matthew 5:38-48. Show your kids the high standards that Jesus sets for His followers. Explain that when people learn to do what Jesus instructs, they find peace of mind that others will never know. Encourage your kids to read through the rest of the Sermon on the Mount (in reasonable increments) during the next week or so. It's a good starting place for people trying to find out what Christianity is all about.

STEP 4

If your kids are like most people, they'll insist that what you're saying isn't fair. If so, ask: **Do you think the world would be a better place if everything were always absolutely fair? Would you want to be punished every single time you did something wrong? Or would you rather have time to think about what you'd done and then ask forgiveness?** Differentiate between *justice* (eye-for-an-eye fairness), *mercy* (not being punished for something we deserve to be punished for), and *grace* (receiving positive gifts that we don't deserve and could never earn on our own). Explain that God is absolutely just, but because Jesus has sacrificed Himself for our sins, God can also be merciful and gracious to us. And since we receive God's mercy and grace in abundance, we should willingly pass it on to other people who offend *us* from time to time.

STEP I

Have kids form teams of three or four. Give each team a stack of magazines or other printed materials that contain advertisements. Give the teams two assignments: (1) Find as many ads as possible that encourage people to "watch out for number one." (2) Find as many ads as possible that show people sacrificing for the good of someone else or giving to someone else. Award prizes to the team that finds the most appropriate ads. Then say: **Our society is very focused on "watching out for number one," which develops proud, selfish people. What do you think are some results of pride and selfishness?** If no one mentions it, suggest that fighting is a result.

STEP 4

Use the following activity to help kids take the focus off themselves and put it on God and others. Give each person a piece of paper and a pencil. Instruct kids to make two columns on the sheet. Say: **In the first column, write as many good things as you can think of about your best friend. In the second column, write as many good things as you can think of about God.** Allow kids a few minutes to work. Then encourage kids to spend some time in prayer, thanking God for creating a friend with so many good attributes and offering adoration to Him for His own attributes.

STEP 3

After looking at Abram's example of conflict resolution in Genesis 13, present your girls with the following scenario and discuss possible positive ways to resolve it. Say: **Annie borrowed Mary Jane's favorite sweater to wear to the fall dance. Annie kept forgetting to return it to Mary Jane. When she finally returned it a month later, the sweater smelled like smoke. Both of Annie's parents smoke. What should Mary Jane do?**

STEP 4

After your girls have completed Repro Resource 7 and have shared their responses, ask them to think of a recent quarrel they've had. Say: **In that situation, which of these rights could you have given up to avoid the quarrel? How might that have changed the outcome?** After a few minutes, ask volunteers to share their stories and solutions. Be ready with an example of your own, if possible.

STEP 2

Before your guys fill out Repro Resource 6, try to get some true stories out of them. Some guys are likely to take pride in some of their previous battles. And since you're going to address the topic of pride in Step 3, this is where you can "set up" your guys. For each category listed on Repro Resource 6, try to find at least one person willing to talk about a time when that specific thing led to a disagreement or fight with someone. Your guys may be surprised to see how many things they can "personalize." After seeing how real some of these things are, have kids begin to prioritize the likelihood of each thing causing a disagreement.

STEP 4

You should probably address the issue of "manliness" if you're telling your guys to give up their rights in order to avoid an argument. Teenage culture says to stand up for your rights. Guys are especially likely to feel uncomfortable if they voluntarily allow others to take advantage of them. Before you close the session, ask: **What do you think other people will think about you if they see you give up something to stay out of a fight? Do you care what other people think as long as you feel good about yourself? Can you walk away from a fight and feel good about yourself? Does it take more strength to let someone else have his way in an argument, or to get into a fight about it? Why? Should you always yield your rights to other people? If not, what guidelines can you use to know when to let go and when to stand fast?**

STEP 1

After the sumo pillow fight, but before you explain the topic of the session, pull out a nicely wrapped gift. Explain that "a fine prize" is in the package, and that the team who is in possession of the gift when you give the signal will get to keep it. Then begin a keep-away game of sorts, using the teams already established for the pillow fight. Short of inflicting physical harm on one another, participants should make an anything-goes effort to get the package. After possession has changed hands several times, give a signal to stop. Let the winners open their prize. Inside should be something that is sure to be a letdown for the winners (a nickel, a picture of you, or whatever). Explain that many times we fight extremely hard to maintain our "rights," only to realize too late that our efforts were all but wasted.

STEP 2

On individual slips of paper, write out the list of things that cause fights between friends (from Repro Resource 6). Call two volunteers at a time to the front of the room. Let them draw one of the slips and *immediately* begin an impromptu fight over that topic. If you wish, have some prizes ready for the people who do the best job. You may be surprised at how quickly some of these things can generate some intense feelings. Even though the volunteers won't actually be fighting, they will draw from times in the past when these items were genuine sources of friction in their relationships.

STEP 2

Instead of having kids rank the items on Repro Resource 6, show a couple of the following video clips (after prescreening them yourself). Have kids mark any of the eighteen items on the sheet that apply to the relationships depicted in the scenes. Let kids add items to the list as needed.

• *Teenage Mutant Ninja Turtles.* Show a scene in which the personalities of the sewer-bred dudes clash.

• *The Three Stooges.* Play a scene in which the Stooges get on each other's nerves (and possibly your own).

• *Grumpy Old Men.* Show one of the many scenes in which longtime acquaintances played by Jack Lemmon and Walter Matthau display their inability to get along.

• *Planes, Trains, and Automobiles.* Play a scene in which the uptight Neal (Steve Martin) is forced to travel with the tiresome Del (John Candy).

STEP 4

As kids work on Repro Resource 7, play a contemporary Christian song that points out how Jesus gave up His rights for our sake. Possibilities include "The Coloring Song" (Petra), "Why" (Michael Card), "Man in the Middle" (Wayne Watson), and "Forgiven" (David Meece).

STEP 1

Skip Step 1. In Step 2, have kids form pairs. Give each pair a copy of Repro Resource 6. Explain that the members of each pair have two minutes to rank the eighteen items. The partners should work together, trying to reach a consensus on how the items should be ranked. Then, instead of having kids share how they ranked all eighteen items, just ask about #1 and #18. Ask: **Was this activity frustrating? If so, how? Did you argue? Did one person always give in to the other? What do you do in real life when you and a friend disagree? How do you keep your friendship together when you don't agree?**

STEP 3

Instead of studying Abram and Lot, a story which requires background explanation, look at the familiar parable of the prodigal son (Luke 15:11-32). Discuss how the father forgave the son and took him back, even though pride could have kept the father from doing so. Note that pride could have kept the son from returning too. Call attention to the elder son as an example of a person who insists on his rights and won't make peace with someone who doesn't "deserve" it. In Step 4, instead of having kids try to come up with friendship rights, write your own on Repro Resource 7 before copying it. (Examples might include the following: "Friends have the right to know each other's secrets"; "Friends have the right to expect never to be put down by each other"; "Friends have to the right to eat off each other's plates"; "Friends have the right to expect presents from each other on birthdays"; "Friends have the right to be late without being criticized for it.") Discuss the sheet as time allows.

STEP 2

Rather than using Repro Resource 6, ask kids to brainstorm a list of comments that might cause an argument or fight between friends. Comments might include things like "When are you going to pay me the money you owe me?" and "Were you flirting with my girlfriend [or boyfriend]?" After kids have listed several such comments, discuss as a group what kinds of situations are most likely to cause conflict between friends. Perhaps you could make a top-ten list of your kids' responses. When you're finished, move on to Step 3.

STEP 3

Ask group members to share some examples of arguments between friends that escalated into major conflicts, perhaps resulting in longtime feuds or even physical violence. Some of your kids will probably be aware of such situations in their neighborhood. If possible, be prepared to share an example of your own. Ask: **What might the two friends have done to prevent the situation from reaching a boiling point? Why do you suppose they didn't do it?** Use your discussion to introduce what the Bible says about conflict and quarreling.

STEP 2

After group members have completed Repro Resource 6, list the items on the board. Then ask your high schoolers: **Do any of these items, or the order in which you ranked them, change between junior high and high school? If so, explain.** Allow time for discussion. Point out that though some of the specific reasons for fighting may change, the one element (pride) that is behind them all doesn't change—whether you're in junior high, high school, or you're an adult.

STEP 3

As you're discussing the issue of pride, ask: **What's the difference between being proud and having a healthy self-esteem? Is having a healthy self-image biblical?** Encourage several kids to respond. Then point out that pride, as mentioned in Step 3, is the false confidence that you're right and that your way is the only or best way. Pride leaves no room for God. Having a healthy self-esteem or self-image is knowing that we are children of God, that we are loved eternally by Him, and that our accomplishments are achieved with His strength. It's feeling good about who we are and what we do because of who God is and what He's done for us. It's viewing ourselves through His eyes.

STEP 1

If you're concerned that the sumo pillow fight might get out of hand with your sixth graders, try a different opener. Have kids form pairs. Give each pair a large rubber band. If possible, make sure that all of the rubber bands are of the same size and strength. Explain that the pairs will be competing to see which one can stretch its rubber band furthest before it breaks. You'll need a yardstick or some other measuring device to determine which rubber band gets stretched furthest. Award prizes to the winning pair. Use this activity to introduce the idea that sometimes friendships get "stretched" and face more tension when conflicts arise. If the conflicts aren't handled properly, the friendship might "break."

STEP 4

As you wrap up the session, give your kids an opportunity to write a note to a friend with whom they've had a conflict. In their notes, kids should incorporate some of the principles you talked about in the session. Explain that the purpose of the note is to restore a friendship or to resolve a conflict that's starting to cause some problems. After a few minutes, close the session in prayer. As kids leave, encourage them to deliver their notes.

DATE USED:

Approx. Time

STEP 1: *Sumo Pillow Fight* _____
- ❏ Small Group
- ❏ Large Group
- ❏ Fellowship & Worship
- ❏ Extra Fun
- ❏ Short Meeting Time
- ❏ Sixth Grade
- Things needed:

STEP 2: *Friction Fuel* _____
- ❏ Extra Action
- ❏ Large Group
- ❏ Mostly Guys
- ❏ Extra Fun
- ❏ Media
- ❏ Urban
- ❏ Combined Junior High/High School
- Things needed:

STEP 3: *The Problem of Pride* _____
- ❏ Heard It All Before
- ❏ Little Bible Background
- ❏ Mostly Girls
- ❏ Short Meeting Time
- ❏ Urban
- ❏ Combined Junior High/High School
- Things needed:

STEP 4: *The Bill of Rights* _____
- ❏ Extra Action
- ❏ Small Group
- ❏ Heard It All Before
- ❏ Little Bible Background
- ❏ Fellowship & Worship
- ❏ Mostly Girls
- ❏ Mostly Guys
- ❏ Media
- ❏ Sixth Grade
- Things needed:

"I Did It"

YOUR GOALS FOR THIS SESSION:

Choose one or more

- [ ] To help kids see how David took responsibility for his actions.

- [ ] To help kids understand that taking responsibility for their actions is part of growing up.

- [ ] To help kids practice making decisions and projecting the consequences of those decisions.

- [ ] Other:_____
_____

Your Bible Base:

2 Samuel 11:2-17;
12:1-10, 13

It's Your Choice

(Needed: Cut-apart copy of Repro Resource 8, prizes)

As group members arrive, have them form four teams. Before the session, you'll need to cut apart a copy of "Share It, Do It, Sound Like It, or Give It" (Repro Resource 8). Place the cut-apart cards in four stacks—"Share It," "Do It," "Sound Like It," and "Give It"—at the front of the room. Explain that the activity is very simple. One at a time, each team will send a contestant to the front of the room. That person will draw a card from one of the stacks and then follow the instructions on the card. If the person carries out the assignment wholeheartedly, with excitement and enthusiasm (you'll be the judge), his or her team gets a point. If the person carries out the assignment halfheartedly, his or her team gets a half point. If the person refuses to carry out the assignment, his or her team loses a point. Continue until everyone in the group has had an opportunity to draw a card or until all of the cards have been drawn. The team with the most points at the end of the game is the winner. Award prizes (perhaps a bag of candy) to the members of the winning team.

Afterward, ask: **Who decided whether you would carry out the instructions on the card(s) you drew?** Most group members will probably agree that ultimately, the decision was theirs. Use this activity to introduce the topic of taking responsibility for one's own actions.

STEP
2

The Mouse Test

(Needed: Two signs)

Ask: **How many of you have heard the expression "Are you a man or a mouse?"** Get a show of hands.

What do you think the expression means? If no one mentions it, suggest that the expression usually refers to someone who's kind of wimpy about taking responsibility for his actions.

Explain: **I'm going to describe several junior highers. I want you to decide whether their actions make them a mouse or a man—or woman.**

Before the session, you'll need to make two signs—one that says "Mouse" and one that says "Man/Woman." Tape the signs on opposite walls of your room. Have your group members stand up. Explain that after you read a description, they should move toward the sign that best represents the character. The descriptions are as follows (feel free to add some of your own):

• **Mike threw a baseball through the front window of his house and blamed it on his little brother. Mouse or man?**

• **Janice ate the last piece of cake in the refrigerator without realizing that it was her brother's. To make up for it, she bought him some Hostess Cupcakes at the supermarket. Mouse or woman?**

• **Marcella borrowed her friend's sweater and then lost it. She never mentioned it to her friend, who seems to have forgotten about the sweater. Mouse or woman?**

• **Tyrone chose to go camping with some friends rather than play in the last baseball game of the season. He called his coach a week in advance to let him know about his plans. Mouse or man?**

• **Thomas was talking in church during the sermon when an old woman in front of him turned around and asked him to be quiet. Thomas whispered, "I wasn't talking." Mouse or man?**

• **Jennifer totally forgot to do her homework. She admitted to her teacher that she forgot to do it and then asked for a one-day extension. Mouse or woman?**

Ask volunteers to explain their responses for each scenario.

STEP 3

Response-o-rama

(Needed: Bibles)

Ask: **Why do you think some people often aren't willing to take responsibility for their actions?** (Perhaps it's because they don't want to face the consequences for their actions—or at least what they think the consequences might be.)

What are some ways that people avoid taking responsibility for their actions? (Lie about it, make an excuse, pretend it never happened, blame someone else.)

Explain: **We're going to look at someone in the Bible who made some huge mistakes, and we're going to focus on how he responded to those mistakes. The name of this great mistake maker is David.**

Ask group members to turn in their Bible to 2 Samuel 11. Have someone read aloud verses 2-17. Afterward, ask: **What were David's mistakes here?** (He committed adultery. He tried to cover up his adultery with deceit. He had Uriah killed.)

Have someone read aloud 2 Samuel 12:1-10. But don't let group members read David's reaction to Nathan yet. Have kids reassemble into the teams they formed in Step 1. Assign each team one of the following possible responses of David. Instruct the members of each team to consider what David might say to Nathan based on their assigned response. Then have each team choose two representatives, who will play the roles of Nathan and David, to act out the response for the rest of the group.

The four possible responses are as follows:

1. David blames someone else for everything he did.
2. David makes up an excuse for what he did.
3. David tries to ignore what he did.
4. David takes responsibility for his actions.

Give the teams about five minutes to work. During this time, walk around the room, offering help to those who need it. When everyone is finished, have each team present its scenario.

After all four scenarios have been performed, read aloud 2 Samuel 12:13. Explain that David's remorse for his actions is well documented in the Bible. In fact, one of David's psalms—Psalm 51—deals with David's great sorrow as a result of this incident. David also took responsibility for Bathsheba from that point on.

O P T I O N S

EXTRA ACTION

SMALL GROUP

LITTLE BIBLE BACKGROUND

MOSTLY GIRLS

MOSTLY GUYS

SHORT MEETING TIME

URBAN

Face the Consequences

(Needed: Copies of Repro Resource 9, pencils)

Explain: **Part of growing up is learning how to take responsibility for your actions. The most immature adults are usually the ones who try to pass off their actions as someone else's fault or the ones who are always making excuses for the things they do. People who won't take responsibility for their actions often have a hard time in the adult world.**

Part of the solution is thinking about the consequences of your choices before you make them, and then deciding if you're willing to accept those consequences. If you're not willing to face the consequences of a decision, it might be wise to make a different choice. Let's look at some examples of this.

Hand out copies of "Take the Consequences" (Repro Resource 9) and pencils. Read the first situation aloud. Have group members write down what they would do in that situation and what the consequences of their actions might be. Then read the follow-up scenario and have group members write down what they would do in that situation and what the consequences might be. When everyone is finished, ask several volunteers to share what they wrote. Let other group members suggest consequences that the volunteers may not have considered. Continue with the second situation on the sheet in the same way.

As you wrap up the session, encourage your group members to start considering consequences before they make decisions. Then close in prayer, asking God for courage for your group members to take responsibility for their actions.

Share It, Do It, Sound Like It, or Give It

Share It	Do It	Sound Like It	Give It
Share something about yourself that no one else in this room knows.	Do an Elvis impersonation.	Sound like a rap artist.	Give someone of the opposite sex your phone number.
Share the name of someone you like.	Do an impression of a famous celebrity singing the national anthem.	Sound like a top-40 radio DJ.	Give someone some money.
Share your favorite color.	Do a square dance.	Sound like a squealing pig.	Give someone a hug.
Share something embarrassing that has happened to you.	Do an impression of a bodybuilder in competition.	Sound like Barney the Dinosaur.	Give someone a back rub.
Share a funny joke.	Do twenty-five jumping jacks.	Sound like a chicken laying an egg.	Give someone a pat on the back.
Share the name you'd pick for yourself if you were the opposite gender.	Do an impression of a ballerina giving a performance.	Sound like a horror movie.	Give someone a suggestion.

NOTES

TAKE THE CONSEQUENCES

SITUATION 1

You sit next to this kid in science class who is really annoying. He's always passing you notes and whispering to you while the teacher's talking. Today, for the very first time ever, you send a note back responding to his note. The teacher sees you and asks, "Are you passing notes in my class?"

What do you do?

What might some of the consequences of that choice be?

Follow-up
The teacher calls your parents that night and tells them she caught you passing notes in class. After your dad hangs up the phone, he looks at you and asks, "What do you have to say for yourself?"

What do you do?

What might some of the consequences of that choice be?

SITUATION 2

You have a ton of homework due tomorrow. But your friend's having a killer party tonight.

What do you do?

What might some of the consequences of that choice be?

Follow-up
You went to the party and didn't touch your history reading assignment. Now your teacher springs a pop quiz on you.

What do you do?

What might some of the consequences of that choice be?

NOTES

STEP 3

After reading 2 Samuel 11:2-17 and summarizing David's sins, have kids form two teams—the Cover-up Team and the Uncovering Team. Give the Cover-up Team three smelly items—a plate of fresh, chopped garlic; a cup of vinegar-soaked cotton balls; and a bowl of diced onions. Give this team a spray can of air freshener too. The Cover-up Team's job is to hide the smelly items in your meeting place and to use up to three two-second squirts of air freshener to throw the other team off the track. Send the Uncovering Team out of the room while the hiding and spraying are done. Then bring in the Uncovering Team to search. If the search takes more than three minutes, the Cover-up Team wins. If not, the Uncovering Team wins. Then ask: **How is sin like the smelly things we hid? How do we try to cover up our sins? Does it really work?** Then proceed with the rest of David's story in 2 Samuel 12:1-10.

STEP 4

Have kids stand in a circle. Give one person a dollar. Instruct him or her to pass the dollar to the next person in the circle, who will pass it to the next person, and so on. Point out that this is "passing the buck." Make sure kids understand that this means "avoiding responsibility." Then point at someone in the circle and say, **The buck stops here!** The person holding the dollar must keep it—and answer the questions for the first part of Situation 1 on Repro Resource 9. (If you wish, give the buck-holder the option of paying someone else to answer the question.) Make sure kids understand that "The buck stops here" refers to accepting personal responsibility. Repeat the buck-passing, the buck-stopping, and the answering for the rest of the questions on the sheet.

STEP 1

A small group seldom has the luxury of forming four teams. So instead of having kids form teams, randomly number the squares on Repro Resource 8. Then ask each person to give you a number between 1 and 24. Kids must perform the action in the square with the number they chose in it. Be sure to announce the category for each action: Share It, Do It, Sound Like It, or Give It. Don't bother keeping score; the activity will be fun enough in itself.

STEP 3

Again, dividing into four teams may be a problem for your group. Instead, let individuals take on the group responsibilities as described in the session. But rather than creating pressure by having kids respond in turn, let everyone respond simultaneously. As Nathan makes his accusations against David, let all of your group members act out David's potential responses *at the same time.* David #1 will think of someone else to blame. David #2 will come up with all of the excuses he can think of. David #3 will have an easier time ignoring Nathan with all of the others present. And David #4 will begin to take responsibility. The different Davids should not acknowledge each other, but should respond to Nathan instead. Afterward, point out that the scene is not unlike a normal group of junior highers (or even adults) when someone begins making accusations. In any group of people, the four distinct responses are likely to arise.

STEP 1

Rather than using Repro Resource 8, begin the session with a game of "Who Did It?" You will call out a list of famous achievements. When you call out an achievement, group members must tell you who did it. For instance, if you were to call out **Most career home runs in the history of major league baseball,** kids should answer "Hank Aaron." The first person to call out the correct answer gets a point. The person with the most points at the end of the game is the winner. To add some fun to the game, you might call out achievements that are unique to your group. For instance, you might call out **First person to capsize his canoe at last year's retreat** or **Won this year's pie-eating contest.** Use this activity to introduce the idea of taking responsibility for one's actions.

STEP 4

Have kids form teams. Assign each team one of the situations on Repro Resource 9. Instruct each team to come up with a roleplay that illustrates a response to its assigned situation—as well as the consequences of that response. Give the teams a few minutes to work. When everyone's finished, have each team perform its roleplay. Discuss as a group which responses involve taking responsibility for one's actions. If you have time, you might ask each team to come up with a second roleplay—one that illustrates a response to the follow-up scenario.

STEP 2

If your kids will find the situations in Step 2 to be clichéd, try the following ones instead. (1) **Caitlin and her boyfriend, ninth graders who call themselves Christians, have been sexually involved for two months. At first Caitlin felt guilty, but no more. Now she's mostly nervous about getting pregnant. She's decided to "take responsibility" by getting birth control pills from the school-based clinic. Mouse or woman?** (2) **Alan's parents just told him that they're getting a divorce. He's decided to "take responsibility" by trying to get them back together. Mouse or man?** (3) **Ron, 15, has feelings that lead him to think he's gay. He's decided to "take responsibility" for his own life by "coming out of the closet." Mouse or man?** Point out that these cases aren't simple. Caitlin may be taking responsibility for avoiding pregnancy, but she's not taking responsibility for obeying God. Alan is trying to take responsibility for someone *else's* actions—which is impossible and will leave him feeling like a failure. Ron is trying to take responsibility for something he can't be sure of; he needs counseling to help him sort out his feelings, and to help him see that God wants to give him a life that's full—without homosexual activity.

STEP 4

Kids may be tired of lectures on growing up and taking responsibility (and may connect such lectures with commands to take out garbage and feed pets). Take a few minutes to brainstorm some of the *appealing* responsibilities that may await kids: driving, choosing movies and videos, dating, deciding when to go to sleep and when to wake up, picking a church, etc. Note that making solid choices in situations like those on Repro Resource 9 is good practice for handling the responsibilities that kids look forward to.

STEP 3

David's sins in connection to his relationship with Bathsheba are familiar to most church people. However, for kids who are just beginning to read the Bible, 2 Samuel 11:2-17 is a significant passage. Your kids probably know about David and Goliath. They probably know that David was a great king. But that David could be guilty of sins like adultery and murder might be news to your kids. Give kids plenty of time to soak in what you're reading and ask questions. Only after they realize the gravity of David's sins will they be able to appreciate the fact that he accepted responsibility for his sinful behavior. Ask: **When we sin, how do you think our lives would be different if we immediately confessed what we did wrong rather than lying about it, trying to cover it up, or otherwise denying it?**

STEP 4

As you wrap up the session, read Galatians 6:1-5. Ask kids to paraphrase what Paul is saying. Then ask: **Why are we told to carry each other's burdens in verse 2, but to carry our own load in verse 5?** Explain that no one is supposed to "coast" through his or her Christian life. We're supposed to do our share. Yet sometimes we face very strong trials that weigh us down. When we see someone in that condition, it's our responsibility to do what we can to help bear the person's burden. Our turn will come soon enough. Have group members write down one thing they can do during the coming week to take more responsibility for their own Christian life. Then have them write down a specific situation in which they can help "carry the burden" of someone else. Have kids report back next week to see if they actually did what they said they would do.

STEP 1

To begin the session, have kids lie on the floor shoulder to shoulder, forming two straight lines. (Kids need to be squeezed tightly together in order for this activity to work.) Explain that the first person at the end of each line will be "passed" down the line by the others. The person being passed must remain very stiff and proceed head first, face up, down the line. When the first person being passed reaches the end, he or she lies down next to the last person and becomes a "passer." The next person at the beginning of the line is then passed down in the same manner. The first team to pass everyone along is the winner. Afterward, ask: **How did it feel to get passed along?** (Probably not very good, especially if one was dropped!) Point out that the same thing is true about responsibility—people often pass it along to the next person, and that's when things get dropped.

STEP 4

Ask your kids to think about what the world—and their lives—would be like if God weren't a responsible God. Challenge them to think about how different the world would be; then have them create a mural depicting some of their ideas. Read 1 Corinthians 14:33. Then spend a few minutes in prayer, thanking God that He is a God of order and responsibility. Ask Him to help your group members as they begin to accept responsibility for their actions.

STEP 3

To help your girls consider what it's like to be on the other side when someone won't take responsibility for his or her actions, have them put themselves in Bathsheba's place. King David has called her to him, slept with her, gotten her pregnant, tried to make it look like her husband's the father, and then had him killed. Ask them to think about the following questions, and then write their responses as though they're Bathsheba writing in a journal. **How do you feel about King David? What would you like to say to him?** When they've finished writing, talk about the fact that what we do—and how we respond to what we do—can have profound effects on other people's lives.

STEP 4

Ask for volunteers to roleplay the scenarios in Repro Resource 9. You can act out each situation several times, getting different responses and corresponding consequences. Afterward, ask: **Why is it sometimes difficult not only to take responsibility for our actions, but also to choose to do the right thing in the first place? What can we do to help us make wise decisions and become more responsible?**

STEP 2

After you read through the "Man or Mouse" choices, challenge each group member to come up with one example of a time when he was a "Man" and a second example of a time when he was a "Mouse." Let guys share their "Mouse" stories first. (It will probably help everyone feel more at ease if you begin with a story of your own.) Don't let anyone "mouse" out of this part of the exercise. Follow these stories with instances in which guys were "men," and felt good about the decisions they made and the responsibility they took during a difficult time. Challenge your guys to keep both stories in mind in the future. They can learn from their shortcomings as well as their successes.

STEP 3

After the Bible study, ask: **Do you relate more to David or to Nathan? Why?** After your guys respond, point out that David is a dynamic person to relate to, even with all of his failures. He always seemed to be doing something exciting. He was a natural leader. On the other hand, we have Nathan. He too was a dynamic individual—when he needed to be. Have your guys consider what it must have been like to confront the very popular king of God's people and tell him that you knew he had been fooling around. Nathan remained tuned in to God's leading, even when David was drifting away. Suggest that many guys want to be "kings" (leaders), but not many dream of being prophets who stay in the background and serve God. Certainly, God uses Davids and Nathans, but very few of us can be leaders. Many more of us will be called to serve God in small and seemingly insignificant ways. While dreaming of being the guy on top, we must not forget to be guys who serve. When David forgot that, he got into serious trouble.

STEP 1

Play a quick game of Simon Says to begin your session. Make it a difficult round, doing whatever it takes to trip people up. (For instance, change your tone of voice and say, **You guys pull closer together to get out of the doorway.** But if they move without your saying "Simon Says," they're out!) As people are eliminated, listen for complaints and excuses. Don't do anything at this time, but later in the session you can refer to such comments as you discuss the reluctance of some people to take responsibility for their own actions.

STEP 4

At the end of the session, serve some kind of dessert such as cake or cookies. On the dessert should be written the word "Responsibility" in frosting or some other delectable topping. After closing in prayer and asking God for courage for your group members to take responsibility for their actions, point out that sometimes (as in this case) taking "responsibility" isn't nearly as difficult or unpleasant as it might sound.

STEP 1

Plant a hidden video camera in your meeting place—perhaps behind a pile of books, with only the lens uncovered. Switch on the camera and leave the room. Delay your arrival at the meeting; pre-arrange with a volunteer to instigate a prank in your absence (drawing unflattering cartoons of you on the board, putting honey on your chair, etc.). Make sure that the camera is positioned so that it will catch the prank. (Your volunteer should try discreetly to keep other kids from blocking the camera's view too.) When you enter and "discover" the prank, demand to know who's behind it. When no one confesses, reveal your hidden camera and play the tape back. Use this activity to introduce the idea of taking responsibility for one's actions.

STEP 4

Show a clip of one of the following videos (after prescreening it first) to illustrate how failing to take responsibility can lead to big problems. Ask: **How did this person try to avoid taking responsibility? What happened as a result? How do you think this person might have handled the situations on Repro Resource 9 when he or she was in junior high?**

• *All the President's Men.* Show a scene in which President Nixon denies having a role in the Watergate cover-up. Then show the scene in which Nixon has to resign.

• *Parenthood.* Play a scene in which Larry (Tom Hulce) refuses to take responsibility for his child or his gambling addiction, causing trouble for his father (Jason Robards).

• *Three Men and a Baby.* Show a scene in which Jack (Ted Danson) tries to avoid responsibility for the baby he's fathered, then has a hard time taking care of her.

STEP 1

Try a shorter opener. Before the session, fill three clear quart jars with water. Add eight drops of red food coloring to one jar, eight drops of blue to another, and eight drops of green to the third. Stir the water and seal the jars. Then fill three more identical jars with water (no coloring) and seal them. Bring all of the jars and the bottles of food coloring to your meeting. Have kids form three teams. Instruct each team to choose a representative. Give each team one of the colored-water jars, the corresponding bottle of food coloring, and a clear-water jar. Each representative must decide in thirty seconds how many drops of coloring to put in his or her team's jar to match the color intensity of the premixed jar. The decision may be made after consulting with other team members, but must be made *before* putting the drops in the water. The team that comes up with the closest match gets a prize. Afterward, ask the representatives how it felt to make the final decision alone. Use this activity to introduce the issue of taking responsibility. In Step 2, skip the cases of Tyrone and Jennifer.

STEP 3

Instead of having kids create and perform roleplays about what David might have said, simply say to the group: **Let's say that David blames someone else for what he did. What do you think he might tell Nathan? Or maybe he makes an excuse for what he did. In that case, what might he tell Nathan?** After hearing responses, move to the last paragraph of Step 3 in the session plan. In Step 4, use only one of the situations on Repro Resource 9.

STEP 3

Ask your group members to share some examples (without using any names) of situations they know of in which someone didn't take responsibility for his or her actions. Ask: **What happened as a result? What might have happened if the person had taken responsibility for his or her actions?** If possible, be prepared with an example of your own.

STEP 4

Replace Situation 1 on Repro Resource 9 with the following:

• While you're hanging out with a group of friends, someone dares you to throw a rock from an overpass at the cars below. Not wanting to look like a wimp in front of your friends, you take the dare. You throw the rock, hoping to miss any cars. No such luck. As your friends run away, you hear the sound of screeching tires and breaking glass. What do you do? What might some of the consequences of that choice be? *Follow-up*—The next Sunday in church, you overhear your pastor talking about someone in the church who was injured by a rock thrown from an overpass. The pastor asks you if you know anything about the incident. What do you do? What might some of the consequences of that choice be?

STEP 2

Ask for volunteers from among your high schoolers to talk about times when they've been in situations similar to those listed in Step 2 and how they reacted. If they accepted the responsibility, what happened? If they didn't accept the responsibility, what happened? Encourage your junior highers to ask questions (though you may need to control the questioning so that it doesn't turn into prying). If none of your high schoolers are willing, be prepared to share some examples of your own.

STEP 4

Make the following changes to Repro Resource 9:

• *Situation 1*—Your English teacher has assigned the following topic for your next term paper: "The Bible—Mythology at Its Best." You don't feel right about agreeing that the Bible is just a myth. What do you do? What might be some of the consequences of that choice? *Follow-up*—You write the paper, agreeing that the Bible is great literature, but arguing that it is truth—and not a myth. Your paper comes back with an "F" on it and a note saying, "This was a well-written paper, but not the right topic." What do you do? What might be some of the consequences of that choice?

STEP 1

Rather than using Repro Resource 8, begin the session with a variation of the game "Seven Up." Ask for three or more (depending on the size of your group) volunteers to come to the front of the room. Have the rest of your group members close their eyes. (You might also ask them to cover their eyes with their hands to make sure that none of them peeks.) Instruct each of your volunteers to wander around the room and tag one person on top of the head. Then have the volunteers regather at the front of your room. Instruct the rest of the kids to open their eyes. Those who were tagged must try to guess which of the volunteers tagged them. If a person guesses correctly, he or she takes the volunteer's place at the front of the room. If not, the original volunteer remains. Play as many rounds as you have time for. Afterward, use the "Who did it?" angle of the game to introduce the idea of taking responsibility for one's actions.

STEP 2

After you go through the scenarios in Step 2, ask: **Have you ever taken responsibility for an action, even though you knew that you'd probably get in trouble for it? If so, why did you do it? How did you feel after you took responsibility for the action? What might have happened if you hadn't taken responsibility for the action?** Encourage several kids to respond. If possible, be prepared to share an example of your own. Then move on to Step 3.

S-U-C-C-E-S-S

YOUR GOALS FOR THIS SESSION:

Choose one or more

☐ To help kids recognize the temporal nature of the world's definition of success.

☐ To help kids understand the difference between the world's definition of success and God's definition of success.

☐ To help kids choose one action that will move them toward success according to God's definition.

☐ Other:_____

_____

Your Bible Base:

Joshua 1:1-9
Mark 9:33-37

Burst Out

(Needed: Prizes)

OPTIONS

Have kids form two teams. Explain that one at a time, you will give each team a category. After you've read the category, the team will have one minute to call out as many items in that category as possible. The team will get one point for each item it comes up with that matches one of the answers on the following master list. If possible, enlist an assistant (perhaps an adult volunteer) to help you listen for answers. This activity can get pretty hectic!

After you announce the first category, give Team 1 one minute to shout out answers. Keep track of how many items on the master list the team names. When time is up, announce the team's score, identifying which items on the master list were named and which were missed. Then announce the second category for Team 2 and continue the process. (There are four categories, so each team will be able to play two rounds.) The team with the most points at the end of the game is the winner. Award prizes (perhaps bite-size candy bars) to members of the winning team.

The categories and master lists for the game are as follows:

Category #1: Signs of Success
1. Big house
2. Money/wealth
3. Expensive clothes
4. Good job
5. Influence
6. Power
7. Investments
8. Fame
9. Nice car
10. Exotic vacations

Category #2: Successful Actors and Actresses
[NOTE: This list was compiled in 1994. You may need to modify it to accommodate current popular actors and actresses or to eliminate people who are no longer popular.]
1. Mel Gibson
2. Tom Hanks
3. Julia Roberts
4. Harrison Ford
5. Sylvester Stallone
6. Arnold Schwarzenegger
7. Kevin Costner
8. Alec Baldwin
9. Meg Ryan
10. Jodie Foster

Category #3: Successful People in History
1. Winston Churchill
2. Henry Ford
3. Albert Einstein
4. Babe Ruth
5. Abraham Lincoln
6. Thomas Edison
7. Charles Lindbergh
8. John F. Kennedy
9. Benjamin Franklin
10. George Washington

Category #4: Successful Professions
1. Businessperson
2. Lawyer
3. Actor/actress
4. Professor
5. Politician
6. Doctor
7. Rock musician
8. Banker
9. Professional athlete
10. Judge

Use this activity to lead in to a discussion on what success is.

Success Is . . .

(Needed: Bibles, copies of Repro Resource 10, copies of Repro Resource 11, pencils)

Hand out copies of "Success Rebus"(Repro Resource 10) and pencils. Let kids work in pairs or small groups to solve the rebus puzzles on the right side of the sheet and then match them with the correct names on the left side of the sheet.

Give group members a few minutes to work. When everyone is finished, go through the sheet as a group, asking kids to shout out their responses. The correct answers are as follows: Howard Hughes—making tons of money; the Wright Brothers—being the first to fly; Michelangelo—painting ceilings of churches; Joshua—knowing and doing what God said.

Afterward, ask: **How many of you were surprised to find Joshua's name included on a list of successful people? After all, as far as we know, Joshua wasn't a wealthy man and he didn't invent anything.** Get a few comments from your group members regarding Joshua's success.

Say: **Before we get too far into our discussion, maybe we'd better decide what success is. After all, not everyone agrees on what it means to be successful. Let's take a quick look at the difference between the world's definition of success and God's definition of success.**

Hand out copies of "What's Success?" (Repro Resource 11). Ideally, your group members should still have their pencils from filling out Repro Resource 10.

Ask: **If you could narrow down the world's definition of success to three words, what words would you choose?** Entertain any answers that group members come up with.

Then refer kids to the three rebuses in the "World's Definition" section of Repro Resource 11. The rebuses are pretty simple. Have kids shout out the answers as soon as they figure them out. The correct answers are "money," "power," and "fame." Have group members write these three words next to the appropriate rebuses on the sheet.

Ask: **Why do you think our culture has decided that these are the things that make someone successful?** (Perhaps because these things appear to give people the freedom or ability to do whatever they want.)

Is there anything wrong with having these three things?
(Not necessarily—it depends on how you use them.)

Say: **Let's take a look at what Jesus said to some guys who were searching for this kind of success.**

Have group members turn in their Bibles to Mark 9:33-37. Ask someone to read the passage aloud. Then ask: **What were the disciples arguing about?** (They were arguing about which of them was the greatest.)

How did Jesus respond to them? (He said that whoever wants to be first must be last, the servant of all.)

Say: **It seems from Jesus' response that God's definition of success must be very different from the world's definition. But that doesn't mean God defines success as being poor, wimpy, and unknown. Let's look at the example of Joshua.**

Ask group members to turn in their Bibles to Joshua 1:1-9. Have someone read the passage aloud. Emphasize that the end of verse 8 says that Joshua will be successful if he follows the Lord's commands.

Refer group members to the "God's Definition" section of Repro Resource 11. Explain that the Lord's definition of success is "knowing and doing what God says." Three examples of this can be found in Joshua 1:6-8. Give group members a few minutes to read the passage and then fill in the blanks on Repro Resource 11. When everyone is finished, ask volunteers to share their responses. The correct answers are as follows:

   • Be strong and courageous (1:6-7)
   • Obey God (1:7b)
   • Read and study the Bible (1:8)

Mark 9:33 (-37)   Romans 12:2   Luke 11:28

Joshua 1:1 (-9)   1 Chr 22:13   Phil 2:13

STEP 3

Compare and Contrast

Use the following questions to help your group members better understand the differences between the world's definition of success and God's definition. During this discussion time, keep in mind that the successes of the world are pummeled into kids' brains daily by every aspect of their culture. And to be honest, God's definition of success can look fairly dull to a culturally brainwashed junior higher.

Ask: **What do you have to do to maintain success in the world's eyes once you get it?** (Be lucky; be careful to do exactly the right things.)

How easy is it to lose success in the world's eyes? Explain.

What do you have to do to maintain success in God's eyes once you get it? (Continue doing the things that gave you success in the first place.)

How easy is it to lose success in God's eyes? Explain.

Which definition of success will bring you more real happiness? Encourage kids to respond honestly here. They may have a hard time with this. They'll know they should say "God's," but might not really think so.

If you have success in the world's eyes, what do you have to worry about? (Losing your money or fame or having it taken from you; people who have more power than you do; people deciding that you're not famous anymore.)

If you have success in God's eyes, what do you have to worry about? (Nothing.)

Why might God's definition of success not always sound as good as the world's definition?

How long does success in the world's eyes last? (Anywhere from a moment to most of a lifetime.)

How long does success in God's eyes last? (Forever.)

My Step toward Success

(Needed: Index cards, pencils, chalkboard and chalk or newsprint and marker)

Instruct your group members to brainstorm a list of things they can do to move toward God's definition of success. Write their ideas on the board. These ideas might include reading the Bible regularly, learning what some of the hard-to-understand passages of the Bible mean, standing up for God at school, and obeying parents.

After you've gotten several ideas listed, hand out an index card to each person. The kids should still have pencils, though the writing utensils may have disintegrated into small shards of wood and graphite by now!

Ask your group members to choose one idea from the list on the board or to come up with an idea of their own. Then have them write on the index card "My step toward success is . . . ," filling in the idea on their cards.

As you wrap up the session, allow for a few minutes of silent prayer, during which time group members can ask God for courage and discipline to follow through with their idea. When the prayer time is over, suggest to your kids that they put their card on their dresser, in the corner of their bedroom mirror, or somewhere else where they'll see it regularly.

SUCCESS REBUS

Solve the word puzzles on the right; then match
them with the correct person on the left.

THIS PERSON ...   BECAME SUCCESSFUL BY ...

Howard
Hughes

 SEAL + RINGS– R; DOVE – D;

The Wright
Brothers

 +  ;  ; OF;

Michaelangelo   NO + –K; AND; + ; ; 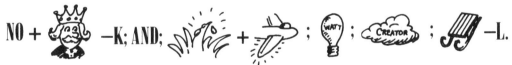 ; –L.

Joshua    + –R; THE;  ;2;

NOTES

WHAT'S SUCCESS?

WORLD'S DEFINITION

1.

2.  **+ R**

3. $$- L$$

GOD'S DEFINITION

1. __ __   _____ ___   ___   _____

2. ____   ___

3. ____   ___   _____ ___   _____

NOTES

STEP 1

Bring in a package of plastic shower curtain rings. Dump the rings in the middle of the floor. Have kids take off their shoes and sit in a circle around the pile of rings. Say: **Have you ever heard the expression "going for the brass ring"?** Explain that the expression refers to putting everything you've got into a chance to be successful. Then say: **Here are the brass rings. Your goal is to get as many rings on your toes as you can in 30 seconds—using only your feet. The person wearing the most rings in 30 seconds wins. No kicking. Go!** After the contest, discuss what kids' real "brass rings"—their symbols of success—are.

STEP 3

Have kids form two teams. Explain that Team A members will try to push each other aside to get a bag of cookies in the middle of the room. The winner keeps all of the cookies. Members of Team B, using another bag, will then serve one cookie to each "loser" from Team A. Finally, reward each person from Team B with two cookies from a third bag. Ask: **Which team got the better deal? Why? Which suffered more stress? How is Team A like those following the world's idea of success? How is Team B like those following God's idea?** In Step 4, let each person choose either a "valuable" Styrofoam ball (which you've painted gold) or a "lowly" Ping-Pong ball (which you've smudged with dirt). Then let kids throw the balls against an outside wall to see which kind bounces better. Use this as a reminder that when we reach for God's idea of success, we bounce back from failures more easily than when we strive for fame and fortune.

STEP 2

After you discuss Joshua and his success, ask: **What do you think made Joshua a success to begin with?** Perhaps someone will be familiar with Joshua's personal history as one of the spies who were sent by Moses into the promised land to check things out. When the 12 spies reported, only Joshua and Caleb advised the people to move ahead. They had faith that God would continue to take care of the people as He always had. But Joshua and Caleb were outnumbered, outvoted, and almost put to death by their own people (Num. 13:26–14:10). Point out that it took the faith of a small group—a *very* small group of two people—to get to the point where the session picks up with Joshua's life. Encourage members of your own small group to remain faithful even though their numbers are somewhat low. Like Joshua, they will eventually be rewarded if their faith remains strong.

STEP 3

Rather than having kids respond as individuals to the questions about success in this step, ask the questions in terms of your entire small group. Discuss God's success and worldly success in terms of your group. The world is looking for big numbers and big budgets to determine success. But is that what God is looking for? Discussing the group as a whole is a lot less threatening than asking junior highers to examine themselves. But after you deal with the entire group, kids should be better able to shift the discussion to a personal level.

STEP 1

Begin the session with a team spelling contest. Have kids form two teams. Explain that one at a time, you will give each team a word to spell. But rather than spelling the word out loud, team members must form the letters of the word with their bodies by lying on the floor in various positions. Every team member must be involved in the spelling of the word. Award a point for each word that is spelled correctly and recognizably (you be the judge). The team with the most points at the end of the game is the winner. Make sure that the last word you use for the spelling contest is "success." After the contest, go through Step 1 as written.

STEP 2

Rather than having kids fill out Repro Resource 10, give them an opportunity to create their own "success rebuses." Draw the rebuses from Repro Resource 10 on the board to give your kids an idea of what you're looking for. Then let volunteers come to the board one at a time to draw their own rebuses that describe how famous people became successful. See how long it takes the rest of the group to decipher each rebus and figure out who's being described. After several volunteers have had an opportunity to draw, move on to the Repro Resource 11 activity.

STEP 2

Kids may yawn at the revelation that they should be strong and courageous, obey God, and study the Bible. If so, write these actions, along with "be a servant," on the left side of the board. Then brainstorm a list of things a person must do to be successful in the world's eyes (get rich, become a great athlete, be born with good looks, practice a skill for hours every day, beat everyone competing against you, etc.); write these things on the right side of the board. Ask: **How many people in this group can do the things on the right side?** (Few, if any.) **How many can do the things on the left side?** (Everyone can, to the best of his or her ability.) Point out that under God's definition, everyone can be a success. If the definition sounds boring, maybe that's because God's idea of success is within our reach—if we belong to Him and rely on His power.

STEP 3

When the alternatives are fortune and fame, how can you get kids to consider a life of servanthood and obedience? Try asking kids how many of these former top-of-the-charts performers are still big today: Milli Vanilli, The Bee Gees, George Michael, Boy George, Irene Cara, Herb Alpert, Lulu, The Archies, and New Kids on the Block. Ask: **What happens to celebrities as they get older?** (Many fade into obscurity, even poverty.) Bring in one to three older people from your church who are still vital and happy about serving God. Interview these people about whether they feel their lives have been worthwhile so far. What are their definitions of success? Would they trade their experiences as Christians for a few years of fame? Do they wish they'd spent more time making money? What are their goals for the future?

STEP 2

Focus on the varying opinions regarding success in this step; back up what you're saying with the Joshua 1:1-9 passage. Save the Mark 9:33-37 passage for the next step. After group members give their definitions of success, have them individually read Joshua 1:1-9. Ask: **Based on what God is telling Joshua in this passage, would you consider yourself to be a success? What would you need to do in order to become more "successful"? What promises does God make to Joshua? What does God expect from Joshua in return?** If your group members don't know this story, don't rush through it. Help them learn to read and absorb important spiritual truths on their own.

STEP 3

If you postponed the Mark 9:33-37 passage from Step 2 (see the "Little Bible Background" option for Step 2), use it here. Some of your kids may be surprised to discover that Jesus' own disciples got into arguments about who was number one. Ask: **Have you ever been in an argument in which you tried to prove that you were better than someone else? If so, were you successful? What are some ways we can serve the other people in this group rather than trying to demand our own way? What do you think Jesus saw in little children that caused Him to use one as a model for how we should behave?**

STEP 1

Have kids form teams. Give each team a piece of newsprint large enough for members to draw a life-sized body. Explain that you're going to have a contest to find the most successful person in the world, whom the teams are going to create. Provide the members of each team with creative supplies and have them prepare their "person" for success. After a few minutes, have each team describe its individual and what it is about the person that makes him or her successful. Afterward, ask: **What is success?** Get several responses. **What do you think God's definition of success is?**

STEP 4

Have kids reassemble into the teams they formed for the "most successful person in the world" contest (see the "Fellowship & Worship" option for Step 1). Provide teams with creative supplies again. This time, instruct the members of each team to portray what they think God would consider to be a success. Encourage them to think creatively; they might portray anything from a sunset that God created to a person helping someone in need. You may wish to read Matthew 6:25-33 as food for thought while they work. After a few minutes, review the new collages; then thank God for His perspective on success.

STEP 1

Substitute the following categories for your opening activity:

• *Category #2: Successful Actresses—* (1) Julia Roberts; (2) Meg Ryan; (3) Meryl Streep; (4) Jodie Foster; (5) Susan Sarandon; (6) Sharon Stone; (7) Winona Ryder; (8) Glenn Close; (9) Melanie Griffith; (10) Juliette Lewis

• *Category #3: Successful Women in History—*(1) Joan of Arc; (2) Florence Nightingale; (3) Marie Curie; (4) Mother Teresa; (5) Margaret Thatcher; (6) Emily Dickinson; (7) Susan B. Anthony; (8) Cleopatra; (9) Queen Esther; (10) Babe Didrikson Zaharias

STEP 3

Have kids form groups of three or four. Give each group paper and pencils. Instruct each group to list the names of women in the Bible who were successful and explain why each woman was a success. Challenge the groups to list as many women as possible. After a few minutes, have each group share its list. Then say: **There's nothing in the Bible that says you must be a man to be a success!** Encourage your girls to live lives that are successful for the Lord.

STEP 2

Rather than having your guys fill out Repro Resource 10, ask them to spend the next few minutes acting "successful." Whatever they think the word entails, they should do what they can to act it out. Watch them to see if some try to boss others around, begin to swagger across the room, or do anything else that reflects a shallow, worldly concept of success. After a few minutes, announce that you want to reward the ones who did the best job of acting out "success." Give prizes to those who didn't automatically become obnoxious and offensive to those around them. Then move on to Repro Resource 11.

STEP 4

Most guys are competitive by nature. But they've already seen from Mark 9:33-37 that competing to be number one is not something that pleases God. If you think your guys can handle the competition without missing the point, challenge them to conduct a servanthood contest during the following week. As they brainstorm ways to be more "successful" from God's perspective, see if you can foster a little good-natured rivalry among your guys. If John sets a goal to be "twice the servant" that Bill is, and Bill takes the challenge, spiritual growth can be fun for guys. You do need to be careful, however, that all glory from the competition goes to God. You want your guys to grow in grace, and not develop a false sense of pride for their efforts.

STEP 1

Since you opened the session with a homemade version of the game Outburst, be aware that "Bible Outburst" also exists (a trademark of Hersch & Company, © 1989, produced in the U.S.A. by Western Publishing Company). If your group members enjoy this kind of competition, find the game and let them play before or after the session. It's also an excellent resource to pull out from time to time when you need to fill periods of time and haven't prepared anything. And if you pay attention while kids are playing, you may be able to determine what areas of Scripture kids may be weak in, allowing you to prepare more effective sessions in the future.

STEP 4

As a conclusion or follow-up to this session, show a video that portrays the life of a truly successful person such as Corrie ten Boom *(The Hiding Place)* or Eric Liddel *(Chariots of Fire)*. It's one thing to talk about being successful for God by serving others, but seeing what it can accomplish can have a much stronger effect on junior highers.

STEP 1

During the week before the session, use your VCR to record the closing credits—just the credits—of several shows. Include some "rolling" credits from TV movies. Record a total of about one minute of credits. Before playing them back for the group, hand out paper and pencils. Say: **Many people would say that working in Hollywood makes you a success. I'm going to show you the names of some of these successful people. As you watch, write down the ones you think are the biggest successes.** After showing the tape, have kids share what they wrote. Ask: **How did you decide who the biggest successes were? If your name was in these credits, would you feel like a success? Why or why not? Would it make a difference if your name was bigger than other names, or on the screen longer? What do you think makes a person a success?**

STEP 3

Play and discuss one or more contemporary Christian songs that contrast the world's view of success with God's view. Possibilities include "Meltdown (At Madame Tussaud's)" (Steve Taylor), "People in a Box" (Farrell and Farrell), "Gotta Have the Real Thing" (Rick Riso), "Not of This World" (Petra), "Ordinary People" (Danniebelle Hall), "Losing Game" (Dallas Holm and Praise), and "God's Own Fool" (Michael Card).

STEP 1

Try a shorter opener. Bring five paper plates that you've numbered (on the bottom, out of sight) from one to five. Bring a large bag of candies, too. Place the plates randomly on the floor. Let each person find a unique object (a coin, sock, etc.) to represent himself or herself. Explain that each plate is numbered on the bottom, and that the number stands for the number of candies that will be won for tossing an item onto that plate. Standing back from the plates, kids should decide which one to toss their items onto. After items are thrown, have kids form two teams. *Then* look under the plates to see how many candies each person won. Award the candies. Then give *extra* candy to the team whose members already won more candy. Ask: **Was this a game of skill or chance? Who was a success in this game? Is being successful in life a matter of skill or chance? Why? How can you tell who's a success in life?**

STEP 4

In place of Step 4, brainstorm three mistakes that a kid could make at school (tripping in the lunch line, studying the wrong chapter for a test, etc.). Ask: **If you're aiming for the world's idea of success, how could mistakes like these really mess you up?** (Clumsiness could put you on the "geek" list; a bad grade might hurt your chances of getting into college and making lots of money later; etc.) **If you're aiming for God's idea of success, would mistakes like these be so serious?** (No, because we could still grow in our ability to obey Him and serve others.) Close by encouraging kids with the thought that aiming for God's idea of success can make it easier to bounce back from goofs and failures.

STEP 1

Rather than using the "Burst Out" game, begin the session with an activity called "What Is Success?" Explain that you will read a list of items one at a time. If group members think that an item indicates success, they should stand; if they don't think that an item necessarily represents success, they should remain seated. Among the items you might name are "having an article written about you in the newspaper," "getting a standing ovation in front of a large crowd of people," "getting a job," "becoming a parent," "being loved by someone of the opposite sex," "owning a large house," "being able to do whatever you want whenever you want," and "winning the lottery." (Feel free to add any other items that you can think of.) Afterward, ask: **How would you define success?** You'll want to refer to group members' responses later in the session when you talk about the difference between the world's definition of success and God's definition of success.

STEP 2

Rather than using Repro Resource 10, try another option. Before the session, make "celebrity flash cards" by writing the names of various successful people on large index cards, one name per card. As you hold up the cards one at a time, ask kids to call out what each person is successful at. For instance, Michael Jordan is successful at basketball; Rosie Perez is successful at acting; Anita Baker is successful at singing; Nelson Mandela is successful at fighting apartheid. Make sure that the last flash card has "Joshua" written on it. See if your kids know what this Bible character was successful at. If no one mentions it, point out that he was successful at knowing and doing what God said. Then move on to the Repro Resource 11 activity.

STEP 1

At the end of Step 1 (and in lieu of using Repro Resource 10 in Step 2), ask: **What do you think the world's definition of success is?** Get several responses; then write a condensed summary of your kids' definitions on the board. Ask: **Who are some people you can think of, living or dead, who fit this definition?** Get several responses. Then ask: **What do you think God's definition of success is?** Write a condensed summary of your kids' definitions on the board. Then brainstorm as a group some people who fit that definition. Spend a few minutes discussing the differences between the world's definition of success and God's definition. Also discuss how difficult (or easy) it was to name people who offer an example of God-honoring success.

STEP 2

Skip Repro Resource 11. Ask: **If you could narrow the world's definition of success to three words, what words would you choose?** After you've gone through Mark 9:33-37, have someone read aloud Matthew 6:14-21. Point out that the verses from Matthew can be applied to the world's three symbols of success. Verses 14 and 15 refer to forgiving others. Often when we don't forgive, we do so because we think that will give us power over someone else. Verses 16-18 refer to fame. The hypocrites wanted to be noticed, wanted the spotlight, wanted recognition. And verses 19-21 are obviously about money and wealth. Based on Matthew 6:14-21 and Mark 9:33-37, have your kids come up with three words to summarize God's definition of success.

STEP 2

Rather than using Repro Resource 10 with your sixth graders, try another activity. Before the session, you'll need to gather pictures of several famous and successful people throughout history. At this point in the session, hold up two of the pictures at a time. Ask: **Which of these people is more successful? Why?** Emphasize that you're not asking which person is more famous or which person is better liked; you're asking which person is more successful. It should be interesting to hear your kids' views as to what makes someone successful. Lead in to a discussion on the difference between the world's definition of success and God's definition of success.

STEP 3

After you've gone through Step 3 as written, ask your kids a few more questions: **Have you ever been successful in the world's eyes? If so, at what? Have you ever been successful in God's eyes? If so, at what?** Group members' responses should let you know whether they understand the difference between the world's definition of success and God's definition.

DATE USED:

Approx. Time

STEP 1: *Burst Out* _____
- ❏ Extra Action
- ❏ Large Group
- ❏ Fellowship & Worship
- ❏ Mostly Girls
- ❏ Extra Fun
- ❏ Media
- ❏ Short Meeting Time
- ❏ Urban
- ❏ Combined Junior High/High School

Things needed:

STEP 2: *Success Is …* _____
- ❏ Small Group
- ❏ Large Group
- ❏ Heard It All Before
- ❏ Little Bible Background
- ❏ Mostly Guys
- ❏ Urban
- ❏ Combined Junior High/High School
- ❏ Sixth Grade

Things needed:

STEP 3: *Compare and Contrast* _____
- ❏ Extra Action
- ❏ Small Group
- ❏ Heard It All Before
- ❏ Little Bible Background
- ❏ Mostly Girls
- ❏ Media
- ❏ Sixth Grade

Things needed:

STEP 4: *My Step toward Success* _____
- ❏ Fellowship & Worship
- ❏ Mostly Guys
- ❏ Extra Fun
- ❏ Short Meeting Time

Things needed:

NOTES

Unit Two: Riding Those Mood Swings

Talking with Junior Highers about Up-and-Down Feelings

by Rich Van Pelt

Skip was the stereotypical junior high guy. He could regularly be found bouncing off a wall or hanging from a chandelier. His energy and enthusiasm made him fun—but extremely exhausting—to be with. Skip's mom wondered whether it was possible for parents to survive their kids' adolescence.

One day I called to see if Skip was interested in going to the movies with a group of guys.

"Hey, Skip, how's it going?"

"Uh . . . OK, I guess."

"What's goin' on?"

"Not a whole lot . . ."

It wouldn't have taken Dick Tracy to discern that something was wrong. The tone of his voice was noticeably troubled. He spoke quietly and slowly. Something was up. I continued.

"Anything wrong?"

". . . Nah."

"You sure?"

"Well . . . she dumped me!"

After considerable hesitation, three simple words said it all: *"She dumped me!"* Skip was reeling from his first heartbreak. After three long months of building up the courage to ask Missy if they could "go out" and a few short weeks of adolescent bliss, Missy decided to "go out" with Skip's best friend. Skip was certain his world had come to an end.

The junior high years have been characterized as the "wonder years," but they weren't always wonderful. The physical, sexual, intellectual, psychological, and emotional changes of early adolescence require more of junior highers than the majority of them believe they have to give. In fact, at a time in their lives when most want nothing more than simply to be "normal," the only constant seems to be change. As a result, emotions appear supercharged. Everything is either the very best or the very worst. There doesn't seem to be an "in-between."

Which is where we enter the picture. Kids like Skip need adults in their lives who are willing to be with them in the up and the down times—adults who will take them seriously and help them understand that what they are experiencing is both normal and survivable. Let me offer a few suggestions on how we can be of assistance. What does it take to talk with junior highers about up and down feelings?

Focus on Building Relationships

Several years ago, a major study was funded for the purpose of identifying the most effective curriculum for implementation in junior high schools nationwide. Survey results demonstrated that student-teacher relationship, not curriculum, is of paramount importance. Without quality student-teacher interaction, the best program or curriculum drowns in a sea of disinterest. Listen to a typical group of junior highers discuss their first week of school. Little attention is given to the subjects they will study, but major importance is placed on what teachers they will have. Kids respond to adults who like them and respect them. As trust develops, they will even risk sharing feelings.

Cultivate a Climate of Openness

Don't naively assume that because the subject is "up-and-down feelings," kids in your group will feel safe enough to join in the discussion. Intentionally cultivate a climate where group members feel comfortable sharing from personal experience. Here are some ways to make that happen.

- Establish ground rules for the class or group.

  (1) What is shared in the group stays in the group. Group members need assurance that anything they say will not be used against them! Unless kids believe that their opinions will be treated confidentially, they will be guarded in what they choose to share. As a result, little vulnerability will be exercised. In most cases, confidentiality should not be violated unless a student's life or the life of another is in jeopardy.

  (2) Everyone has a right to speak—or remain silent. No one will be put on the spot. Each person may choose to share or to respectfully decline.

  (3) No put-downs are allowed. It is imperative that the opinions of all be respected and protected. Group members inclined to discredit others will be invited to change—or leave.

  (4) One person speaks at a time. Respect is non-negotiable. We communicate honor and value to each other by listening to what each other has to say.

  (5) Everyone has equal status in the group. Personal value and the right to share has nothing to do with age, class, race, etc.

- Model transparency.

  Leaders influence the tone of any group process. If honesty and transparency characterize our personal sharing, group members are more likely to follow suit. We've got to remember, however, that our goal is to talk as little as possible. In our role as facilitator, we work at drawing students into the discussion.

- Address real-life issues.

  Up-and-down feelings are prompted by real-life issues. Riding Those Mood Swings honestly faces real issues that contribute to the feelings junior highers experience. Provide a place where they can freely explore and talk about any and all of those feelings.

Listen Empathetically

Suicide is the second-leading cause of death among teenagers in America because too many of us believe that young people should be "seen and not heard." Statistics reveal that the average household in America with teenagers living in it spends 14.5 minutes a day communicating—with 12.5 of those minutes consumed by negative communication. The average teenager in America, therefore, can expect about 14 minutes a week of positive communication with mom and/or dad. Fourteen minutes a week of talking and listening is simply not enough. Youth workers, Sunday school teachers, and youth ministry volunteers must cultivate a climate in which kids feel safe enough to speak, and then take time to listen empathetically.

Someone once said, "Empathy is feeling your pain in my heart." For some time I've entertained a love-hate relationship with the TV series The Wonder Years. Love, because the early episodes so accurately and poignantly portray life in junior high school, and hate for the same reason. I find it nearly impossible to watch an episode without being reminded of my own junior high experience—a time I, like many others, would rather forget. To be effective in ministry with junior highers and speak credibly with them about the realities of up-and-down feelings requires that we be willing to remember what it was like to be an early adolescent. When we remember how difficult those years and struggles were for us, we have greater capacity to genuinely come alongside kids on a gut level. There is a difference, however, between *empathy* and *arrogance*. Arrogance says, "I understand exactly what you are feeling," based solely on the premise that because I lived through a similar experience I can understand what you are going through. Empathy, by contrast, is coming alongside someone on a gut level, and taking the time to listen so that understanding may result.

Avoid "Adultisms"

Most adults remember a time in their childhood when they swore never to repeat something a parent said or did when they themselves bacame parents. For many, that commitment involved never hammering their children with phrases like:
- "You think *you* have it bad?"
- "Why don't you act your age?"
- "Just wait until you're a parent."
- "When I was your age . . ."
- "It's only puppy love."

We remember hating those messages because they seemed to discount what we were feeling. After all, puppy love is real to puppies! Noted child and adolescent psychologist Stephen Glenn says, "An adultism occurs any time an adult forgets what it is like to be a child and then expects, demands, and requires of the child who has never been an adult to think, act, understand, see and do things as an adult" (*Raising Self-Reliant Children in a Self-Indulgent World,* H. Stephen Glenn and Jane Nelsen, p. 91).

Offer Sound Biblical Advice

Developmentally speaking, the early adolescent years represent a time of increased spiritual openness. Junior highers are eager to embrace the Christian faith, but they want to know how that faith relates to the real world in which they live. They need to know that the Christian faith is a faith of mountain tops *and* valleys, of highs *and* lows. They will be encouraged to learn that the God of the Bible meets people where they are—that great Bible characters like David, Job, Peter, and others struggled with feelings of loneliness, fear, anger, and abandonment. Junior highers should be encouraged that even in the worst of times, God offers peace and joy through His presence.

Know Your Limits

These are tough times in which to be a kid. When given an opportunity to share about life's ups and downs, situations may surface that require specialized professional help. In an attempt to anesthetize their pain or lessen the demands of living, unprecedented numbers of young people are turning to high-risk activities like drinking or drugging, sexual promiscuity, eating disorders, and suicidal behavior. Learn to go with your gut. Whenever you sense that a young person's struggle is beyond your level of comfortability or training, seek professional assistance. Referral is a sign of strength, not weakness. Ask the advice of your supervisor or senior pastor, or contact a local mental health professional.

Rich Van Pelt is president of Alongside Ministries in Denver, Colorado. A 25 year veteran of youth ministry, Rich is the author of Intensive Care: Helping Kids in Crisis, *co-author of* The Compassion Project, *and a regular contributor to various youth ministry journals and perodicals. Rich is also a popular speaker at youth events, youth worker training conferences, and parent workshops nationwide.*

The images on these two pages are designed to help you promote this course within your church and community. Feel free to photocopy anything here and adapt it to fit your publicity needs. The stuff on this page could be used as a flier that you send or hand out to kids—or as a bulletin insert. The stuff on the next page could be used to add visual interest to newsletters, calendars, bulletin boards, or other promotions. Be creative and have fun!

Why Do Our Moods Change?

You know the feeling—one minute you're on top of the world, and not much later you're down in the dumps.
For the next few weeks, we'll be looking at our up-and-down emotions in a new course called *Riding Those Mood Swings*.
Hang on—it's going to be a wild ride.

Who:

When:

Where:

Questions? Call:

Is it wrong to be angry?

How do you try to cheer up?

Come and see what's cooking.

(Write your own ideas in the signs.)

Come and have a good/lousy time—
the choice is yours!

Why Do I Feel This Way?

YOUR GOALS FOR THIS SESSION:
Choose one or more

☐ To help kids recognize that emotions are a natural part of us—we were created with them.

☐ To help kids understand God's "emotions"—including His love, His anger, and His jealousy.

☐ To help kids choose a strategy for including God in their emotional lives

☐ Other:_____
_____

Your Bible Base:

Genesis 1:27
Exodus 20:5
Numbers 32:13
Ecclesiastes 3:1-8
John 3:16

Emotions on Display

(Needed: Copies of Repro Resource 1)

As group members arrive, distribute copies of "A Trip to Grandmother's House" (Repro Resource 1). Assign the roles of the narrator, the young girl, the mother, the young man, and the stranger. (If you don't have many volunteers for the roles, you could double up on some of the parts.)

Explain that the actors will read the lines of the skit, while the rest of the group makes the noises called for in parentheses. Point out that a "cute sound" could be any sound people make when they see a cute baby or puppy dog ("awhhh," for instance). A "crying sound" could be anything from a sniffle to a bawling fit. A "yummy sound" could be any sound people make when they taste a food they like. "Boo, hiss" could be any sound members of an audience make when they don't like what they're seeing. "Applause" could be any sound members of an audience make when they like what they're seeing.

Encourage both the actors and the rest of the group members to "ham it up" in their assigned roles.

Afterward, point out: **The sweet young girl in this skit went through several different emotions. What were some of them?** (Sadness, fear, relief, happiness.)

Have you ever had a day in which you experienced several different emotions in a short period of time? Encourage several group members to share their experiences. If you think they'd be comfortable talking about it, ask them to explain what events and circumstances influenced their emotions that day. You may want to be prepared to share an example from your own life to "break the ice."

STEP 2

Circumstances

Ask: **What usually causes your emotions to change? For instance, if you're feeling sad, what might cause you to feel happy?** Help group members recognize that events and circumstances play a large role in determining our emotions.

Explain: **I'm going to read a list of different situations. After I read each one, let me know what emotions you would probably feel in that situation and how strongly you would feel them.** Group members will indicate their emotions by calling them out to you. They will indicate how strongly they would feel those emotions by the volume of their voices. Whispers will indicate that their emotions wouldn't be very strong. Shouts will indicate that their emotions would be overpowering.

The situations are as follows:

(1) Your teacher is passing out a test that you haven't studied for at all. (Possible responses: Nervousness, fear, regret, etc.)

(2) Your teacher is passing out a test that you've studied hard for all week. (Possible responses: Confidence, happiness, excitement, etc.)

(3) You're sitting in a dentist's chair, and your dentist is getting ready to drill a hole in your tooth. (Possible responses: Nervousness, fear, panic, etc.)

(4) You've just been caught in a lie by your parents. (Possible responses: Nervousness, fear, regret, etc.)

(5) You just found out that the person at school you have a crush on tried to call you last night while you were out with your family. (Possible responses: Excitement, nervousness, regret, etc.)

(6) Your best friend just moved to another state to live. (Possible responses: Sadness, fear, regret, etc.)

Afterward, ask: **Are emotions good or bad?** Get responses from as many group members as possible.

Then say: **That's like asking whether arms and legs are bad, or hair and hands. Emotions are just part of us. We were created with them.**

OPTIONS

SMALL GROUP

FELLOWSHIP & WORSHIP

MOSTLY GIRLS

MOSTLY GUYS

EXTRA FUN

SHORT MEETING TIME

URBAN

JR. HIGH / HIGH SCHOOL COMBINED

SIXTH GRADE

In Whose Image?

(Needed: Bibles)

Have group members turn in their Bibles to Genesis 1:27. Read the verse aloud together as a group.

Then ask: **Who created the man and woman?** (God.)

According to this verse, how were the man and woman created? (In God's image.)

If we're created in God's image, and we have emotions, does that mean God has emotions too? If so, which emotions do you think God experiences? Encourage several group members to offer their opinions.

Have someone read aloud John 3:16. Then ask: **What emotion is God identified with in this verse?** (Love.)

Is this the same kind of love we feel for others? (Human love is often conditional. We love people who love us or who do nice things for us. When we speak of God's love, we're really talking about more than a feeling. It is the attitude or will that seeks the best for us. God's love is a perfect, unconditional love. It's not based on anything we do for Him. Romans 5:8 tells us that even when we were sinners, God loved us enough to send His Son to die for us.)

Have someone read aloud Numbers 32:13. Then ask: **What emotion is God identified with in this passage?** (Anger.)

Is this the same kind of anger we feel for others? (Human anger is usually based on revenge. When someone does something to us, we get angry and usually desire to "get back" at the person. Because God is holy and perfect, His anger is directed at sin. His anger is not based on revenge or other insecure human emotions.)

Have someone read aloud Exodus 20:5. Then ask: **What emotion is God identified with in this passage?** (Jealousy.)

Is this the same kind of jealousy we experience? (Human jealousy is based on insecurity. When people get jealous, it's usually because their fragile egos have been wounded. It's tough to accept that people prefer others to us. God's jealousy is based on His perfection. God created us; God is perfect; and God is the one, true God. For these reasons, He alone deserves our worship. When we put other "gods" in His place—after all He's done for us—we are denying His rightful authority and position. Therefore, His jealousy is justified.)

Point out that if God's emotions are perfect and ours are imperfect, God might be a good source to turn to when we have questions about or problems with our emotions.

STEP 4

A Time for Everything

(Needed: Bible, paper, pencils)

Distribute a piece of paper and a pencil to each group member. Then give the following instructions: **Tear this sheet of paper into four sections. On one section, write down an everyday situation or event that could cause you to get *angry*. On another section, write down an everyday situation or event that could make you *happy*. On another section, write down an everyday situation or event that could make you *sad*. On the final section, write down an everyday situation or event that could make you feel *scared*.**

After group members have written their responses, have them label the back of each section ("angry," "happy," "sad," and "scared"). Collect the slips of paper, keeping each emotion category separate.

Have group members form four teams. Assign each team one of the emotion categories, and give that team three slips of paper from the corresponding stack. If possible, look through the slips before you distribute them. Make sure you don't distribute any slips that are too personal or that would identify the people who wrote them.

Instruct the members of the "angry," "sad," and "scared" teams to read their situations and then come up with ideas for how God could help someone facing those situations. For instance, let's say the "scared" team is assigned the following situation: "Every day I'm afraid that I won't have anyone to sit with at lunch." Team members may suggest that God could help someone facing this situation by bringing a group of friends into this person's life or by giving the person the courage to sit with people he or she doesn't know.

Instruct the members of the "happy" team to read their situations and then come up with ideas for how God could be honored and praised in those situations. For instance, let's say the team is assigned the following situation: "Buying new clothes makes me happy." Team members may suggest that God could be honored if the person would

OPTIONS

EXTRA **ACTION**

LARGE GROUP

HEARD IT ALL **BEFORE**

LITTLE BIBLE BACKGROUND

FELLOWSHIP & **WORSHIP**

MOSTLY GIRLS

SIXTH GRADE

WHY DO I FEEL THIS WAY ?

take a certain percentage of his or her clothes money and give it to the church or to the needy.

Give the teams a few minutes to work. When they're finished, have each team share its situations and responses with the rest of the group.

Afterward, say: **Think about the ideas we've just heard for including God in our emotional lives. Choose one idea that sounded good to you. Make a commitment to use that idea the next time you get angry, happy, sad, or scared.** Give group members a minute or two to consider the ideas. If you have time, ask a couple of volunteers to share the ideas they chose.

As you wrap up the session, have someone read aloud Ecclesiastes 3:1-8. Ask group members to call out other suggestions for this passage—perhaps suggestions that are relevant to their everyday experiences.

For instance, group members might suggest that there is
- a time for studying and a time for goofing off;
- a time for being excited and a time for being reserved;
- a time for getting angry and a time for patching things up;
- a time to feel scared and a time to feel confident.

Emphasize that there is a time for every emotion and a time to ask for God's help with those emotions.

Close the session in prayer, thanking God that He created us with the ability to experience a wide range of emotions and that He's always available to help us with our emotions.

NOTES

A TRIP TO
GRANDMOTHER'S HOUSE

NARRATOR: One day, many years ago, a sweet young girl (**CUTE SOUND**) was sitting at the breakfast table talking with her kind and caring mother (**CUTE SOUND**).

MOTHER: Oh, my sweet young daughter (**CUTE SOUND**), I have terrible news for you. Your grandmother is feeling ill (**CRYING SOUND**). She needs you to take her some soup (**YUMMY SOUND**).

YOUNG GIRL: What kind of soup (**YUMMY SOUND**) shall I take her?

MOTHER: Her favorite—cream of mustard (**YUMMY SOUND**).

NARRATOR: Before the sweet young girl (**CUTE SOUND**) left the house with the hot, homemade cream of mustard soup (**YUMMY SOUND**), her mother said…

MOTHER: Be careful on your way to Grandmother's house. Do not talk to any mean and terrible strangers (**BOO, HISS**). You know that mean and terrible strangers (**BOO, HISS**) love soup (**YUMMY SOUND**). They may hurt you (**CRYING SOUND**) if you refuse to give it to them.

NARRATOR: With this warning, the sweet young girl (**CUTE SOUND**) left. On the way to her grandmother's house, who should appear before her but a mean and terrible stranger (**BOO, HISS**)!

STRANGER: Give me that hot, homemade soup (**YUMMY SOUND**) or I'll bite your nose off!

YOUNG GIRL: No, no, I must not—for if I do, my grandmother will have nothing to eat (**CRYING SOUND**). And she so loves her cream of mustard soup. (**YUMMY SOUND**)

STRANGER: Cream of *mustard* soup (**YUMMY SOUND**)?

NARRATOR: Just then, a strong and noble young man (**APPLAUSE**) came along.

YOUNG MAN: Away with you, you mean and terrible stranger (**BOO, HISS**).

NARRATOR: The mean and terrible stranger (**BOO, HISS**) ran away, fearing for his life. As he ran, he yelled back over his shoulder…

STRANGER: I don't even like cream of mustard soup (**YUMMY SOUND**)! Why don't you teach your mother to make something normal, like chicken noodle soup (**BOO, HISS**) or beef stew (**BOO, HISS**)?

NARRATOR: The moral of this story is "Never talk to mean and terrible strangers (**BOO, HISS**)—especially when you're a sweet young girl (**CUTE SOUND**) carrying hot, homemade cream of mustard soup (**YUMMY SOUND**) to your grandmother (**APPLAUSE**)!

NOTES

STEP 1

Have a sound-effects contest along with the skit. Before the actors begin, have the rest of the students form Teams A and B. Give them time to look over the skit and figure out how to make each sound effect unique every time it is used during the skit. For example, unique ways to say the cute "ahhh" sound would be for a team to whisper it or to sing it in harmony. Have teams take turns going first.

STEP 4

Write the following emotions on index cards: happy, angry, excited, confident, sad, scared, nervous, jealous, and vengeful. Have group members form teams. Give one index card to each team along with a stack of newspapers, old magazines, and tape. Have each team use the supplies to creatively "dress" one of its members to look like the emotion that is written on the team's index card. For example, to make a person look angry or vengeful, kids could wrap their teammate like a mummy and tape long horns made out of crushed, rolled-up newspaper to his or her head. Have each team's "dressed up" member stand, walk around, or act while each team member describes an every-day situation or event that could cause him or her to feel the emotion printed on the card. If the emotion is negative, have kids come up with ideas for how God could help them in those negative situations; if the emotion is positive, have them come up with ways to honor or praise God in those situations.

STEP 1

Skip the skit. Instead, have kids "chart" their emotions for a day or a week. Distribute pencils and paper. Have kids draw two intersecting lines near the lower left corner of their papers. Along the vertical line, they should write numbers one through five, with one at the bottom (representing not much emotion) and five at the top (representing hit-the-ceiling emotion). Along the horizontal line, they should write key words or draw symbols to represent people or events that elicited an emotion last week (in the order in which the events happened). Some graphs may resemble wild roller coaster rides; others may resemble gently rolling hills. Ask volunteers to explain their charts. Then have them make separate charts that represent what they wish their emotional charts would look like. Ask: **How is your made-up chart different from your real one? What things tend to cause you to feel really emotional? What kinds of things don't bother you much?**

STEP 2

A small group of kids may feel put on the spot by all of the questions in this step. So cut down on the number of situations you describe that ask kids to identify their emotional responses. Just read a few of the six situations. Choose a mixture of negative and positive ones. Or simply read some of the emotions and have kids supply events in life that might lead to those particular emotions.

STEP 3

Involve more kids by creating small groups and having them look up more Scripture passages about God's emotions. Have them answer these questions for each passage: **What emotion is God identified with in this passage? Is this the same kind of emotion we experience? Why or why not?** Suggested passages include John 2:13-17 (anger, enthusiasm); Romans 15:13 (hope); Zephaniah 1:18; Exodus 34:14; Deuteronomy 6:15 (jealousy); Jeremiah 33:9 (joy); Proverbs 6:16-19 (hate); Matthew 18:12-14 (happiness); Nahum 1:2 (vengeance); Hebrews 1:9 (hate, joy); Exodus 20:6; Matthew 3:16, 17 (love).

STEP 4

A creative way to help a large group relate more to the closing prayer is to have someone bring in a baby just before you pray. Have kids watch the baby for a few minutes while it plays, interacts with its mother or father, or cries about something it needs or wants. After the baby leaves, have everyone settle down. The baby will have reminded your kids in a fresh way of the range of emotions that God gave us, which might help them to better tune in to the prayer.

HEARD IT ALL BEFORE

LITTLE BIBLE BACKGROUND

FELLOWSHIP & WORSHIP

STEP 3

What do you do with kids who think, "Emotions? Made in God's image? So what! Image schmimage!"? You get kids with this attitude to create a skit in which earthlings try to describe various emotions to an emotionless alien like Spock from *Star Trek*. To get them started, you could tell them to build a skit around a description of rage, like this: **Rage feels like a river of pain pulsing through your body after you step on 10 sharp nails that pierce deep into your foot. The river of rage races up your legs, into your chest, through your neck, and explodes out of your head like a nuclear blast. Hate and anger spurt from your mouth and fingernails, forever staining, even maiming, anyone or anything near you.** Have kids take turns trying to describe emotions, like fear, love, joy, surprise, sorrow, pity, etc. Discuss Scripture passages that talk about how our emotions have been warped by sin (Rom. 1:28-32) and how God can help us deal with overwhelming emotions (Ps. 71:20-21; Rom. 8:18-27).

STEP 4

Don't let the closing prayer go by unnoticed at the end of this step. Make it a special time by suddenly changing the pace of the session. Encourage kids to stop rustling papers, shifting in their seats, or whispering. Remind them that they are about to approach God's throne. You may even want to pray in hushed tones to bring attention to the fact that something very important is going on. You might turn off the bright lights and light a candle or bring a small lamp that sheds a soft light.

STEP 3

To give your kids a little more background about what it means to be created in the image of God, read aloud this updated version of a passage from Martin Luther's *Commentary on Genesis*. Point out that much of it is speculation on Luther's part. **When God created Adam, He created a beautiful, excellent, noble creature. Adam wasn't sick from sin. All of his senses were perfect and pure. His mind was clear, his memory was complete, his will was sincere. He didn't fear death and didn't worry about anything. Adam was strong and beautiful physically. He was greater than any other creature God made. I believe that before Adam sinned, his eyesight was so good that his vision was more powerful than that of the lynx. I believe that Adam was so strong that he could handle full-grown lions and bears as if they were cubs. I also believe that food tasted better to Adam before he sinned.** Ask kids if they agree or disagree and why.

STEP 4

By now your kids will have learned that God has emotions. But some of your kids may not know much else about God. So they might not feel comfortable when you encourage them to turn to a stranger (God) for help when they feel emotionally distraught. If you suspect that some of your kids feel this way, you may want to take time to talk about who God is and what He has done for us. You can refer to the classic *Knowing God* by J. I. Packer (InterVarsity Press), which examines the nature and character of God. Draw a few key concepts from it. Or, to explain the Gospel clearly and succinctly, read and discuss the following verses: Jeremiah 31:3; Romans 3:23; 6:23; John 3:16-17; Romans 10:9; 1 Corinthians 15:3-4; 1 John 5:11; John 10:10.

STEP 2

In large print, write down colors and associated emotions on separate sheets of paper. (For example: red/angry, blue/sad, black/depressed, yellow/happy, etc.) Post the sheets around the room. If possible, assign kids to groups based on a color they are wearing. Randomly shift kids around if some groups are larger than others. Give someone in each group a pencil and paper to record the group's response to this question: **What kinds of things have caused you to experience the emotion you have been assigned?** Also have group members come up with Scripture verses that describe people (or God) experiencing a similar emotion. Each group should present its personal stories and Bible stories to the other groups.

STEP 4

At the end of your session, give kids a chance to relax and eat together while continuing to teach them something about emotions. Set a table for them to eat at. Then tell them that you are going to provide them with a wonderful snack. Bring out a bowl of brussels sprouts, lemon wedges, or lima beans. After the protests die down, bring out the real snack—something kids will like. In a low-key way, you can talk about the difference between feeling disappointed or angry and satisfied or happy. Encourage kids to tell God about their disappointments *and* their joys.

STEP 2

As you talk about whether group members think of emotions as being either "good" or "bad," ask if they know why they answered as they did. Say: **Since emotions are just a normal part of us, does this mean we can use our emotions in either a "good" way or a "bad" way? Can you think of an example of someone using a normal emotion in an appropriate way? In an inappropriate way? Is it possible for girls to use emotions as an excuse to justify wrong behavior? If so, give some examples.**

STEP 4

After the members of the teams have been given their situations, ask them to plan a skit to demonstrate at least one positive way someone could handle that situation and one negative way to handle it. If possible, provide some materials for props. After a few minutes, have the teams present their skits.

STEP 1

If you have mostly guys in your group, you may need to loosen them up a bit so that they are more willing to talk about emotions. The skit may help you do that because it is lighthearted enough to be nonthreatening. Guys may also like it if you create a more competitive atmosphere by having auditions for the skit parts and for the privilege of making the sound effects. The more creative and expressive they are, the more likely they will be awarded a part or sound effect.

STEP 2

Some guys may feel uncomfortable answering the first question because it is personal. You might want to generalize the question in this way: **What usually causes someone's emotions to change? For instance, if someone is feeling sad, what might cause him or her to feel happy?** Here are some other situations you might want to use:

• **Your favorite baseball team just choked and lost the final play-off game.**

• **A bunch of guys are teasing you about your voice changing.**

• **It's a beautiful day outside and the church service looks like it's never going to end.**

• **It's really stormy outside and the sirens go off because a tornado (or hurricane) is moving your way.**

STEP 1

Add a fun twist to the skit by assigning the male roles to girls and the female roles to guys. Guys should try to talk in a higher voice while the girls talk in lower voices. The guy who plays the sweet young girl could pretend he has long hair that he twists around his finger when he talks. The girl who plays the stranger could talk with a tough accent and flex her muscles. Add a crazy twist to the narrator's part by having two narrators take turns reading every other word. Or add to the fun with props like a picnic basket or soup tureen, wigs, skirts for the guys, a trench coat, fake mustaches, etc.

STEP 2

Create an atmosphere in which kids feel all kinds of emotions. Pump kids up by promising unusual or outrageous prizes (if you dare), then playing a few high-energy, very competitive, challenging relays. You could promise the winning team a concert or sports outing. Or before the games begin, you could have all players sign contracts promising to personally serve the winners for a day or a week. Losers could promise to make the winners' beds, do their laundry, make meals or treats, etc. If personal weekday contact is impossible, kids could sign contracts to make a complete dinner for the winners at your next session. After the games, talk about the different emotions kids may have felt as they played (excitement, disappointment, anxiety, etc.).

STEP 1

During the week, videotape a dozen or so brief segments from TV shows or movies that show people expressing various emotions (being careful to avoid sexually explicit or gory scenes, of course). When you play the tape, have kids identify each emotion and give a thumbs-up signal if it is a healthy way to express emotion or a thumbs-down signal if it is unhealthy. Then ask: **Have you ever had a day in which you experienced several different emotions in a short period of time?**

STEP 3

Play a current secular love song about disappointment, miscommunication, conditional love, or regret. You can use the song to compare and contrast the world's concept of love with God's love as expressed in John 3:16. Or clip a review of a popular movie that represents unhealthy ways in which people deal with anger. (A good example is a scene from *Batman Returns*. In revenge, Catwoman gives her boss a deadly kiss.) Compare and contrast God's anger with human anger.

STEP 1

Combine Steps 1 and 2. Read the following scenario: **A company has just invented a button that changes color to show whatever emotion you are feeling at the time—red means you're angry, blue means your depressed, green means you're jealous, and so on. Your school just bought a bunch of the buttons and kids are required to wear them whenever they're on the school grounds.** Have group members form teams to answer these questions:

• **What would be the positive things about the emotion buttons?**
• **What would be the negative things about the emotion buttons?**
• **When would/wouldn't you want to wear the buttons?**
• **What colors would your button have been during your most recent school day?**

As you discuss the circumstances in Step 2, continue to refer to the buttons and their changing colors.

STEP 2

If you don't even have time for the button exercise described above, skip Step 1 entirely. Have kids stand up. Explain to them that they're going to get some exercise. It's a new concept called "Facial Aerobics." When you call out an emotion (or a circumstance), kids are to demonstrate that emotion with a facial expression or some other body movement. Here are some emotions you might use: fear, disgust, joy, surprise, anger, and sadness. You might also use these situations:

• **You're about to take a test you haven't studied for.**
• **You wake up and find out that school's been canceled.**
• **Your best friend just told you he or she is moving to another state.**
• **Your favorite team just won the championship.**

STEP 2

For an urban group, you might want to use the following situations:

(1) The car you borrowed has just been stolen.

(2) A home pregnancy test has shown that you (or your girlfriend) are positively pregnant.

(3) The doctor orders you to stay home for ten days because you have chicken pox. Now you can't go to the amusement park tomorrow.

(4) You just received $5,000 for turning in a wanted fugitive.

(5) The fugitive you turned in just escaped from prison.

(6) You broke a window while playing stickball.

(7) You get punched in the eye and mouth while trying to break up a fight.

STEP 3

After answering the questions associated with Numbers 32:13, mention that our anger and God's anger are often pointed in two different directions. Ours tends to involve revenge, while God's involves renewal. We take sin against us personally and try to harm. God seeks to reconcile the sinner to not do it again. Read the following anger scenarios and have teens decide how they could respond with reconciliation, not vengeance.

• **You are ticked off because someone just cursed at your mother and said degrading things about her. You're steaming. How do you respond?**

• **The $80 watch you just bought is missing. You saw it last in your locker, but overheard who stole it. How do you respond?**

STEP 1

Be sensitive to junior high kids who might feel uncomfortable acting in the skit in front of high schoolers. You could help them feel more comfortable by offering junior highers small roles (such as the mother or the noble young man) or roles that don't require any acting (such as the narrator). Or you could have junior highers serve as some of the props. For example, a high schooler could play the sweet young girl and could carry a junior higher who has the word *soup* pinned to his or her shirt. If high schoolers think the skit is beneath them, have them create skits of their own in which a person experiences as many emotions as possible in a very short time. Suggest one or more of the following scenarios: the first day of school; a kid applying to a college; a spectator at a football game; a driving instructor.

STEP 2

Give kids the opportunity to interact with someone their own age by pairing up high schoolers with high schoolers and junior highers with junior highers. Then have the partners tell each other their answer to this question: **What usually causes your emotions to change? For instance, if you're feeling sad, what might cause you to feel happy?** Tell them to come up with responses that weren't discussed earlier.

STEP 2

As you discuss the different situations, make a list on the board of the emotions named. Ask your sixth graders to describe and define the words and talk about their experiences with these emotions. Ask: **Have you experienced most or all of these emotions? How about in the last 24 hours? Can you choose which emotions you will experience? Why or why not?**

STEP 4

Instead of asking all of your sixth graders to write about four different emotions, have them tear their papers into two sections and write about two emotions. Ask one half of the group to write about an event that could cause them to be angry and about something that would make them happy. Have the others write about events that would make them sad and events that would make them scared. Collect the papers, keeping each emotion category separate, and continue the activity as described.

DATE USED:

Approx. Time

STEP 1: *Emotions on Display* _____
- ❏ Extra Action
- ❏ Small Group
- ❏ Mostly Guys
- ❏ Extra Fun
- ❏ Media
- ❏ Short Meeting Time
- ❏ Combined Junior High/High School

Things needed:

STEP 2: *Circumstances* _____
- ❏ Small Group
- ❏ Fellowship & Worship
- ❏ Mostly Girls
- ❏ Mostly Guys
- ❏ Extra Fun
- ❏ Short Meeting Time
- ❏ Urban
- ❏ Combined Junior High/High School
- ❏ Sixth Grade

Things needed:

STEP 3: *In Whose Image?* _____
- ❏ Large Group
- ❏ Heard It All Before
- ❏ Little Bible Background
- ❏ Media
- ❏ Urban

Things needed:

STEP 4: *A Time for Everything* _____
- ❏ Extra Action
- ❏ Large Group
- ❏ Heard It All Before
- ❏ Little Bible Background
- ❏ Fellowship & Worship
- ❏ Mostly Girls
- ❏ Sixth Grade

Things needed:

Sad, Glad, and Back Again

YOUR GOALS FOR THIS SESSION:
Choose one or more

☐ To help kids recognize which situations cause them to feel certain emotions.

☐ To help kids understand how God can help us with any emotion we experience.

☐ To help kids choose a promise from God's Word that will help them understand His role in their emotions.

☐ Other:_____

_____

Your Bible Base:

Psalm 31

A Lot of Hot Air

(Needed: Balloons, markers, chalkboard and chalk or newsprint and marker [optional])

Ask: **How many different emotions would you say you experience in an average day?** Encourage group members to name the different emotions they might experience. You may want to list the emotions on the board as they are named. Among the emotions that might be named are happiness, sadness, anger, disappointment, fear, anxiety, jealousy, revenge, hatred, etc.

Do you think it's normal to go through so many different emotions in one day? (Yes. Our emotions are usually our reaction to events and circumstances in our lives. As those events and circumstances change, our emotions usually change.)

Say: **Let's take a closer look at four of the most common emotions we face.**

Have group members form four teams. Distribute a balloon and several markers to each team. Assign each team one of the following emotions: happiness, sadness, anger, and disappointment. Instruct the teams to come up with a brief scenario, using the balloons, to illustrate their assigned emotions.

For instance, members of the "anger" team might inflate their balloon (without tying it), draw a scowling face on it, and then deflate it. Then they could brainstorm several different events and circumstances that could make a person angry.

When they make their presentation, they could hold up their balloon and say, "This is Bob Balloon. He's not having a very good day today. This morning his little brother ate all the Cap'n Crunch, so the only cereal left for Bob was Bran Flakes." Then someone could blow up the balloon a little to indicate Bob's anger. "On the way to school, Bob was walking too close to a mud puddle in the street when a car went by. Bob was soaked from the waist down. He didn't have time to go home and change, so he had to wear the wet clothes to school." Then someone could blow up the balloon a little more to indicate Bob's growing anger. The team could continue blowing up the balloon little by little, until it explodes.

Give the teams several minutes to work. When everyone is finished, have each team make its presentation. Lead the group in a round of applause after each presentation.

Collect the balloons after the presentations have been made, so they don't become a distraction later in the session.

Say What You Feel

(Needed: Two sheets of newsprint or poster board, markers, masking tape)

Have group members form two teams. Give each team a sheet of newsprint or poster board and several markers. Instruct the members of one team to create a sign with the following words on it: "Happy," "Wonderful," "Great," and "Awesome." They should use bright colors and cheerful designs (smiling faces, sunshine, etc.) for the sign.

Instruct the members of the other team to create a sign with the following words on it: "Terrible," "Rotten," "Difficult," and "The Worst." They should use dark colors and depressing designs (frowning faces, storm clouds, etc.) for the sign.

When the teams are finished, have them tape the signs on opposite sides of the room. Then have everyone gather in the middle of the room.

Explain: **I'm going to read a list of questions. After I read each one, I want you to go to the side of the room that best answers that question.**

For instance, I might ask, "How was your last trip to the dentist?" If your last visit to the dentist's office was happy, wonderful, great, or awesome, you would stand on that side of the room. Point to the appropriate side of the room. **If the visit was terrible, rotten, difficult, or the worst, you would stand on that side of the room.** Point to the other side of the room. **If the visit was kind of good, kind of bad, or just so-so, you'd stand somewhere in the middle of the room to show that.**

Use as many of the following questions as are appropriate for your group. You may even want to come up with some questions of your own.

- **How was your day at school today** (or **Friday**)?
- **How was your lunch today?**
- **How did you do on the last test you took at school?**
- **How was the last conversation you had with one of your parents?**

- **How is your relationship with the guy or girl you're interested in?**
- **How is your relationship with your best friend?**
- **How is your relationship with your brothers and sisters?**
- **How do you feel about life in general?**

Afterward, ask: **How much of an influence do circumstances and events have on a person's emotions?** (Circumstances and events have a direct impact on a person's emotions. If things are going well for the person, he or she is usually happy. If things aren't going well, his or her emotions usually will reflect it.)

STEP
3

Emotional Rescue

(Needed: Copies of Repro Resource 2, colored pens or markers)

Ask: **If circumstances and events have such a big influence on us, does that mean we're helpless to control our emotions? For instance, when we're sad, do we have to wait for something good to happen before we can get happy again?** Get responses from as many group members as possible.

Where can we find help for our emotions? (From God, from the Bible.)

Hold up a Bible. Ask: **Have you ever thought of this as an "emotional" book?** Get a few responses.

Point out that probably every emotion we will ever experience is addressed in the Bible—whether it's practical advice for dealing with a specific emotion ("Do not let the sun go down while you are still angry" [Eph. 4:26]) or stories about how certain Bible characters handled their emotions.

Explain: **Probably one of the most emotional books of the Bible is the Book of Psalms. Most of the Psalms were written by David, a man who was very close to God. As part of his closeness with God, David often shared his innermost emotions and feelings in his writings. From these writings, we can get an idea of how God feels about our emotions.**

Have group members form pairs. Distribute copies of "Emotions in Motion" (Repro Resource 2) and several colored pens or markers to each pair.

Instruct the pairs to read through the sheet (which is the text of Psalm 31) and circle any words that have to do with emotions. Instruct

O P T I O N S

EXTRA
ACTION

LARGE
GROUP

HEARD IT ALL
BEFORE

LITTLE
BIBLE
BACKGROUND

FELLOWSHIP &
WORSHIP

MOSTLY
GIRLS

SIXTH
GRADE

the pairs to use different colors to indicate different kinds of emotions. For instance, they might use yellow to indicate happy or joyful emotions; they might use blue to indicate depressed or sad emotions; they might use green to indicate jealous or envious emotions; they might use purple to indicate hateful emotions; they might use red to indicate angry emotions; etc.

Give the pairs several minutes to work. When they're finished, go through Repro Resource 2 as a group. Have volunteers take turns reading Psalm 31 aloud. As a volunteer reads each verse, the other group members will call out any emotion words they circled in that verse, and explain what color they used and why.

Among the words that might be circled are "shame" (vs. 1), "hate" (vs. 6), "glad and rejoice" (vs. 7), "anguish" (vs. 7), "distress" (vs. 9), "sorrow" (vs. 9), "grief" (vs. 9), "anguish" (vs. 10), and "shame" (vs. 17). In addition, verses 11-13 seem to address emotions like worthlessness and fear.

Why do you think David shared his emotions with God? (Perhaps it made him feel better to know that God knew what he was feeling. Perhaps he wanted God's help in dealing with his emotions.)

What phrases in Psalm 31 describe the kind of comfort David was looking for from God during David's time of emotional distress? ("In you, O Lord, I have taken refuge," "let me never be put to shame," "deliver me in your righteousness" [vs. 1]; "turn your ear to me," "come quickly to my rescue" [vs. 2]; "lead and guide me" [vs. 3]; "Be merciful to me, O Lord, for I am in distress" [vs. 9]; "let me not be put to shame" [vs. 17].)

Do you think God answered David's requests? (By the number of praises in David's psalms and the thankful tone of his writing, it's probably safe to say that God answered David's requests.)

If you were feeling angry or sad or even happy, do you think sharing your emotions with God would help you feel any better? Explain your answer. Encourage group members to respond honestly.

STEP 4

Help from a Friend

(Needed: Different-colored balloons, strings, slips of paper, pencils, tape, copies of Repro Resource 2)

OPTIONS

EXTRA ACTION

HEARD IT ALL BEFORE

LITTLE BIBLE BACKGROUND

FELLOWSHIP & WORSHIP

MOSTLY GIRLS

MOSTLY GUYS

EXTRA FUN

MEDIA

SHORT MEETING TIME

URBAN

SIXTH GRADE

Say: **Just like David, we can find comfort and help from God when our emotions get the better of us. In fact, we can probably find that comfort and help in David's writings.**

Set out several different-colored balloons, pieces of string, slips of paper, and pencils. Instruct each group member to choose a balloon whose color represents an emotion he or she would like to take to God. For instance, if someone wanted God's help for sadness or depression, he or she might choose a blue balloon; if someone wanted God's help for anger, he or she might choose a red balloon; etc.

After a group member has chosen a balloon, he or she should blow it up and tie a piece of string to it. Then he or she should look through Repro Resource 2 and find a verse or statement that could provide comfort or help for dealing with his or her chosen emotion. (For instance, verse 9 might be a good prayer for someone who is sad or depressed. Verse 22 might be a helpful reminder for someone who is scared or lonely. And verse 7 could be a source of comfort for practically any troubling emotion.)

Have each group member write his or her verse on a slip of paper and then tape the paper to the balloon string.

Encourage group members to take their balloons home as reminders of God's willingness to help us with our emotions. Then, whenever they feel overwhelmed by their emotions, they can look at the verse they wrote down for comfort.

Close the session in prayer, thanking God for comforting us and helping us with our emotions.

EMOTIONS IN MOTION

PSALM 31

1 In you, O Lord, I have taken refuge; let me never be put to shame; deliver me in your righteousness.

2 Turn your ear to me, come quickly to my rescue; be my rock of refuge, a strong fortress to save me.

3 Since you are my rock and my fortress, for the sake of your name lead and guide me.

4 Free me from the trap that is set for me, for you are my refuge.

5 Into your hands I commit my spirit; redeem me, O Lord, the God of truth.

6 I hate those who cling to worthless idols; I trust in the Lord.

7 I will be glad and rejoice in your love, for you saw my affliction and knew the anguish of my soul.

8 You have not handed me over to the enemy but have set my feet in a spacious place.

9 Be merciful to me, O Lord, for I am in distress; my eyes grow weak with sorrow, my soul and my body with grief.

10 My life is consumed by anguish and my years by groaning; my strength fails because of my affliction, and my bones grow weak.

11 Because of all my enemies, I am the utter contempt of my neighbors; I am a dread to my friends—those who see me on the street flee from me.

12 I am forgotten by them as though I were dead; I have become like broken pottery.

13 For I hear the slander of many; there is terror on every side; they conspire against me and plot to take my life.

14 But I trust in you, O Lord; I say, "You are my God."

15 My times are in your hands; deliver me from my enemies and from those who pursue me.

16 Let your face shine on your servant; save me in your unfailing love.

17 Let me not be put to shame, O Lord, for I have cried out to you; but let the wicked be put to shame and lie silent in the grave.

18 Let their lying lips be silenced, for with pride and contempt they speak arrogantly against the righteous.

19 How great is your goodness, which you have stored up for those who fear you, which you bestow in the sight of men on those who take refuge in you.

20 In the shelter of your presence you hide them from the intrigues of men; in your dwelling you keep them safe from accusing tongues.

21 Praise be to the Lord, for he showed his wonderful love to me when I was in a besieged city.

22 In my alarm I said, "I am cut off from your sight!" Yet you heard my cry for mercy when I called to you for help.

23 Love the Lord, all his saints! The Lord preserves the faithful, but the proud he pays back in full.

24 Be strong and take heart, all you who hope in the Lord.

NOTES

EXTRA ACTION

Step 3

Instead of having pairs of kids circle emotional words on "Emotions in Motion" (Repro Resource 2), have teams of three or more kids do something a little different with it. Assign each team three to five verses from the sheet. Have the members of each team present their verses by standing up and linking arms. As a volunteer from the team reads the verses aloud, the rest of the team should demonstrate each emotion with their faces or with gestures (arms still linked). They should say the word aloud and softly until another emotional word is read. For example, team members assigned the first group of verses might hang their heads and softly say, "Shame, shame, shame . . ."

Step 4

Distribute a balloon, a long piece of string, a slip of paper, and a pencil to each group member. Instruct each group member to write an emotion on his or her slip of paper and then insert the slip into the deflated balloon. Then have each kid blow up his or her balloon, tie one end of the string to the balloon, and tie the other end of the string to his or her ankle. Have a contest in which kids try to pop each other's balloons by stepping on them. If a person pops someone else's balloon, he or she collects the slip of paper that was inside. The object of the game is for group members to get as many different emotions as possible. Afterward, briefly discuss the various emotions that were written on the slips. Then go through Step 4 as written.

SMALL GROUP

Step 1

Depending on how small your group is, you might want to have kids work in pairs instead of teams to come up with the balloon scenarios. Or you might have only two teams each address an emotion. If you use only two teams, make sure you assign one of them "happiness," so that there's a balance between a positive emotion and a negative one.

Step 2

Instead of having two teams create colorful signs that might take a lot of teamwork and artwork, give each group member three index cards. On one card, group members should write "happy," "wonderful," "great," or "awesome." On the second card, they should write "so-so" or "OK." On the third card, they should write "terrible," "rotten," "difficult," or "the worst." Then, instead of having kids move from one side of the room to the other in response to the questions you ask, they can hold up their individual cards to show how they feel.

LARGE GROUP

Step 1

Set up two "emotion stations" in the room. You'll need a table, a chair, several rolls of tape, and a box at each station. Fill one box with slips of paper on which you've written instructions (one per slip) that will make kids happy. (For example: "Get a dollar from your leader." "Get a free soda on our next outing." "Get two compliments from your leader.") Fill the box at the other station with instructions that will irritate kids. (For example: "Give a quarter to your leader." "Keep your hands on your knees for the next five minutes.") Ask for one or two volunteers to work at each station. Divide the other kids into two teams; assign each team to one of the stations. Instruct kids to draw a slip from the box, read it, tape it to their shirts, and do what it says (if applicable). The station leader should initial the papers as kids follow through on them. Afterward, talk about how happy or irritated groups members felt about their instruction. Then introduce the topic of emotions.

Step 3

Get kids to open up about the emotions they feel by creating teams. Give a bowl filled with nuts or small candies to each team. Say: **David felt a lot of different emotions, and so do we. But we don't always get to talk about our feelings. Take as many pieces of candy as you want. But you will have to talk about one emotion you felt this week for every piece you take.**

STEP 3

Kids who have spent a lot of time in church may have heard plenty of statements like these: "God knows how you feel." "He can help you when you are upset." "A lot of people in the Bible expressed their emotions to God." Grab the attention of your skeptics and make this session even more relevant to them by challenging them with this simulation: **The year is 2141. You have just been appointed the leader of a country that is in terrible trouble. No one in this country has talked about his or her emotions for decades. No one has said "I'm angry," "I'm sad," or "I'm happy" for 30 years. Some people are starting to feel as if they are going to explode because they have bottled up their feelings for so long; others are too depressed to even think about exploding. As the new leader, you are called upon to solve this problem. What do you do and why?**

STEP 4

Jaded kids may not have thought seriously about why it's important to seek God's help in dealing with their emotions. Present two extreme ways of mishandling emotions and have kids list their consequences. The first extreme is keeping emotions bottled up. Instead of asking kids how to solve this problem, have them identify and discuss the consequences of living this way. The second extreme is expressing emotions without restraint. What if everyone who was angry screamed all of the time at the top of his or her lungs? What if everyone who was happy was sickeningly joyful for brief periods? What if people felt so much hate that there was no room for any other emotion? Some of the consequences of out-of-control emotions are exhaustion, depression, or even violence. Discuss what life would be like if all people were overly emotional. Then talk about how to strike the right balance.

STEP 3

Give a little more background on David. Help kids understand that he experienced all kinds of wonderful and terrible things throughout his life that resulted in feelings of great joy, sorrow, fear, and worry. Read or briefly describe highlights of his life, such as these: I Samuel 16:1, 13 (David is anointed king); I Samuel 18:6-11 (Saul tries to murder David); 20:16, 41-42 (Jonathan and David's friendship); 27:1 (David is afraid of being murdered); 2 Samuel 1:11-12 (David mourns Jonathan); 7:8-9 (God promises David great things); 11:1-5 and 12:15-22 (David commits adultery); 19:1-4 (David mourns Absalom).

STEP 4

Some kids may not understand how God's Word—particularly the Psalms—can be a source of comfort and help to them. Reassure them that these ancient thoughts and feelings do apply to their lives today. Have them highlight the following phrases from "Emotions in Motion" (Repro Resource 2). Rephrase each statement in contemporary terms in the form of a question. For example, have kids highlight "put to shame." Then ask: **Have you ever seen someone humiliated? What happened? What does it feel like to be humiliated?** You can have kids highlight these phrases or others that you think apply to their lives: "free me from the trap that is set for me" (Ps. 31:4); "I will be glad and rejoice in your love" (vs. 7); "I am in distress . . . sorrow . . . grief" (vs. 9); "I am the utter contempt of my neighbors . . . a dread to my friends" (vs. 11); "I hear the slander of many" (vs. 13); "they conspire against me" (vs. 13); "I was in a besieged city" (vs. 21).

STEP 3

After kids examine Psalm 31, have them stand in a circle, hold hands, and close their eyes. Ask each kid to use one word to identify one emotion that he or she felt during the past week. Have kids say their words in order around the circle. Ask a few volunteers to explain what events caused their emotions.

STEP 4

Have kids pair up. Instruct them to choose an encouraging verse from "Emotions in Motion" (Repro Resource 2) or any passage in the Bible to write out and present to their partners. Then have the partners pray for each other, thanking God for being available to comfort and help us with our emotions. Before they pray, they might ask their partner for specific prayer requests concerning struggles the partner may be having in the area of emotions. Challenge kids to pray for their partners during the week.

STEP 3

After completing "Emotions in Motion" (Repro Resource 2), ask your group members to respond to the following statement: **Many people say that girls are more emotional than guys, so how could David write a psalm like this one?** You might also ask your group members to comment on the statements listed in the "Mostly Guys" option for Step 4, adding one final question:

(6) If guys had to deal with PMS and other woman-stuff, they'd be more emotional.

STEP 4

Talk about Psalm 31:1 and God's power to keep us from "being put to shame" or embarrassed. Ask: **What are some ways our changing emotions can embarrass us? How do you handle embarrassing situations? What could you do to help you remember to pray for God's help when you need more self-control with your emotions?**

STEP 2

Guys will probably enjoy an opportunity to move around the room. They might also enjoy an added challenge. After group members move to the appropriate part of the room in response to each question, let one volunteer challenge someone else who is standing nearby. He should say something like this: "I think that my lunch today was better (or worse) than yours." Then the two have to describe their lunches. The rest of the group will decide whose lunch was better (or worse).

STEP 4

If you're not sure how the balloon activity will go over with your group, give a short true-false test.

(1) Real men don't cry.

(2) Guys aren't as emotional as girls.

(3) It's not cool to show too much emotion.

(4) If you're angry, it's better to explode and get it off your chest than to let it eat you up inside.

(5) It's hard for most guys to talk about their emotions.

After giving the test, discuss each answer in more detail. Ask: **How do you think David would have answered this question? Why?**

STEP 1

Before the session begins, have a "Roller Coaster of Emotions" contest. Invite daring volunteers to sign up for these contests: Screaming Meemies, Laugh 'Til You're Sick, and Real Tears. You might want to limit the sign-ups to three people per contest. Announce the contests like a game show host. **Do you scream well? Well enough to make someone's blood curdle? Then here's your chance to sign up for the Screaming Meemies contest. The winner will receive a fantastic, wonderful, amazing, fabulous, incredible candy bar.** Figure out how to decide on the winners. Award small prizes in categories like the most unusual scream (not necessarily the loudest), the funniest laugh, and the most convincing tears. Then move on to the rest of Step 1 as it's written.

STEP 4

Balloons are always more fun when they're filled with helium. Rent a helium tank from a party shop and let kids take home helium-filled balloons (with Scripture verses taped to the balloon string). You may also want to buy higher quality balloons that will last a while and festive ribbon instead of string. Or buy balloons in unusual colors or with encouraging messages preprinted on them. You may also want to buy more than one balloon for each kid.

STEP 1

Create a powerful presentation by video-taping the expression of a series of opposite emotions back-to-back. Scan your television guide for programs that might be good sources. Or get ideas from your own video library or a friend's. For example, tape a scene of a joyful, frenzied audience at a rock concert followed by a scene of a single, weeping person. Or tape a news story that shows an angry, screaming mob followed by a scene in which a mother is gently singing to her baby. Or show a scene in which someone is screaming at his or her spouse followed by a scene of a big brother gently pushing a little brother in a swing. Or show a war scene followed by a comedy routine. Use this video to kick off the session. Have kids identify the emotions they saw. Then move into Step 1.

STEP 4

Close the session in a lighthearted way. Bring in a supermarket tabloid and have kids react as you read some of the headlines aloud. Read through a couple of the stories that most interest kids. Skip the questionable stuff. Talk about the emotions that kids felt as they listened to the headlines.

STEP 1

If you are short on time, skip the balloon activity in Step 1. Just ask the first two questions from Step 1; then go right into Step 2. This way, kids won't miss the brief review of the last session, which is brought out in Step 1. And Step 2 is lighthearted enough to give them time to warm up to the idea of discussing "emotions."

STEP 4

If you are short on time, don't skip reading Psalm 31 aloud during Step 3. It will be good for kids to read Scripture together as a group after they've worked on it in pairs. Instead, you can save time in Step 4 by having the balloons already blown up with strings attached. Then all kids have to do is find an appropriate verse, write it down, and tape it to the balloon.

STEP 1

Use the following option to illustrate how we should control our emotions. Blow up two balloons. On one of the balloons, tape an "X" with two pieces of transparent tape. Stick a pin in the untaped balloon. Of course, it will pop. Then, with the taped balloon, stick the pin *straight* into the crossed section of the tape and through the balloon's skin. If the tape is firm, with no air bubbles, the balloon will not pop. (Have other balloons ready just in case!) Let group members observe that it isn't a trick. Then pull the pin out *slowly* and watch the balloon. The air will slowly leak out of the balloon. Afterward, draw parallels, helping kids recognize that the force (emotion) pent up in the balloon (us), when protected by the tape (Holy Spirit), is able to be released in a calm and directed manner (self-control).

STEP 4

Distribute one balloon and a slip of paper to each group member. Instruct kids to write down some specific steps they could take toward resolving one emotional issue. The steps should be practical enough that they could be accomplished in the next few days. Then have each kid fold his or her paper, stuff it into the balloon, blow up the balloon, and tie it tight. Say: **Before this balloon deflates, you must keep your promise and take the steps toward resolving your emotional issue.**

STEP 1

As much as possible, try to have a balanced mix of junior highers and high schoolers on the teams. High schoolers will probably be a little more comfortable with this activity because it requires more creativity and an ability to translate emotions into an unusual object lesson. Working alongside high schoolers should help junior highers feel more comfortable during the brainstorming and presentation of the stories.

STEP 2

If your junior highers tend to hold back to see what your high schoolers do, you'll need to handle the regular activity differently. Instead of having kids move from one side of the room to the other to answer questions, pair them up with someone their own age. Then they can privately share their responses to your questions with their partner. They can go into more detail by talking, rather than only moving around the room. And they may feel freer to talk about their struggles, rather than trying to appear positive to a roomful of people.

STEP 3

Have your sixth graders work in teams of three or four on "Emotions in Motion" (Repro Resource 2). As they are marking the different kinds of emotions, ask the teams also to choose one of the emotions to describe to the rest of the group and tell of a time when that emotion might be present. Ask: **What are some other ways, besides writing a psalm, that we can express our emotions to God?**

STEP 4

If some of your sixth graders aren't sure which emotion they want God's help with, suggest that they write down Psalm 31:14. Talk about why God is worthy of our trust and how His unchanging character and unconditional love is a good example to follow, especially when our emotions are unpredictable. Ask some of the following questions to wrap up the session:

• **As you get older, is it getting easier or harder to handle your emotions? Why?**

• **At what age do you think people are best able to handle their emotions? Why?**

• **Some people say the teen years are an emotional roller coaster. From what you've seen so far, do you think they're right?**

• **What fears do you have about being a teenager?**

DATE USED:

Approx. Time

STEP 1: *A Lot of Hot Air* _____
- ❏ Small Group
- ❏ Large Group
- ❏ Extra Fun
- ❏ Media
- ❏ Short Meeting Time
- ❏ Urban
- ❏ Combined Junior High/High School

Things needed:

STEP 2: *Say What You Feel* _____
- ❏ Small Group
- ❏ Mostly Guys
- ❏ Combined Junior High/High School

Things needed:

STEP 3: *Emotional Rescue* _____
- ❏ Extra Action
- ❏ Large Group
- ❏ Heard It All Before
- ❏ Little Bible Background
- ❏ Fellowship & Worship
- ❏ Mostly Girls
- ❏ Sixth Grade

Things needed:

STEP 4: *Help from a Friend* _____
- ❏ Extra Action
- ❏ Heard It All Before
- ❏ Little Bible Background
- ❏ Fellowship & Worship
- ❏ Mostly Girls
- ❏ Mostly Guys
- ❏ Extra Fun
- ❏ Media
- ❏ Short Meeting Time
- ❏ Urban
- ❏ Sixth Grade

Things needed:

SESSION 3

What to Do with Anger

YOUR GOALS FOR THIS SESSION:
Choose one or more

☐ To help kids discover that anger is not necessarily a negative emotion.

☐ To help kids understand that there are God-honoring ways to express anger and sinful ways to express anger.

☐ To help kids choose healthy, God-honoring ways to deal with their anger.

☐ Other:_____
_____

Your Bible Base:

Matthew 18:15-17
Ephesians 4:26-30

Sticky Emotions

(Needed: Name tags with different emotions written on them)

Before the session, you'll need to prepare several name tags (one for each group member) by writing a different emotion on each one. Among the emotions you might use are happiness, sadness, anger, fear, jealousy, disappointment, hatred, and revenge. If you have a large group, it's OK to use an emotion more than once.

As group members arrive, stick a name tag on the back of each person. Make sure group members can't see what's written on their name tags.

Say: **Each of you is wearing a name tag with a specific emotion written on it. Your job is to find out what your emotion is. To do this, you'll have to pay attention to the way the other people in the group talk to you.**

Explain that when you give the signal, everyone will "mingle" for a few minutes. However, as kids mingle, they must communicate with each other only in ways that illustrate the emotions on each other's name tags. For instance, if you saw someone with a "jealousy" name tag, you might walk up and say, "I wish *I* had that shirt you're wearing. You *always* get all of the nicest clothes." Or if you saw someone with a "revenge" name tag, you might walk up and say, "I'll get you back for what you did to me if it's the last thing I ever do!"

Encourage group members to keep their comments to each other brief—perhaps one or two sentences—and not to be so obvious that the other person figures out his or her emotion right away. If you want to make it more challenging, don't allow any talking. Kids should only communicate nonverbally. After a person guesses his or her emotion, he or she may remove the name tag. Continue until everyone has guessed his or her emotion.

Afterward, say: **We've got a lot of different emotions represented here on these name tags. But today we're going to focus on one in particular—anger.**

Have those group members whose name tag said "anger" come to the front of the room for a brief contest. You may also want to ask for a couple of other volunteers to compete. The object of the game is to see who can pretend to be angriest. Each contestant will have 15 seconds to demonstrate anger through facial expressions, tone of voice, body language, etc. (You may want to emphasize that contestants may not use swearing or personal verbal attacks in their "performances.")

After all of the contestants have performed, vote as a group on which one was the angriest. Then bestow on that person the title "King/Queen of Anger."

A Different Look at Anger

(Needed: Copies of Repro Resource 3, pencils)

Have group members form pairs. Distribute copies of "Abstract Anger" (Repro Resource 3) and pencils to each pair.

Explain: **Use your imagination to answer these questions about anger. Of course, there are no right or wrong answers. We just want to see what kinds of things you associate with anger.**

Give the pairs a few minutes to work. When everyone is finished, go through the questions one at a time and have each pair share its response.

Use the following responses to supplement the pairs' answers.

(1) *If anger were a color, what color would it be?* (Red or hot pink.)

(2) *If anger were a car, what kind of car would it be?*
(A black hot rod with flames painted on the sides.)

(3) *If anger were a shoe, what kind of shoe would it be?*
(A motorcycle boot with spurs on it.)

(4) *If anger were a song, what song would it be?*
(A heavy metal song with lyrics about death and destruction.)

(5) *If anger were a dog, what kind of dog would it be?* (A pit bull.)

(6) *If anger were a sound, what sound would it be?*
(An exploding firecracker.)

(7) *If anger were an odor, what odor would it be?* (Burning rubber.)

(8) *If anger were a food, what food would it be?* (Jalapeño peppers.)

(9) *If anger were a liquid, what liquid would it be?*
(Hot lava spewing from a volcano.)

(10) *If anger were weather, what kind of weather would it be?*
(A lightning storm.)

Afterward, say: **True or false: Anger is a bad emotion.**
Get responses from as many group members as possible.

OPTIONS

LARGE GROUP

HEARD IT ALL BEFORE

LITTLE BIBLE BACKGROUND

MOSTLY GUYS

EXTRA FUN

MEDIA

JR. HIGH / HIGH SCHOOL COMBINED

Have someone read aloud the first six words of Ephesians 4:26 ("In your anger do not sin").

Ask: **If anger were a bad emotion, what would this verse have said?** (Do not get angry.)

Explain: **Ephesians 4:26 tells us not to sin in our anger. That means it's possible to be angry without sinning. So anger is not necessarily a bad emotion. How you** *express* **your anger determines whether it's good or bad.**

STEP 3

Anger in Action

(Needed: Copies of Repro Resource 4, Bibles)

Distribute copies of "Anger: Up Close and Personal" (Repro Resource 4). Explain: **Here are two anger-causing situations. Let's take a look at them and see if we can come up with some positive and some negative ways to respond to them.**

Give group members a minute or two to read the first situation. Then say: **I'm going to read a list of possible responses to this situation. If you think a response is positive, give me a thumbs-up sign. If you think a response is negative, give me a thumbs-down sign. If you're not sure, shrug your shoulders.**

The possible responses are as follows:
- Spread a rumor that Sara cheated on the math test, but was so dumb she still only got a "C–."
- Spray-paint "LIAR" in big letters on the side of Sara's house.
- Tell Richard, the guy Sara's madly in love with, about the time Sara threw up in the middle of McDonald's.
- Trip Sara as she's walking down the hall.
- Don't ever mention the incident to Sara; just deal with it privately.

If no one mentions it, point out that all five responses are negative. The first four are based on revenge. Anger becomes sin when it causes you to do things to "get even" with someone else. The fifth response involves suppressing anger. When anger is not dealt with properly, it can cause some serious problems later.

Have someone read aloud Matthew 18:15-17. Then ask: **According to this passage, what is the first thing you should do when someone makes you angry or hurts you?** (Go and talk to the person one-on-one. Explain to the person how you feel and why you're so angry or upset.)

OPTIONS

EXTRA ACTION

HEARD IT ALL BEFORE

LITTLE BIBLE BACKGROUND

FELLOWSHIP & WORSHIP

MOSTLY GIRLS

MOSTLY GUYS

MEDIA

SHORT MEETING TIME

URBAN

SIXTH GRADE

What might happen if Mary talked to Sara one-on-one about how she's feeling? (Sara might realize how much she hurt Mary, apologize, and admit her lie to Mr. Reed and the other kids in the math class. Sara might also explain to Mary why she did what she did. She might have had some resentment toward Mary that had been growing for some time. In a one-on-one setting, the two of them might be able to work things out. It's possible that Sara won't apologize, but at least Mary took the initiative to make things right.)

Give group members a minute or two to read the second situation on Repro Resource 4. Then ask: **Do you think Jason has a right to be angry in this situation?** (Yes. He was falsely accused and punished for something he didn't do.)

Put yourself in Jason's position. Let's say your mother, after she realized her mistake, came to you crying and apologizing for what she did. What would be some negative ways you might respond to the situation? (Yell at your mother for ruining your weekend; refuse to speak to her for several days; keep reminding her of the incident to make her feel bad; demand that she do special things for you to make up for her mistake; etc.)

Have someone read aloud Ephesians 4:26-30. Then ask: **According to this passage, what should we *not* do when someone makes us angry?** (Allow our anger to last more than a day without resolving it; give the devil a chance to take advantage of our anger; talk "unwholesomely" about the person who made us angry.)

Based on this passage, what should Jason do with his anger toward his mother? (Talk to her about how angry he is; resolve the situation before he goes to bed that night; avoid yelling or being sarcastic to his mother when he talks to her; etc.)

How could the devil get a "foothold" in this situation? What might happen if he did? (If Jason decided to sulk and stay mad at his mother for several days, the devil could cause Jason to doubt whether his mother really cares about him. That might lead to a *serious* relationship problem between Jason and his mother.)

Dealing with Anger

(Needed: Balloons, straight pin)

Quickly blow up a balloon and hold it by the nozzle. Explain: **There are several different ways to deal with anger. One way is to throw a fit or go into a rage.** Let go of the balloon's nozzle, and send the balloon flying through the air.

Blow up another balloon and hold it by the nozzle. Say: **Another way to deal with anger is to gripe or complain to others.** Pinch the nozzle as you let the air out of the balloon, so that the escaping air makes a squealing noise.

Blow up the balloon and tie a knot in it. Say: **Another way to deal with anger is to hold it in.**

And another way to deal with anger is to explode. Quickly pop the balloon with a pin.

But none of these ways is really helpful. In fact, these methods might cause your anger to turn into sin.

Refer your group members back to Matthew 18:15-17 and Ephesians 4:26-30. Explain: **God tells us that when we're angry with someone, we should go to that person as quickly as possible and talk with him or her one-on-one. We should tell that person exactly how we feel—without using "unwholesome" talk—and work to straighten out the situation. I know it's harder than it sounds, especially when we're angry. But we have God's Word on it that it's the best way to deal with our anger.**

Blow up another balloon. Say: **A minute ago we looked at some negative ways to deal with anger. A more constructive way is to keep your cool, but take whatever steps are necessary to deal with it.** Slowly let the air out, while keeping control of the balloon.

Instruct group members to think of someone they're angry with now or have been angry with recently. Have them consider how they can use the principles in Matthew 18 and Ephesians 4 to resolve the situation. If time permits, ask for a couple of volunteers to share what they plan to do.

Close the session in prayer, asking God to help your group members resolve their anger in ways that are pleasing to Him.

As group members leave, distribute uninflated balloons to help remind them not to deal with their anger in negative ways.

NOTES

Abstract Anger

1. If anger were a color, what color would it be?

2. If anger were a car, what kind of car would it be?

3. If anger were a shoe, what kind of shoe would it be?

4. If anger were a song, what song would it be?

5. If anger were a dog, what kind of dog would it be?

6. If anger were a sound, what sound would it be?

7. If anger were an odor, what odor would it be?

8. If anger were a food, what food would it be?

9. If anger were a liquid, what liquid would it be?

10. If anger were weather, what kind of weather would it be?

Anger: Up Close and Personal

Situation #1

Sara and Mary *used* to be good friends. They played on the junior high tennis team together; they were counselors at summer camp together; and they often studied together. In fact, last week Mary stayed at Sara's house for the entire weekend so the two of them could study for Monday's big math test. (It counted as one-third of the final semester grade.)

On Wednesday, Mr. Reed handed back the tests. Mary got an "A-"; Sara got a "C-." Mary was excited that she'd done so well, but she felt bad for Sara. She tried to talk to Sara after class, but Sara didn't seem to want to talk.

The next day in the cafeteria, Mary overheard a couple of guys from her math class talking about her.

"I always thought she was real straightlaced. I never thought she'd do something like that," one of them said.

"It was probably just an act," another one said. "She knew no one would suspect her, so she could get away with it."

Mary was confused. She couldn't figure out what they were talking about. A few minutes later, Mary ran into Sara and a couple of other girls in the hall. She told them about what she'd heard in the cafeteria.

"Oh, quit pretending, Mary," Sara said disgustedly. "You know you cheated on the math test. So I made sure that everyone else knows—including Mr. Reed. If I were you, I wouldn't get too excited about that 'A-'—if you know what I mean."

Sara and her friends laughed as they walked away. Mary couldn't believe it. Sara was telling people that Mary had cheated on the math test, when she knew it wasn't true. Some friend! Sara was spreading lies about Mary, and those lies were about to get Mary in trouble!

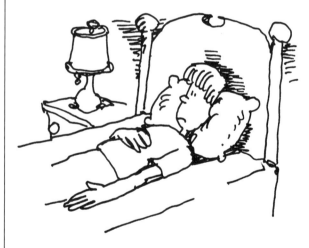

Situation #2

On Thursday morning, Jason's mother discovered five dollars missing from her purse. When Jason's brother, Matt, came home from school for lunch, his mother asked him if he knew anything about the missing money.

"No," Matt said, "but I saw Jason in your room this morning. Maybe he knows something about it."

When Jason got home from school that afternoon, his mother cornered him in the living room.

"Were you in my purse this morning?" she demanded.

"No, I don't think so," Jason said slowly, trying to remember.

"Your brother said he saw you in my room this morning. What were you doing there?" his mother asked.

"Oh, yeah, that's right!" Jason said, suddenly remembering. "I was looking for a pen for school."

"And you just happened to find five dollars instead, right?" his mother added.

"I didn't take any money, Mom," Jason said.

"Don't make things worse by lying!" his mom warned. "You're grounded to your room for the weekend."

"But, Mom, I—" he started.

"Do you want me to make it two weekends?" she threatened.

Jason stopped arguing and went to his room. Over the weekend, he missed his park-district baseball game, going to see the Cubs with one of his friends, and his favorite TV show. It was one of the longest weekends of Jason's life.

Monday morning, as Jason's mom was getting ready for work, she reached for her new pair of earrings. Suddenly she remembered that she'd used the five dollars in her purse to buy the earrings.

STEP 1

Instead of having only a few kids partici-pate in the "show anger" contest, have everyone take part. Bring an instant cam-era and enough film to take two pictures of each group member pretending to be angry. Let kids take home one of their own pictures to remind them of the ses-sion. Provide poster board or newsprint, markers, tape or glue, scissors, etc., so the kids can create a huge poster about anger. Include the remaining photos on the poster. Display the poster for a couple of weeks.

STEP 3

As you describe the five ways Mary might respond in anger to Sara, list the responses on the board. Also list the responses kids come up with for Situation 2. Then have two volunteers roleplay an ending for Situation 1. They can get an idea of possible responses from the list on the board. Tell them to keep acting until you say **Freeze!** (Give them about 15-30 seconds.) Then let the actors choose replacements to roleplay a different ending to the skit. Say **Freeze!** again, and so on. Let several kids do this with Situation 2 also. Then have a couple of kids read Matthew 18:15-17 and Ephesians 4:26-30 aloud. Discuss the principles these verses teach on handling our anger. Have more volunteers act out endings to both situations based on these scriptural guidelines.

STEP 1

If you don't have enough kids to make the name-tag game fun, you may want to use another idea to loosen kids up at the beginning of the session. Pass around a 12-inch ruler, a pair of scissors, and a ball of string. Have each person cut off a foot-long section of string. One at a time, kids should wrap the string around their index finger. With each wrap, they should "fess up" about a time when they lost their temper.

STEP 4

Have kids debate whether they would be able to control their anger for the rest of their lives if they were paid $1,000,000 to do it. Let them define limitations for themselves. Would they never be allowed to glare, yell, scream, swear, etc? Or would it be OK to glare? What if they had to pay back the money if they even just felt angry inside? (A microchip slipped under their skin would alert the authorities to angry feelings.) Find out how much group members picked up in this session by asking them to write down the reference to one of the session's Bible passages on anger. Also have them write down one way in which God wants them to deal with their anger.

STEP 2

Have the group create a huge mural to fill a wall in the room. Base the mural on the comparisons they came up with. ("If anger were a _____, what would it be?") Provide poster board or newsprint, mark-ers, scissors, magazines, etc. for the project.

STEP 4

The object lesson with balloons will be more effective in a large group if you get the kids involved. If it won't break your budget, give each kid a balloon. It's best if the balloons are all the same size. Have kids perform the following activities in groups of eight to 10.

• When demonstrating fits of rage, have each kid blow up his or her balloon, stand behind a certain line, and let the balloon go. The balloon that goes farthest wins.

• When demonstrating griping or com-plaining, see which kid can make the longest continuous noise by pinching his or her balloon nozzle and letting the air out.

• When demonstrating holding anger in, have each kid tie his or her balloon in a knot. He or she should then kick the balloon, alternating feet (left foot, right foot, left foot, etc.). See who can keep his or her balloon off the floor the longest. Throw in some more difficult actions like off the head, backward kick, or kicking with both feet while lying on the floor.

• When demonstrating exploding, have a group countdown, starting at 10. When you say **Blast-off!** have the kids pop their balloons at the very same moment.

• After reviewing the Scripture passages, give each kid one more balloon to blow up. He or she should then slowly let the air out of the balloon. The person can then take this balloon home as a reminder of how to deal with anger constructively.

STEP 2

Even kids who think they've heard it all before may discover something new about themselves as a result of the following activity. Prepare and copy a list of general situations that could evoke anger. Give each kid a copy. Have kids check off the situations that have made them angry in the past. They might be shocked at how many they check off. Here are some examples: being teased by a brother or sister, having to do a chore, being punished, stubbing a toe, getting a poor grade, missing the bus, waiting for someone who is late, etc. Have kids place a star next to the items that have angered them more than once. Then have them circle one item that upsets them the most. After a few minutes, have them share their responses.

STEP 3

If some kids think that anger is no big deal, skip Repro Resource 4. Instead, read the following excerpt from *Gifted Hands* by Dr. Ben Carson, a Christian pediatric surgeon. **"I was in the ninth grade when the unthinkable happened. I lost control and tried to knife a friend. [They were arguing about what radio station to listen to.] In that instant blind anger—pathological anger—took possession of me. Grabbing the camping knife I carried in my back pocket, I snapped it open and lunged for the boy who had been my friend. With all the power of my young muscles, I thrust the knife toward his belly."** Fortunately, the knife hit his friend's big, heavy buckle, saving his life. Carson could not believe that he almost killed his friend. Generally, Carson was pretty patient, but once he got angry, he would go crazy. After this incident, Carson asked God to take control of his temper. He has learned to appropriately express his anger, despite all kinds of stress in his life. Ask: **Do you know anyone who might be capable of this kind of rage? Have you ever felt that you might go out of control with anger?**

STEP 2

Point out that God gets angry too. Ask volunteers to read the following passages as you take a look at various facets of God's anger: Psalm 2:12; 30:5; 78:38; Numbers 14:18; Deuteronomy 29:26-28. Then ask: **How do these passages describe God's anger? What makes God angry? How is our anger like or unlike God's?**

STEP 3

If kids can't figure out what some of the phrases in Matthew 18:15-17 and Ephesians 4:26-30 mean, offer the following explanations.

• "Treat him as you would a pagan or a tax collector"—Jews did not think very highly of pagans (Gentiles) or tax collectors, even though both kinds of people were being saved and were shown compassion by Jesus.

• "Do not give the devil a foothold"—When we don't deal with our anger properly, Satan can use it to create bigger problems.

• "Unwholesome talk"—Hurtful comments, as opposed to encouraging words.

• "Do not grieve the Holy Spirit of God"—When Christians sin, the Holy Spirit who lives in us is saddened. Sin interferes with His purpose in our lives, which is to set us apart for God.

• "Sealed for the day of redemption"— This gives us hope to "hang in there" with God until the day that He has chosen to come for us.

STEP 3

Instead of using Repro Resource 4, invite a visitor (preferably someone from your church that your kids know) to explain his or her struggle with anger and how he or she learned to rely on God for help in dealing with it. Encourage the speaker to quote or read Scripture that applies to the situation. Afterward, let kids ask questions. Invite kids to describe similar struggles in their own lives and to pray for one another. To do so, you might have them form groups of three to complete the following statements:

• "I'm most angry when . . ."

• "The last time I was angry, I . . ."

STEP 4

Here is a good way to get kids to pray for each other about controlling their anger. Give each person a candle. Then have kids sit in a circle in a darkened room (or go outside if it's dark). Explain that you will light the first person's candle. He or she will then pray for someone else in the circle, and then light that person's candle. That person will then pray for someone else, and so on, until everyone in the group has been prayed for. Point out that the candle represents God's light in our lives and His willingness to help us control our anger.

STEP 3

Before distributing "Anger: Up Close and Personal" (Repro Resource 4), ask for some volunteers to act out the situations on the sheet. If possible, get at least five or six volunteers for Situation #1 (with some of the kids playing friends of the main characters). Get three volunteers for Situation #2. (You may need to change names from Jason to Janet and from Matt to Martha.) Ask the volunteers to adjust the events in the situation as they wish. Provide a little planning time; then have the volunteers present the skits. Ask the entire group to contribute to the discussion at the end of each presentation.

STEP 4

As a group, talk about what to do when others around you are angry. Say:
Often we aren't angry until someone responds to us in anger—then we pick up their anger. What do you usually do? What should you do? How would you respond if the following people were really angry?
• **Friends**
• **Parents**
• **Brothers or sisters**
• **Someone that's hard to like**
• **Teachers**
• **A person you'd like to be friends with**

STEP 2

When your guys give their answers to the questions from Repro Resource 3, have them sound as angry and mean as possible—just for fun. Also encourage them to create sound effects whenever possible instead of giving their answers straight. Have the rest of the group try to guess what the answer is based on the sound effect.

STEP 3

Have cans of all kinds of soda on hand. Let two contestants compete to create the loudest burp. Let them choose their sodas, pour equal amounts into glasses of the same size, guzzle, and burp away. Take a vote on the best burp. Then let two more contestants compete. (Open new cans every time.) You may want to give out small prizes to the winners. Draw parallels between burps and anger. Point out that sometimes it is hard to suppress a burp when it really wants to come out. If you don't let it out, you feel uncomfortable. Talk about how uncomfortable it can feel to keep anger bottled up inside. Discuss appropriate and inappropriate ways for letting anger out.

Another good object lesson using soda is to let kids shake up cans and see who can create the biggest explosion upon opening them. This is a lot like people who keep their anger bottled up inside. If you use an object lesson like this, you can skip the balloon activities in Step 4 and spend your time cleaning up!

STEP 2

Have kids form teams of three for a "toilet paper nose relay." Appoint one team member to be an "enemy," another to be a "friend," and the third to be a "contestant." The enemy is to try to prevent his or her "teammates" from winning the relay. The friend is to offer encouragement and advice during the relay. The contestant will actually compete. Give each team a roll of toilet paper. Designate a finish line on the other side of the room. When you blow the whistle, the contestant on each team should roll the paper toward the finish line with his or her nose. The first team to reach the finish line wins. During play, the "enemy" should discourage the other two players by contradicting instructions and encouragement given by the "friendly" teammate, blocking the view, making noise, etc. No one is allowed to touch anyone else or to stop the contestant from rolling the toilet paper. Award a prize to the winning toilet paper roller and the "friend" on his or her team. Afterward, have kids talk about whether they felt angry at any point during or after the game, and why.

STEP 4

Have two teams compete to see which can make the most popcorn in 10 minutes. If you can't borrow air poppers that are exactly alike (so the competition is fair), and if you have access to a stove, give each team a pot, plenty of oil and popping corn, and a few large paper sacks to put the popped corn in. Award prizes to the winners if you want. While kids eat the popcorn, discuss parallels between the popping corn and anger. There are two analogies you could make: (1) Some of the kernels did not "explode," despite the hot oil. Compare this to controlling one's temper. (2) Some of the kernels never popped, so they're no good to eat. Compare this to people who don't deal with their anger. Have kids describe what it's like to be around a person with a bad temper and a person with a good temper.

STEP 2

Follow up your last statement in Step 2 with the following activity. Bring in current newspapers or newsmagazines. Have kids cut out and discuss stories that involve anger. Ask: **What is this story about? What role do you think anger played in it? How could this problem have been averted if the anger had been dealt with according to the guidelines found in Matthew 18:15-17 and Ephesians 4:26-30?**

STEP 3

If some of your kids are heavy metal or grunge fans, you could borrow almost any tape or CD they have, and find songs with a theme related to anger or its by-product—hate. During the session, play excerpts from a song or two. If you can, type up the lyrics for the excerpts you use and display them on an overhead projector. You could also do a little research on the lifestyles of the band members. (For information, you might check *The Guide to Periodical Literature* at your local library.) Ask: **What message does this band/person/song communicate? How does this message oppose the guidelines for dealing with anger that are given in Matthew 18:15-17 and Ephesians 4:26-30?**

STEP 1

To save some time, skip the name-tag contest and go right to the contest in which kids compete to see who can act angriest. You may have to throw out a few challenges to inspire volunteers. Say: **I need a couple of people who are in the mood to do something crazy—people who are willing to do this crazy thing in front of the whole group. If you do this crazy thing the best, you'll (a) win a prize, (b) have the respect of the whole group, or (c) look weird.**

STEP 3

Have students look up Matthew 21:1-13. Instruct them to reenact the scene from verses 12 and 13. You could provide props like a plastic "kiddy" table, stuffed animals, play money, etc. Students should mingle about, barter, and eat food that was "bought" with the play money. After Jesus clears the temple and the money changers react, bring the group together. Ask: **What triggered Jesus' anger? When is it appropriate to get angry? Was Jesus' response appropriate?** Ask various students how they felt as they played their parts—Jesus, sellers, buyers, innocent bystanders, etc.

STEP 3

Have group members form two to four teams. Instruct the members of each team to discuss responses to the following situations, focusing on how anger might be expressed in a positive way and in a negative way for each situation.

(1) You were just slapped in the face by someone who hates you.

(2) You found out that the person who set your apartment building on fire is in your class.

(3) You keep getting teased that you're gay because you like ballet (if you're a guy) or sports (if you're a girl).

(4) You know the person who spray-painted a racial slur on your locker.

After group members discuss these situations, point out that anger is an emotion that helps make us aware of injustice and move us to action. Ask: **What are some things that happen in the city that are unjust and make you angry?** List responses as they are given, and discuss how some of them could be acted upon.

STEP 4

The best way to deal with anger caused by others is to learn how to confront those people lovingly. Distribute paper and pens. Challenge kids to write down three starting phrases that can help them lovingly confront someone who has angered them. Examples might include "May I speak with you privately?" or "There's something I'd like to talk with you about." Point out that sometimes love needs to be tough, so the statements shouldn't let people off the hook too easily. For example, the following statement wouldn't be effective: "I'm sorry you tried to burn down my apartment building. But hey, that's OK. We all have our little faults."

STEP 2

The following activity is a good way to get kids of different ages to interact. Have each person write out a question he or she has about dealing with anger. The question should involve a personal struggle. Collect the questions and mix them up (keeping them anonymous). Then have group members form teams that include both junior highers and high schoolers. Give each team one or more of the questions. Each team must come up with an answer for its assigned question(s). Each answer must include a principle from the Bible. (For help, the teams could look up "anger" or "angry" in a Bible concordance.) When everyone is ready, have each team read its question(s) and share its answer(s).

STEP 4

Invite people with different physical or mental disabilities to talk to the group about their frustrations and how they try to deal with them. After each presentation, let kids ask questions. Then talk about how out-of-control anger can be a disability. Follow up with the discussion in Step 4.

STEP 3

As a group, discuss "Anger: Up Close and Personal" (Repro Resource 4). Then ask for suggestions of other situations that make people angry. Ask for volunteers to act out the situations, demonstrating both inappropriate and appropriate responses. Afterward, have other kids comment on what they might do in similar situations.

STEP 4

Have your sixth graders form teams. Give each team a gummy worm; a rubber band; a short, strong wooden or aluminum rod; a braided cord; a lightweight plastic bucket with a handle; and a brick. Have each team conduct an experiment. Instruct each team to put the brick in the bucket and try to hang the bucket from each item, beginning with the gummy worm. After kids conduct their experiments, have them talk about the result of each one. Then ask how they think each test relates to anger. (Explain that the brick in the bucket represents anger and the rest of the objects represent ways we deal with anger.) Help kids see that a gummy worm will always give in to the weight of anger; a rubber band might bear the weight for a moment, until it snaps; a rod and a cord can both bear the weight of anger (although a cord is more flexible than a rod). Ask: **Which of these objects best describes how you deal with anger?**

After the object lesson, write the principles from Matthew 18:15-17 and Ephesians 4:26-30 on the board. Then ask: **When are these guidelines hard to follow? How can your relationship with God help make doing these things easier?**

DATE USED:

Approx. Time

STEP 1: *Sticky Emotions* _____
- ❑ Extra Action
- ❑ Small Group
- ❑ Short Meeting Time

Things needed:

STEP 2: *A Different Look at Anger* _____
- ❑ Large Group
- ❑ Heard It All Before
- ❑ Little Bible Background
- ❑ Mostly Guys
- ❑ Extra Fun
- ❑ Media
- ❑ Combined Junior High/High School

Things needed:

STEP 3: *Anger in Action* _____
- ❑ Extra Action
- ❑ Heard It All Before
- ❑ Little Bible Background
- ❑ Fellowship & Worship
- ❑ Mostly Girls
- ❑ Mostly Guys
- ❑ Media
- ❑ Short Meeting Time
- ❑ Urban
- ❑ Sixth Grade

Things needed:

STEP 4: *Dealing with Anger* _____
- ❑ Small Group
- ❑ Large Group
- ❑ Fellowship & Worship
- ❑ Mostly Girls
- ❑ Extra Fun
- ❑ Urban
- ❑ Combined Junior High/High School
- ❑ Sixth Grade

Things needed:

How Can I Feel Better?

YOUR GOALS FOR THIS SESSION:

Choose one or more

☐ To help kids recognize that seeking happiness through artificial means (things like alcohol, drugs, sex, and food) is a bad idea.

☐ To help kids understand how to find real happiness, based on principles from God's Word.

☐ To help kids choose creative, God-honoring ways to help themselves feel better when things aren't going so great.

☐ Other:_____
_____

Your Bible Base:

Psalm 100

Always Read the Instructions

(Needed: Copies of Repro Resource 5, pencils, prize)

To begin the session, distribute copies of "No Shortcuts, Please" (Repro Resource 5) and pencils. Place the sheets facedown in front of group members as you pass them out.

Explain: **We're going to begin our session today with a brief quiz. When I say "Go," you will turn your papers over and follow the directions on the sheet. You may not talk with each other while you take the quiz, and you may not look at anyone else's sheet. As soon as you're finished, raise your hand. The first person to correctly complete the quiz will receive a prize. Ready, go!**

Walk around as group members work, paying attention to who follows the directions and who doesn't. Those who follow the directions will answer only numbers 2, 5, and 8. Award a prize (perhaps a candy bar) to the first person who answers these three questions. When other group members question or complain, refer them to number 20 on the sheet.

Afterward, ask: **How many of you took the "shortcut" and wrote your responses before you read all of the instructions?** Get a show of hands.

What are some other shortcuts that people take? (Drivers often take side streets and back roads as shortcuts to their destinations. Kids doing homework often take shortcuts by "half-answering" questions and by not checking their answers. Building contractors sometimes take shortcuts to save money by using inferior materials, ignoring safety guidelines, etc.)

Explain: **Sometimes when we take shortcuts, we think we're making things easier for ourselves. But shortcuts aren't always the best way. Today we're going to be talking about shortcuts that some people take to become "happy"; then we'll compare those shortcuts with God's way for us to be truly happy.**

Cookie Time

(Needed: Blindfolds, plastic spoons, homemade chocolate chip cookies, chalkboard and chalk or newsprint and marker, several plastic containers—each containing one ingredient for chocolate chip cookies)

OPTIONS

[NOTE: The following activity will require a little more preparation than most of the other activities in this book. If you don't have time to prepare, you can simply describe the gist of the object lesson. It won't be as effective as actually performing the activity, but it will still work.]

Before the session, you'll need to make (or have one of your group members make) a batch of chocolate chip cookies. You'll also need to bring in several plastic containers. Each one should contain an ingredient for chocolate chip cookies. Among the ingredients you might use are butter, sugar, brown sugar, vanilla, eggs, flour, baking soda, salt, and chocolate chips. [NOTE: It's important that you bring in only all-natural ingredients and that you use only all-natural ingredients when you make the cookies.]

Ask for three or four volunteers to participate in a "taste test." Blindfold the volunteers, and give each one a plastic spoon. Put each volunteer in front of a container. Instruct the volunteers to dip their spoons into the containers (you may need to guide them), taste what's inside, and then describe the taste to the rest of the group. Some of the ingredients—like the sugar and chocolate chips—will taste good. Others—like the flour and baking soda—will taste bad.

Lead the group in a round of applause for your brave volunteers, and then have the volunteers take their seats.

Explain: **The items in these containers are ingredients— ingredients for chocolate chip cookies. When you taste the ingredients on their own, some of them are pretty gross. However, when you mix the ingredients together, the results can be pretty tasty.** Pass out homemade chocolate chip cookies. (You might want to give extra cookies to your taste-test volunteers.)

As group members enjoy their cookies, say: **You could say that our lives are like these cookies—they're made up of ingredients. Some of the ingredients of our lives are good, and leave a sweet taste in our mouth. These would be the times when we're happy and enjoying life. Some of our lives' ingredients aren't so good, and leave a bitter taste in our** mouth. These would be the times when we're depressed or sad, and not enjoying life very much.

What would happen if you tried to make chocolate chip cookies without baking soda, or flour, or salt, or butter, or any of the other bad-tasting ingredients? (The cookies would be incomplete. They wouldn't turn out right.)

By the same token, what would our lives be like if we didn't have down times—times of depression or sadness? (Our lives would be incomplete.)

Summarize: **Of course, probably none of us have ever wished for depressing or sad times—even if they do make our lives complete. If we had our choice, most of us would probably choose to be happy all of the time.**

What are some things that make you happy? (Being with friends, laughing, watching TV, listening to music, participating in sports, etc.) List group members' responses on the board as they are named.

Shortcuts and Artificial Ingredients

(Needed: Chalkboard and chalk or newsprint and marker)

O P T I O N S

EXTRA **FUN**

SHORT MEETING **TIME**

SIXTH GRADE

Draw another analogy from your cookie activity. Say: **We used only all-natural ingredients for our chocolate chip cookies. We didn't have to; we could have used imitation butter, imitation salt, artificial sweeteners, artificially flavored chocolate, etc. But what would that have done to the cookies?** (It might have made them taste strange—or at least not as good.)

In the same way, some people use "artificial ingredients" in their lives. They try to take "shortcuts" to happiness. What are some shortcuts people take to try to find happiness? What artificial ingredients do they use to make themselves happy? (Alcohol, drugs, sex, the pursuit of money or material possessions, power, etc.) List these responses on the board as they are named.

Can these things really make a person happy? (Only temporarily. Their effects wear off after a short time. So the person must constantly be looking for new ways to make himself or herself happy.)

Do you know anyone who tries to find happiness through alcohol, drugs, sex, or any other artificial ways? Emphasize that you're not looking for people's names here. **Do these people seem truly happy?** Get a few responses.

STEP 4

Real Happiness

(Needed: Chalkboard and chalk or newsprint and marker, paper, pencils)

Say: **We've seen where we can find artificial happiness. But where can we find real happiness?** (In God's Word.)

Have someone read aloud Psalm 100. Then ask: **How would you describe this psalm?** (Happy, joyful, full of thanksgiving.)

What is the psalmist so happy about? (He knows that the Lord is good and that His love and faithfulness endure forever.)

What are some of the instructions the psalmist gives in this psalm? Have group members call them out to you while you write them on the board. Responses should include the following:

• "Shout for joy to the Lord" (vs. 1).
• "Worship the Lord with gladness" (vs. 2).
• "Come before him with joyful songs" (vs. 2).
• "Know that the Lord is God" (vs. 3).
• "Enter his gates with thanksgiving" (vs. 4).
• "Give thanks to him" (vs. 4).
• "Praise his name" (vs. 4).

Ask: **Do you think any of these instructions could be helpful to us when we're feeling down? If so, how?** You might want to have group members pair up and work together on these questions. Give the pairs a few minutes to discuss; then have each one share its responses.

Use the following information to supplement the pairs' responses.

• Shouting for joy to the Lord, worshiping Him, and praising His name involve thinking about His greatness. When we're depressed or sad, reflecting on what a great God we serve can cheer us up.

• Singing joyful songs (perhaps hymns or contemporary worship tunes) is another way to overcome depression or sadness.

• If we know that the Lord is God, we know He has the power to lift us out of our depression and sadness.

• Entering His gates with thanksgiving and giving thanks to Him involves thinking about all God has done for us. Reflecting on what He's done for us could cause us to begin to feel special and cared for, and could chase away our depression and sadness.

Distribute paper and pencils. Say: **Imagine that you have a close friend who's been feeling sad and depressed lately. Write this friend a brief letter to cheer him or her up. If possible, give your friend some advice, based on Psalm 100.**

Give group members a few minutes to work. When they're finished, ask volunteers to share what they wrote. You might want to write some of their suggestions on the board as they are named.

STEP 5

Feel-Better Remedies

(Needed: Slips of paper, pencils)

Say: **True or false: Being a Christian means never getting depressed or sad.** (False.)

True or false: **When you're depressed or sad, the only good ways to help yourself feel better are to pray, read the Bible, and sing hymns.** Get several responses.

Distribute slips of paper and pencils. Instruct group members to write down a few things they do to cheer up when they're feeling sad or depressed. Encourage them to be honest in their responses. You're not looking for "religious" answers here. If group members cheer themselves up by watching TV, listening to music, eating, or even by getting drunk or high, they should say so. (You could encourage them to disguise their handwriting if it would make them feel more comfortable.)

Collect the slips, and then read each one aloud. After you read each one, have group members call out whether they think it's a good way or a bad way to cheer up. You may need to emphasize that things like watching TV, listening to music, eating, shopping, and goofing off with friends are not necessarily bad remedies for depression and sadness. Doing things that are fun is not an ungodly way to feel better.

Summarize: **The key is dependence. We shouldn't depend on food or music or even our friends to help us feel better when we're depressed. Our deepest dependence should be on God. These other things are simply diversions. When we're sad or depressed, the first thing we should do is take our feelings to God in prayer and let Him help us.**

Close the session in prayer, thanking God that we can depend on Him to help us when we're feeling sad or depressed.

OPTIONS

LITTLE BIBLE BACKGROUND

FELLOWSHIP & WORSHIP

MOSTLY GIRLS

MOSTLY GUYS

MEDIA

JR. HIGH / HIGH SCHOOL COMBINED

NOTES

NO Short Cuts, Please!

Read each of the following instructions thoroughly. When you've finished reading all of the instructions, go back and write the appropriate responses.

1. Write your full name. _____

2. Write the age you'll be on your next birthday. _____

3. Write the first names of your brothers and sisters. _____

4. Write the names of the cities you've lived in. _____

5. Write the 26 letters of the alphabet in order. _____

6. Write the sum of 23 + 89. _____

7. Write the name of the last store you shopped in. _____

8. Write your address. _____

9. Write the name of your favorite cereal. _____

10. Write the name of your favorite rock group or singer. _____

11. Write your height. _____

12. Write the name of the holiday that falls on December 25. _____

13. Write your shoe size. _____

14. Write the name of your favorite teacher. _____

15. Write the name of your favorite radio station. _____

16. Write the name of your best friend. _____

17. Write the name of your favorite food. _____

18. Write the number of fingers you have. _____

19. Write the name of your favorite TV show. _____

20. Write nothing here. Now that you've read through all of the instructions, go back and answer only numbers 2, 5, and 8. _____

NOTES

STEP 1

Begin the session with a cheering contest. Have group members form teams. Instruct each team to come up with a cheer for God (or for your group). For example: "We love God! Yes we do! We love God! How 'bout you?!" or "Give me a 'G!' Give me an 'O!' Give me a 'D!' What's it spell? GOD! The one and only God of Abraham . . . Isaac . . . Jacob . . . and me!" Invite an impartial adult to pick the winner and runners-up. You may even want to award prizes. Afterward, talk about whether Christians should always be this cheerful. Ask: **If you get depressed, are you sinning?** Acknowledge that even the most mature Christians aren't always cheerful or happy—especially when life becomes difficult. But Christians can experience a quiet joy despite problems. If you wish, take a brief look at 2 Corinthians 1:8, in which Paul sounds anything but cheerful.

STEP 4

Before you identify or read Psalm 100 in this step, have your kids do something a little crazy. Get five volunteers to stand in front of the group one at a time and spell out words in the air with their hips. (It will look hilarious.) Tell the group that the words are part of a psalm being written by someone who is feeling really happy. The rest of the group members should shout out each letter as they recognize it. Assign the following words: *shout, worship, sing, thank,* and *praise.* Then have kids read Psalm 100. Work through Step 4, beginning with the fourth question: **What are some of the instructions the psalmist gives in this psalm?**

STEP 2

If your group is small, you could let everyone taste one or all of the separate ingredients that combine to make good cookies. That way, everyone will be able to personally relate to your comments about how sweet and bitter ingredients make one's life complete.

STEP 4

If you have just a few kids, you may not want to have them work through Psalm 100 in pairs. Instead, you can have them answer this question from Step 4 as a group: **Do you think any of these instructions could be helpful to us when we're feeling down? If so, how?** Let kids call out their answers. Write them on the board as they are named. Since you have fewer kids, you will be able to spend more time listening to the letters they write to depressed friends. Also, group members will have more time to explain their friends' situations before they read their letters aloud.

STEP 1

In a large group, the chances are pretty good that some of the kids will know the trick of Repro Resource 5 and not be fooled by it. Here's another alternative you might use: Pass out several vanilla wafers, or other "unexciting" cookies. Say: **You can have some of these now, or wait until later to have your snack.** Keep track of who takes cookies now. Exclude them from having any of the homemade cookies later in the session. Use this activity to talk about shortcuts people take to try to find happiness.

STEP 4

Have group members form teams. Assign each team a different psalm. (You can still follow up with the questions in Step 4.) Here are some suggested psalms that are similar to Psalm 100: Psalm 103:1-5, 22; Psalm 105:1-5; Psalm 108:1-5; Psalm 113. Skip the letter-writing/advice-giving activity at the end of the step so that you have plenty of time for each team to read its psalm aloud and give its answers. Write these questions on the board so that kids know what to answer: **How would you describe this psalm? What is the psalmist so happy about? What are some of the instructions the psalmist gives in this psalm? Do you think any of these instructions could be helpful when we're feeling down? If so, how?**

STEP 1

If your kids immediately figure out the gist of the shortcut trick from Repro Resource 5 or know it already, try another option. Give a volunteer a choice: he or she can have a candy bar that is sitting on top of an upside-down box or do ten sit-ups and get what might be a better prize under the box instead. The hidden prize should be better than the one in view. (It could be two candy bars.) No matter which choice the kid makes, you can lead into the discussion about short-cuts. If you want to involve the whole group, adapt the "Large Group" option for Step 1 to make a similar point.

STEP 4

Kids who have have heard it all before might benefit from some personal testimonies that will bring to life the concept of God as the source of happiness. Ask a couple of Christians, young and old, to tell your group how they searched for happiness before they found true happiness in God. If you're feeling really gutsy, you could also invite a non-Christian to present his or her views about how to find true happiness. Encourage the group to ask questions, being sensitive to each person's beliefs. After the people have left, discuss what they had to say, especially in light of the teachings found in Scripture. Here are some passages you might use to supplement your discussion: Proverbs 14:12; Romans 15:13; I Peter 1:3-9.

STEP 4

Since this whole session is based on one powerful psalm, you may want to explain the psalm in more detail. It begins with an invitation to anyone and everyone ("all the earth") to have a relationship with God (vs. 1). People who know and love God can be joyful because they have a relationship with the awesome God (vs. 2). It identifies God as Lord (vs. 3). Verse 3 tells us that there are three parts to our relationship with Him: He created us, we belong to Him, and He guides us (like a shepherd). We should praise Him (vs. 4) because He is good, He loves us, and He is faithful to us (vs. 5).

STEP 5

If your group is small, assign the following questions and Scripture passages to individuals; otherwise, have kids work in pairs or small groups.

(1) What are some things we should be joyful about?

• **Luke 2:10** (The Savior's birth.)

• **Acts 17:18** (Christ's resurrection.)

• **James 1:2** (Suffering.)

• **I Peter 1:3-9** (New birth, an inheritance, salvation, eternal life.)

(2) Where does joy come from?

• **Galatians 5:22** (The Holy Spirit.)

• **Psalm 16:11** (God.)

(3) How did people in the Bible express their happiness?

• **2 Samuel 6:14-15** (David danced before the Lord; Israel shouted and blew trumpets.)

• **Acts 16:25** (Paul sang.)

(4) What brings joy?

• **John 15:10-11** (Obeying God.)

STEP 4

Rather than just discussing Psalm 100, have students sing it. There are several different versions. Choose one your kids know, or have them make up their own tune (or change/rearrange some of the words to make the psalm fit a familiar tune). They can also add a clapping pattern and/or gestures to enhance the presentation. Kids can work as one group or in small groups. (Or you might have kids individually write and present their own versions of Psalm 100 based on their personal feelings about God.) Let volunteers present their songs or readings. Follow up with prayer. Remind kids that when they worship God this way, it encourages them to focus on Him instead of on themselves.

STEP 5

Have each group member write out a Bible verse about joy or happiness on a small slip of paper. (You'll probably want to have some concordances on hand for this activity.) Encourage kids to pick verses they especially like. Then have them sit in a circle. Create a more worshipful atmosphere by darkening the room and lighting enough candles to make it possible for kids to read their verses. Have each group member finish both of these sentences aloud:

• "I am really happy when . . ."

• "I would be really happy if . . ."

After each group member finishes, have the person to his or her right read aloud the verse he or she wrote down. Afterward, ask some of the kids how likely it is that they will get what they wished for and how long they think it would make them happy.

STEP 4

Have group members form teams. Give each team one (or more) of the phrases from Psalm 100 that includes an action word (shout, worship, come, know, enter, give, and praise). Ask the members of each team to talk together about how our knowledge of and relationship to God contribute to helping us feel better. Then have each team plan a two-minute (or shorter) skit. In the skit, one team member should play a person needing help. The rest of the team members should then act out what they might say or do to help that person (based on the principles from Psalm 100).

STEP 5

Spend some time talking in more detail about "bad" moods. Ask: **Does it make you angry when someone—especially a parent—asks you to snap out of your bad mood as if it were something you can turn on or off? What do you usually do in response? What would be a better way for someone to ask you to try to stop being so grouchy?**

If it's appropriate for your group, you might want to take some time to discuss how a woman's menstrual cycle affects her emotions. Invite some mature Christian women to share about this with the girls in your group. Be especially sensitive to the different stages your girls are in. Here are some questions you might use to get the discussion going:

• How do your emotions change around your period?

• Do you think women blame too much on PMS? Why or why not?

• What do you do to control your emotions during your period? What have you found helpful?

STEP 4

Instead of having your guys write letters to cheer up their friends, have them just explain what they would say to those friends. If guys complain that the situation you describe is too vague, invite them to describe a real friend's problem (without naming names).

STEP 5

Guys may be less willing than girls to acknowledge their down times or to talk about what they do to cheer themselves up. That's why this session does not specifically ask them if they ever feel down. Instead, it is assumes that they sometimes feel down, which takes the pressure off. No one has to be the first to admit that he gets depressed or to identify what depresses him. Encourage group members to be honest when they write down what they do to cheer themselves up. Explain that their comments will remain anonymous and that they can spread out around the room for a little privacy while they write.

Another way to address the subject is to have guys discuss positive and negative ways to use each of the following things when you're feeling down:

• music
• television or movies
• friends
• religion
• sports or exercise
• food

STEP 1

Divide the group into two or more teams. Line the teams up for a relay race. (You'll need a large room for this activity.) Place baseball bats at the opposite end of the room, one bat per team. Each player has a choice when his or her turn comes. He or she may (1) run the perimeter of the room or (2) run to the bat, put his or her forehead on the tip of the bat, and circle it ten times, keeping the bat perpendicular to and touching the ground at all times. After the completing the activity of his or her choice, the player will run back to the team and tag the next person in line, who will continue the relay. The first team to have all of its members complete the relay wins. Afterward, ask kids how they chose which relay to run. If some say that they thought the bat relay would be quicker than running the perimeter of the room, point out that what appears to be the faster way may not always be the best. Follow up with the last paragraph in Step 1.

STEP 3

After kids answer your questions in Step 3, have them form teams for a relay. Mark straight paths across the room with masking tape, one path per team. Give each team a pencil and a lemon. Each person on the team is to take a turn rolling the lemon across the room and back on the path, using only the pencil. If the lemon rolls beyond the masking tape, the player must start over. When the last player rolls the lemon back to the team, the first player must skin the lemon, eat it, and have an empty mouth upon inspection. The first team to do all of this is the winner. Use the sour expressions of the lemon eaters to lead into a discussion of how God can turn our sorrow into joy. Explain that you are going to read a joyful psalm. Ask: **Do you think any of our lemon eaters would be capable of writing a happy psalm right now?**

STEP 1

Play a few video clips from concerts that show an audience expressing its appreciation for a performance. Start with a tame audience, one that is politely clapping. Then show an audience that is a little more lively. Finally, show an audience going crazy—clapping, cheering, whistling, screaming, and dancing. Draw parallels between these audiences and levels of happiness. Point out that God can give us different kinds of joy—a quiet, calm joy; a hearty-laugh kind of joy; and an intense joy. Explain that true, lasting joy comes only from God. Any other source of happiness is short-lived.

STEP 5

Check out a couple of secular books at your local library on finding happiness. Use them to gather a variety of brief quotes that you can read and discuss with your kids. Ask: **How does this person define happiness? What does this person say is the source of happiness? How is this person's view on happiness different from what is taught in the Bible?** Actually bringing the books to the session, showing kids the covers, and reading quotes directly from the books will help to spark interest in the discussion. Then follow up with the rest of Step 5 as written.

STEP 3

You can save a little time by skipping the first part of Step 3. Say: **Some people try to gain happiness by doing things that only harm them in the end. Can you think of some examples of this?** (Alcohol, drugs, sex, the pursuit of money or material possessions, power, etc.). Then ask: **Can these things really make a person happy?**

STEP 4

If you're short on time, you can skip the letter-writing activity at the end of this step and move right into Step 5. The activity in Step 5 will help your kids personally apply what they've learned. Therefore, they won't miss out on application even if they skip the activity at the end of Step 4.

STEP 2

After the ingredient-tasting activity, say: **Just as there are many bad-tasting ingredients in good-tasting cookies, there are bad characteristics in us and bad situations we encounter, all of which God can use to make us into better and stronger people.** Ask group members to name some other bad-tasting ingredients in good-tasting foods. Then have the group read together James 1:2-4, 12; Mark 9:49; and I Corinthians 10:13. As you discuss the passages, point out that a good chef is an expert at mixing ingredients that might not be too tasty on their own. Then suggest that Jesus is our master chef, the one who can positively blend the most negative ingredients of our personality and cook them at the right temperature in the oven of life to make us into beautiful examples of His expertise.

STEP 4

Point out that all of us at times get depressed and "down." Then use the following activity to illustrate the help we all need to give each other during such times. First, get a thin volunteer and a strong volunteer. The thin one should lie on the floor; the strong one should pick him or her up. Next, try having someone a little heavier lie on the floor. It might take two persons to lift him or her. Then get two heavy people to link arms and lie on the floor. It should take several people to lift them. Point out that the heavier our problem is, or the deeper our depression, the more personal help we need to get back on our feet.

STEP 2

One way to encourage camaraderie is to have small mixed groups of junior highers and high schoolers actually bake their own cookies. After the "ingredients" discussion, give the groups a couple of basic recipes to choose from. Have each group mix up a batch of cookie dough. Let the cookies bake while you work through the next few steps. Then allow kids to enjoy the fruits of their labor at the end of the session.

STEP 5

Collect the slips on which kids have anonymously written how they go about cheering themselves up. As you read them aloud, don't have kids call out whether it's a good way or bad way to cheer up. Instead, find a way to encourage junior highers to express their opinions without holding back until the high schoolers have spoken. One way is to have kids hold up plus or minus signs that they've drawn on the front and back of an index card. Give them a few seconds to think by having them hold up the cards at the same time on the count of five. Make sure kids get to express the reasons behind their opinions.

STEP 3

Write the words "I am happy when I . . ." across the top of the board. Instruct your sixth graders to write their responses to the statement. Collect the responses and read some of them aloud. Then ask group members to name some of the "artificial ingredients" used by kids they know to try to obtain happiness. Help kids focus on the artificial things that are a part of their immediate world. Ask: **In addition to using substances and possessions, how do we use words and actions as artificial means to happiness?** As an example, talk about how we use words to put someone else down so we can feel better about ourselves or look better in front of other people.

STEP 4

After your sixth graders have talked about Psalm 100 and its helpful instructions, discuss the choices we have concerning our emotions. Say: **Although we can't choose when or how we will have an emotional response to something, what are some choices we do have? Is staying in a bad mood a choice you make or do you *have* to stay that way until it wears off? What about a good mood?** Ask kids to think of times when they felt sad, glad, or angry—without having had anything happen to make them feel that way. Ask: **When you realized that nothing had happened to cause you to feel that way, what did you do?**

DATE USED:

Approx. Time

STEP 1: *Always Read the Instructions*   _____
❏ Extra Action
❏ Large Group
❏ Heard It All Before
❏ Extra Fun
❏ Media
Things needed:

STEP 2: *Cookie Time*   _____
❏ Small Group
❏ Urban
❏ Combined Junior High/High School
Things needed:

STEP 3: *Shortcuts and Artificial Ingredients*   _____
❏ Extra Fun
❏ Short Meeting Time
❏ Sixth Grade
Things needed:

STEP 4: *Real Happiness*   _____
❏ Extra Action
❏ Small Group
❏ Large Group
❏ Heard It All Before
❏ Little Bible Background
❏ Fellowship & Worship
❏ Mostly Girls
❏ Mostly Guys
❏ Short Meeting Time
❏ Urban
❏ Sixth Grade
Things needed:

STEP 5: *Feel-Better Remedies*   _____
❏ Little Bible Background
❏ Fellowship & Worship
❏ Mostly Girls
❏ Mostly Guys
❏ Media
❏ Combined Junior High/High School
Things needed:

Emotions out of Control

Choose one or more

☐ To help kids recognize that talking to another person can often help us feel better when we're experiencing emotional turmoil.

☐ To help kids understand how to help people who are experiencing emotional turmoil—and how to ask for help from others when they are experiencing emotional turmoil.

☐ To help kids choose God as a "cord of strength" in their emotional lives.

☐ Other:_____

_____

Your Bible Base:

Psalm 139:1-5
Ecclesiastes 4:7-12

Let's Work Together

(Needed: Two strips of cloth, a spoon, several large marshmallows, a stopwatch, chalkboard and chalk or newsprint and marker [optional])

OPTIONS

EXTRA ACTION

SMALL GROUP

LARGE GROUP

FELLOWSHIP & WORSHIP

EXTRA FUN

Have group members form pairs. Suggest that they pair up with people who are about as tall as they are. Explain that the pairs will be competing in a "three-legged race." The member of each pair will race to a designated point (perhaps the far wall of your meeting area) and back—with their legs tied together.

Have the pairs line up behind a start/finish line. Have the members of the first pair stand side-by-side while you tie their inner legs together. Tie one strip of cloth just above their knees and one strip around their ankles.

Just before you tell the first pair to go, introduce a twist to the contest. Give the members of the pair a spoon with a marshmallow on it. Explain that both members of the pair have to hold on to the spoon and keep the marshmallow from falling off as they race. If the marshmallow falls off, they must stop, pick it up (without falling over), set it back on the spoon, and then continue racing.

You'll need a stopwatch to time the pairs as they race. To make things more "official," you might want to write the times on the board.

After all of the pairs have taken a turn, lead the group in a round of applause for the pair with the fastest time.

Afterward, ask: **What was the key to doing well in this activity?** (Working together and communicating well with your partner.)

What are some other things that require the help of another person? (Lifting a heavy object, moving furniture, playing doubles in tennis, etc.)

If no one mentions it, ask: **What about dealing with our emotions? Does that ever require the help of someone else?** Get responses from as many group members as possible.

With a Little Help from My Friends

(Needed: Copies of Repro Resource 6, pencils)

Distribute copies of "Help Needed—or Not?" (Repro Resource 6) and pencils. Give group members a few minutes to complete the sheet.

When everyone is finished, go through the situations one at a time. Read each situation aloud and have group members hold up one or two fingers to indicate their responses. Then ask volunteers to explain why they responded as they did.

Use the following information to supplement group members' responses.

(1) *Alec just found out he made the school basketball team. He's so excited, he can barely talk.* (Alec could certainly "work out" his happiness on his own, but it would probably be much more enjoyable for him to have someone to share his joy with.)

(2) *Janna's been having weird dreams about being attacked by a stranger. As a result, she's afraid to go anywhere by herself.* (Janna needs someone to share her fears with. She's being "crippled" by her fears if they prevent her from doing normal things.)

(3) *Candy was dumped by her boyfriend two days ago. Now every time she sees him in the hallway at school, she runs to the bathroom and cries.* (Candy eventually may be able to work through her sadness by herself; but having someone to comfort and reassure her would probably speed up the process.)

(4) *Li is really moody. One minute he might be laughing and joking; the next minute he might be yelling at someone for some minor thing. Sometimes he's exciting and fun to be with; other times he's sad and depressing.* (Sudden mood swings may be a symptom of some deeper emotional—or perhaps even physical—problem. Li needs help with his situation.)

(5) *Jeff's been extremely angry since he found out his mother and father are divorcing. He's been getting into fights at school. He yells at his teachers. And he's had a couple of run-ins with the police for vandalism.* (Jeff's anti-social behavior is probably the result of his anger over his parents' divorce. Jeff needs help in dealing with his anger more effectively.)

(6) *Gabrielle made the cheerleading team; Tara didn't. Tara got jealous and started spreading lies about Gabrielle to "get even" with her.* (It's possible that Tara could work through her jealousy on her own.

OPTIONS

EXTRA ACTION

HEARD IT ALL BEFORE

MOSTLY GIRLS

MOSTLY GUYS

SHORT MEETING TIME

URBAN

JR.HIGH HIGH SCHOOL COMBINED

SIXTH GRADE

However, having someone to talk to about her jealousy could speed up the healing process.)

(7) Chenelle is mad at her parents for not letting her go to a concert with her friends. She hasn't spoken to her mom or dad for two days. (It's probably safe to say that Chenelle's relationship with her parents would gradually get back to normal after a few days. However, if Chenelle had someone to talk to about her feelings, it might help clear up the situation for her.)

(8) Gary just found out he and his family are moving to another state. Gary will have to leave behind all of his friends. He's really sad about it. (Gary may be able to work through his sadness on his own. However, not having someone to talk to about his sadness may make the transition very difficult for Gary.)

(9) Last week, Alejandro found out that he has to give a 10-minute speech in front of his English class. Alejandro is afraid of speaking in front of an audience. He hasn't been able to sleep for the past two nights because he's so worried about the speech. (Alejandro may feel better sharing his fears with someone he trusts. Other people also may be able to encourage Alejandro and give him tips for easing his nervousness in front of a crowd.)

(10) At school, Eddie was always being picked on or made fun of. It made him angry, but Eddie usually didn't do anything about it. However, one day when Jeff tripped him in the hallway, Eddie's rage exploded. He jumped up, punched Jeff in the face, and then started kicking him when Jeff fell to the ground. When a couple of girls started yelling at him to stop, Eddie threw his books at them as hard as he could. (Anytime a person's pent-up anger leads to violence or rage, he or she needs help.)

Ask: **Why do we need other people's help for something as personal and private as our emotions?** (Some emotions are so big and so overpowering that it takes more than one person to handle them. Emotions can cloud our judgment; other people can give us a fresh perspective and help see things in a new light.)

A Helping Hand

(Needed: Copies of Repro Resource 7, copies of Repro Resource 8 [optional])

Say: **OK, we've seen that sometimes we may need help from others in dealing with our emotions. By the same token, we may also need to help others deal with their emotions. But how do we do that?**

Have group members form three teams. Before the session, you'll need to cut apart a copy of "Emotional Dilemmas" (Repro Resource 7). Distribute one section to each team.

Give the teams a few minutes to read their assigned situations and come up with ideas for how they could offer emotional assistance to the people in the situations.

Use the following questions and information to guide your discussion of the activity.

Situation #1

What emotions are Kelly and Jay probably experiencing? (Sadness, anger, jealousy, depression, fear, loneliness.)

How could you help Kelly and Jay deal with their emotions? (Encourage them to talk honestly about how they're feeling; listen to them and ask questions to let them know that you really care about what they're feeling; invite them [separately, of course] to do things to take their minds off each other; avoid acting embarrassed or uncomfortable if they share their innermost feelings; calm their fears by reassuring them of their attractiveness; etc.)

If you were Kelly or Jay, what kind of help would you want from your friends as you dealt with this situation? Encourage several group members to respond.

Situation #2

What emotions is John probably experiencing? (Anger, sadness, fear.)

How could you help John deal with his emotions? (Let him know that you're always willing to talk or listen to him if he needs you; call him frequently to let him know you're thinking about him; invite him to do things with you so that he can get away from his parents occasionally; etc.) If no one mentions it, point out that this situation may require the help of a professional counselor. Part of helping John may involve encouraging him to talk to your youth leader or pastor about

his situation. [You'll address the subject of professional help a little later in the session.]

If you were John, what kind of help would you want from your friends as you dealt with this situation? Encourage group members to be honest here. If they would want to be left alone by their friends in this situation, they should say so.

Situation #3

What emotions is Susan probably experiencing? (Depression, sadness, boredom.)

How could you help Susan deal with her emotions? (Encourage her to continue sharing her feelings with you; let her know you're concerned about her; affirm her as often as possible; etc.) If no one mentions it, point out that this situation *definitely* requires the help of a professional counselor. You would need to encourage Susan to talk to your youth leader or pastor about her situation. If she refused, *you* would need to talk to a professional about Susan's situation.

If you were Susan, what kind of help would you want from your friends as you dealt with this situation? Encourage several group members to respond.

Explain: **John's and Susan's situations were a little different from Kelly and Jay's. John's and Susan's situations require the help of a professional counselor. What kinds of emotional situations require professional help?** (Suicidal or self-destructive behavior, violence toward others, wild mood swings, prolonged depression, family abuse problems, etc.)

If you or someone you know needed professional help, what could you do? (Talk to a trusted adult—whether it's your parents, your youth leader, your pastor, a school counselor, or someone else.)

True or false: Needing help with your emotions is a sign of weakness. (False!) Make sure your group members understand that everyone feels overwhelmed by his or her emotions at one time or another.

[Note: We've included "Counseling Q & A" (Repro Resource 8) as an additional resource you might want to use. If you think some group members might benefit from professional counseling, hand out the sheet and briefly review it, or let kids read it on their own. This is a serious subject, and it's hard to do it justice in the short space we have here. The point is for you to open the door for those who might be in serious need of some help. We'll trust your judgment as to whether the information on the sheet is or isn't appropriate for your group.]

STEP 4

Three Strands

(Needed: Bibles, a roll of narrow masking tape, chalkboard and chalk or newsprint and marker)

Say: **Think about one person you would turn to when you need help with your emotions. What qualities does he or she have?** Among the qualities group members might mention are being a good listener, someone who knows you well, someone you can trust, someone you feel comfortable talking to, etc.

Have someone read aloud Psalm 139:1-5. Then ask: **Who is being described in this passage?** (God.)

Point out that God is a good listener, He knows us well, and He's trustworthy. In other words, He's the perfect person to go to when we experience emotional turmoil.

How could God help us when our emotions get the better of us? (He might provide a calmness in our lives in the midst of our emotional upheaval. He might help us find a relevant passage of Scripture that gives us advice for dealing with our emotions. But perhaps the most likely thing He would do is provide someone here on earth for us to talk to about our situation.)

Have your group members read aloud Ecclesiastes 4:7-12 together. Then ask for a volunteer to come to the front of the room to help you illustrate the principle of the passage.

Have the volunteer sit in a chair facing the group. Ask the person to put his or her palms together. Wrap his or her hands once with masking tape.

Say: **A cord of one strand—someone who tries to handle his or her emotions alone—is easily broken.** Ask the volunteer to pull apart his or her hands. The tape should break quite easily.

Wrap the person's hands with two layers of tape. Make sure you wrap the second layer directly on top of the first layer.

Say: **A cord of two strands—someone who asks for help from a friend or a professional in handling tough emotional situations—is a lot stronger than a cord of one strand.** Ask the volunteer to pull apart his or her hands. The tape should be stronger, but still should be able to be broken.

Wrap the person's hands with three layers of tape. Make sure you wrap each layer directly on top of the previous one.

OPTIONS

LARGE GROUP

HEARD IT ALL BEFORE

LITTLE BIBLE BACKGROUND

FELLOWSHIP & WORSHIP

MOSTLY GIRLS

MEDIA

SIXTH GRADE

Say: **A cord of three strands—someone who trusts God to bring other people into his or her life to handle tough emotional situations—is virtually unbreakable.** Ask the volunteer to pull apart his or her hands. He or she should not be able to.

Explain: **God *wants* to be a cord of strength in our lives. He is always available when we ask for His help. Think about an emotion or situation that you're having problems with. Ask God for His strength and help in dealing with the situation. Ask Him to be the cord of strength in your life and in this situation.**

Give group members a few minutes to pray silently; then close the session by praying aloud.

NOTES

Help Needed—or Not?

Read each of the following situations. If you think the situation is something the person could work out alone, write "1" in the blank. If you think the situation is something that might require the help of another person, write "2" in the blank.

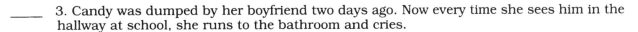

_____ 1. Alec just found out he made the school basketball team. He's so excited, he can barely talk.

_____ 2. Janna's been having weird dreams about being attacked by a stranger. As a result, she's afraid to go anywhere by herself.

_____ 3. Candy was dumped by her boyfriend two days ago. Now every time she sees him in the hallway at school, she runs to the bathroom and cries.

_____ 4. Li is really moody. One minute he might be laughing and joking; the next minute he might be yelling at someone for some minor thing. Sometimes he's exciting and fun to be with; other times he's sad and depressing.

_____ 5. Jeff's been extremely angry since he found out his mother and father are divorcing. He's been getting into fights at school. He yells at his teachers. And he's had a couple of run-ins with the police for vandalism.

 _____ 6. Gabrielle made the cheerleading team; Tara didn't. Tara got jealous and started spreading lies about Gabrielle to "get even" with her.

_____ 7. Chenelle is mad at her parents for not letting her go to a concert with her friends. She hasn't spoken to her mom or dad for two days.

_____ 8. Gary just found out he and his family are moving to another state. Gary will have to leave behind all of his friends. He's really sad about it.

_____ 9. Last week, Alejandro found out that he has to give a ten-minute speech in front of his English class. Alejandro is afraid of speaking in front of an audience. He hasn't been able to sleep for the past two nights because he's so worried about the speech.

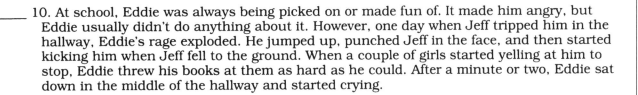

_____ 10. At school, Eddie was always being picked on or made fun of. It made him angry, but Eddie usually didn't do anything about it. However, one day when Jeff tripped him in the hallway, Eddie's rage exploded. He jumped up, punched Jeff in the face, and then started kicking him when Jeff fell to the ground. When a couple of girls started yelling at him to stop, Eddie threw his books at them as hard as he could. After a minute or two, Eddie sat down in the middle of the hallway and started crying.

Emotional Dilemmas

SITUATION #1

Jay and Kelly had been going together for almost a year. They were one of the most popular couples in school. Their relationship was really starting to get serious. Unfortunately, Kelly's parents thought the relationship was getting *too* serious. They made Kelly break up with Jay.

Now Kelly and Jay aren't allowed to see each other at all. At school, Kelly's not allowed to sit with Jay at lunch or even talk to him in the halls.

You're friends with both Kelly and Jay; you've seen the emotional turmoil they've both been going through since the break-up. Kelly is obeying her parents' demands, but she's very angry with her parents. She also cries a lot at school—especially when she sees Jay talking to other girls. Jay, on the other hand, is angry at Kelly for "choosing her parents over him." He mopes around a lot and certainly isn't the fun guy he used to be.

SITUATION #2

John's parents have always fought a lot. When you used to stop by his house after school, you could usually hear his parents yelling at each other in their bedroom. But things have gotten a lot worse lately. John has hinted that his mother and father may be hitting each other.

John doesn't talk much about his parents anymore. In fact, he doesn't talk much at all anymore. He seems angry and irritable.

The last time you went over to his house, he met you at the front door. "I don't want to stay here," he said. "Let's go over to your house."

When you tried to ask him what was going on with his parents, he exploded. "Can we just drop it, please?" he said. "Just forget about my parents! It's my business and I'll deal with it myself!"

SITUATION #3

Susan, the girl who sits next to you in English class, is usually pretty quiet. But lately she's been talking to you a lot. She asks weird questions—things like "Are you afraid of dying?" and "Do you think anyone would miss you if you died?"

She also talks about how much of a pain it is to get up in the morning and face another day. She's always seemed sad and depressed, but her mood has gotten even darker in the past couple of weeks. You're afraid she might be considering suicide—but you're not absolutely sure.

COUNSELING Q & A

Many people struggle with tough issues—things like drug or alcohol addiction, eating disorders, sexual addiction, homosexuality, physical or sexual abuse, unwanted pregnancy, and suicide. All of us can benefit from the counsel of others, but those with special needs should consider formal counseling. Here are some questions people might ask about counseling:

1. What should I do first? After praying about it, seek out a trusted Christian adult (perhaps a youth worker, pastor, or school counselor) to talk to. Be very honest with this person about your struggles, and trust this person to help you. Maybe that person can counsel you, or perhaps he or she can refer you to a professional.

2. When should I seek help? It's best to seek help right away, especially if you can relate to any of these signs of danger: sense of losing control of your life, loss of interest in activities, withdrawal from friends and family, depression, too little (or too much) sleep, loss of appetite, poor school performance, aggressive or violent behavior.

3. Will counseling solve my problems? No, but it can help. Ultimately, only God can meet your deepest needs, but a counselor can help get you to the point where you can better face your situation.

4. Should I see a Christian counselor? Again, it's best to start by talking with a trusted Christian adult. You can then explore your options together, basing future counseling requirements on your particular needs, and people that are available to help.

5. What if I can't afford it? Financial concerns should never prevent you from getting the help you need. Many professional counselors have a sliding-scale fee structure to make it more affordable. It's possible that some of the expense is covered under a parent's medical plan. Check it out.

6. If I need counseling, does that mean I'm crazy? Absolutely not—but you might be crazy *not* to seek help. Counseling is not a sign of weakness; if anything, it's healthy to get help when you need it.

7. Do my parents need to know? In most cases, it's probably best that they do know, so they can support you, and possibly get help themselves if they are contributing to your problem. So much depends on your unique situation. This is an issue you'll want to discuss with your trusted adult friend.

8. If I have a relationship with God, why get professional help? Good question. Maybe God can use the skills of a counselor to bring about some healing and growth in your life. Don't view counseling as a substitute for God, view it as one tool He gives to help us.

NOTES

STEP 1

Even though the three-legged race suggested in the session is active, you might want to try a less common activity that helps kids work together. Have kids form teams. Give one team 10 red balloons, another team 10 blue balloons, and so on. Also give each team a can of shaving cream or whipped cream and 10 pennies. Place a trash can in the center of the room. Explain that no one may go within 10 feet of the can. When the whistle blows, kids should squirt a little cream into each balloon, put a penny in each one, blow up the balloons, tie them off, and throw them into the trash can (from a distance of 10 feet). Balloons must be inflated to a minimum size. (You may want to display a sample balloon.) To determine the winning team, dump the balloons from the trash can, separate them by color, eliminate the ones that don't meet the minimum size requirement, and count the ones that are left. The team with the most balloons wins. Afterward, have each team explain its system. Did kids work as teammates or did individuals take over?

STEP 2

Cut apart the 10 situations from Repro Resource 6. Put the 10 slips of paper into a bag. Have someone pull one of the slips from the bag, read the situation, and act out a reaction as if he or she were alone with no one else to confide in. Then have another student come on the scene to share the first kid's burden or joy. Discuss which "scene" the kids preferred: handling a situation alone or with a friend. Do the same with as many situations as you have time for.

STEP 1

Play the three-legged race with a twist if you have a small group. Rather than having group members pair up, have them stand in line next to each other. Tie their legs together, forming a multi-legged chain. Place obstacles around the room to make it more difficult for the group to move. Also, assign various disabilities to slow the group down, such as blindness, muteness, paralysis in both legs, etc. Someone in line should hold the spoon with the marshmallow on it. Instead of racing, the goal is to get past the obstacles and to the other side of the room without dropping the marshmallow. Afterward, ask kids to describe how they felt during the activity. Talk about how they had to work together and communicate despite obstacles. Follow up with the last three questions from Step 1.

STEP 3

If you don't have enough kids to create three teams, work through Repro Resource 7 as a group. You might also want to work through only two of the situations instead of all three. If your group is small, you probably have a good sense as to whether any of your kids would benefit from the information on Repro Resource 8. If you think it might help some kids, distribute a copy to everyone in the group. You might even want to ask group members some of the questions on the sheet *before* passing it out. This will give you an idea of what your kids think about professional counseling.

STEP 1

If your group is large, you might want to have two pairs race against each other at a time. This should make it easier to determine who the winners are. You won't have to keep track of a long list of times. If you think the race will take up more time than you're willing to give it, try this: Invite a volunteer to come forward for a ballet demonstration. Ask him or her to jump up and click his or her heels together five times before hitting the ground. After a few attempts, invite two other volunteers (preferably two of your stronger group members) to come forward and assist the person. Now see if the person can click his or her heels together five times. It should be simple, if the two volunteers hold him or her up. Use this activity to lead into the questions at the end of Step 1 about relying on other people to help us work through our emotions.

STEP 4

Instead of using the activity with masking tape, have group members form two kinds of teams—Helpers (with four members each) and Hurters (with two members each). Make sure you have an equal number of Helpers and Hurters teams. Tie the members of each Hurters team together back-to-back at the waist. Have them start at the wall opposite the Helpers. Assign one Hurters team to each Helpers team. The Hurters should try to stop the Helpers from getting to the other side of the room. The Helpers can run only when three of them are carrying a fourth teammate. The Hurters should chase the Helpers and try to tag the one that is being carried. If the person is tagged, the Helpers have to start over again. The game ends when the first Helpers team makes it across the room. Afterward, compare the strength of the larger teams of Helpers to the strength of the three cords or strands mentioned in the Ecclesiastes passage.

STEP 2

Ask for five volunteers to perform some brief roleplays. Assign each volunteer one of the following roles: friend, parent, pastor, counselor, and psychiatrist. Instruct each volunteer to explain to the group why his or her character would be helpful to someone who is upset or has a problem. Volunteers should assume the roles of their characters and speak in the first person. For example, the "parent" might say: "I am a parent and I could be helpful to someone who is upset. I've raised five kids and dealt with all kinds of problems and emergencies. So I have lots of ideas, patience, and calmness to offer." Then select several of the situations from Repro Resource 6 and have the volunteers explain how their characters could help. Situations 2, 3, 4, 5, and 10 might work best for this activity.

STEP 4

The following activity may help sensitize kids who have heard the principles contained in this step before. Have group members choose a word from Psalm 139:1-5. Write the word vertically on the left side of the board. Turn the word into an acronym by making each letter the first letter of a word or phrase that has to do with the session topic. Each word or phrase should deal with turning to other people for help when we experience emotional turmoil, helping others who are hurting, or choosing God as a cord of strength in our emotional lives. For example, *hand* could be used in the following way:

• Help others.

• Always be there.

• Never turn someone away.

• Don't forget to lend a hand.

STEP 3

You might want to provide some additional scriptural background to encourage your kids to help others who are in need. Here some passages you might want to use:

• Luke 10:30-37 ("He went to him and bandaged his wounds. . . . Go and do likewise.")

• I Corinthians 12:27-28 ("those able to help others")

• Ephesians 4:29 ("only what is helpful for building others up according to their needs")

• Colossians 3:12-14 ("clothe yourselves with compassion, kindness, humility, gentleness and patience"; "Bear with each other"; "put on love")

• Hebrews 13:15-16 ("do not forget to do good and share with others")

STEP 4

Why should kids who don't know God very well trust Him in tough situations? Have your group members look up Job 38. It's a long passage, but it describes an amazing God. Ask: **What amazing things does this passage say that God knows or has done?** (Among other things, He created the earth, the oceans and seas, the light, darkness, death, snow, hail, lightning, winds, rain, thunderstorms, deserts, grass, dew, ice, frost, the stars and constellations, clouds, and food.) Say: **The same great God who created the heavens and the earth and all of the secrets of science and who knows all of the things mentioned in Job 38 is the same God who gently invites people to come to Him when they are in need.** Have kids look up a couple of God's invitations: Matthew 11:25-30 and Psalm 9:9-10.

STEP I

Have group members sit in a circle (preferably on chairs). If you know of close friends within the group, quietly ask them to sit across from each other, not next to each other. Hand a large ball of yarn (or string) to someone in the circle. That person should hold on to the end of the yarn and throw the ball to someone else. Each time the ball of yarn is passed, the person who receives it should share an experience in which another person really helped him or her during a tough time. No one should receive the ball of yarn twice. After everyone is holding on to a piece of yarn, talk about how the people in your group can support each other emotionally. Discuss the emotional strength that can be created in the group. Then read aloud Romans 12:9-16 and discuss how it applies to helping one another emotionally.

STEP 4

After the discussion in Step 4, have your group members create personal welcome mats from heavy-duty poster board. Provide colorful markers, scissors, paints, pieces of fabric, old magazines, etc., so that kids can get creative. Explain that the welcome mats will symbolize their willingness to help others in times of crisis. On the other side of their mats, they should symbolize their willingness to be helped by others in times of turmoil. Afterward, have kids explain the meaning of the symbols they chose. Encourage them to keep the mats in their rooms as a reminder to be available to help others, and to be willing to ask for help. Then have a time of prayer in which kids can tell God that they want to become part of His "support network." Let kids act on their prayers by pairing them up to discuss how they can make themselves available to each other for support during good times and times of crisis.

STEP 2

After you've discussed the situations on "Help Needed—or Not?" (Repro Resource 6), talk about the emotions of guys and girls. Ask: **Do the guys you know have some of the same problems controlling their emotions that girls do? Is it easier for you to ask for help or to keep your emotions inside? Is it easier for you to be open about your feelings or to keep them private? What about guys? What can you do to be more sensitive to the guys you know as they are learning to understand the appropriate ways to express their emotions?**

STEP 4

Distribute paper and pencils. Ask your group members to vote in response to the following statements by writing "yes" or "no" on their papers. **(1) I can always tell when my emotions are out of control and whether I need help. (2) I can always tell if a friend's emotions are out of control and whether that person needs help.** Collect and tally the votes; then discuss the results. Ask: **What is your responsibility in helping someone or in getting help for someone who needs it? What is your responsibility in getting help for yourself?** Mention some specific adults who would welcome the opportunity to be of help to any of your group members (and their friends), if needed. This discussion might make a good tie-in to the information on Repro Resource 8 concerning professional counseling.

STEP 2

Bring in a set of barbells. Briefly train kids on how to lift safely (using the legs, not the back). Make sure that one barbell is so heavy that no one can lift it. Let a volunteer see how far he can get in picking up the barbells one at a time, beginning with the lightest one. Let other kids try the same thing. Then have kids try to guess how many people it would take to lift the heaviest barbell two inches or so off the floor. Let a couple of volunteers attempt it. (Make sure you have spotters to help if there is a problem.) Use the activity to lead into a discussion on how important it is to be open to accepting help from others when you are struggling. Also point out that it is important to be available to help others when needed.

STEP 3

Often guys are encouraged to rely on themselves and to hide their vulnerability from others. Encourage your group members to be more reliant upon others and more transparent. Add the following situation to your discussion of Repro Resource 7: **Doug goes to your church. He's kind of quiet, but seems like a nice guy. You start spending some time with him and become friends with him. He doesn't usually talk about his feelings, but you get the sense that he doesn't like himself very much. He puts himself down and always tries to change the subject when you ask him anything that's even remotely personal. One day, he opens up and says he wishes he were you because you're more outgoing, better-looking, more fun to be with, and not afraid to talk to girls. What do you say?** After discussing the situation, ask: **Why is it hard for a lot of guys to talk about their feelings? What could happen to someone who never cries? What could happen to someone who never shows weakness?**

STEP 1

Have someone bring a puppy, kitten, or some other baby animal to the session. Ask the person to describe all of the ways in which he or she takes care of the animal. Then have kids brainstorm ways in which caring for an animal is similar to caring for one another. Ask how people's emotional needs differ from animals'. You could also have new parents bring their baby to the session. Have them describe all of the ways in which they take care of the baby, including some of the dangers they protect the baby from. Then, as a group, brainstorm some ways in which kids could help take care of the baby— spiritually, emotionally, socially, and even physically when necessary. Challenge them to have the same concern for everyone in the group.

STEP 3

Place a dozen or so paper milk cartons on a table and number them. Fill six of them with items that stink, such as vinegar, fertilizer, rotten eggs, a cigarette butt, used cat litter, etc. Fill the other six with pleasant smelling items such as perfume, half of a lemon or orange, a sweet-smelling flower, chocolate, maple syrup, etc. Cover each carton by taping a thin sheet of paper towel over the top. This will prevent kids from seeing what is inside, but will still let the odors escape. Have kids sniff the cartons and write down their guesses as to what's inside each one. You might want to award small prizes to the kids with the most correct guesses. Afterward, have someone read aloud Philippians 4:18-19. Explain that in this passage, the apostle Paul is thanking the Philippian church for sending gifts that met his needs. Point out that if our acts of kindness to others had an odor, they would smell pleasant to God. You might also say that our reluctance to help others might smell bad to God.

STEP 3

Discuss only one of the emotional dilemmas from Repro Resource 7 so that there's time to watch clips you've recorded from TV shows and movies that show people helping others who are in need. You might show scenes of someone listening sympathetically to a troubled person, someone giving advice or first aid, someone protecting a helpless person, and/or someone calming down a distressed person. If you show several clips, you might want to add some fun to the activity by letting a volunteer try to recall and describe each scene in order—after you've shown all of the clips. If the first volunteer mentions a clip out of order, go to another volunteer. Afterward, ask kids if they've been in similar situations—as either the helper or the person being helped.

STEP 4

When you're finished discussing the "cord of three strands" activity, play "When You Need Someone" from The Kry's album of the same name. The Kry is a Christian rock band with a sound that your kids should enjoy. Use the song to create a worshipful atmosphere just before you close in prayer.

STEP 2

To save time, have group members work only on the first five situations from Repro Resource 6. Then ask: **When kids are having emotional problems, what do they usually do to deal with those problems? Do most kids keep quiet about them? When kids do seek someone else's help, who do they usually go to first?**

STEP 3

Instead of discussing the situations from Repro Resource 7, ask the following questions: **Do you think that needing help with your emotions is a sign of weakness? If your best friend was upset, would you think he or she was weak for getting help? Is it OK to get help from a friend? A parent? Some other adult? A pastor? A counselor? A psychiatrist? A psychiatric hospital?** Make sure each group member offers his or her opinion (even if it's just by nodding his or her head) for each question. These questions could be used as an introduction to Repro Resource 8.

STEP 2

Ask two people to come to the front of the room and make a tight bond by linking arms. Place a mattress or a stack of pillows or blankets behind them. Then ask for a volunteer to try to push the two over. The volunteer may or may not be successful. If he or she is unsuccessful, bring up other volunteers to try to push the two over. For the second round, make the activity more challenging by having kids try to knock down a group of three. Continue adding more people to the group until the rest of the kids give up. You can use this activity to point out that the bigger the problem, the more help we need to bring it down.

STEP 3

Here are some additional "Emotional Dilemmas" you might use with your urban group:

Situation #1
BaeBae's mother has been out of a job for over a year. The family has very little money. Today when BaeBae got home from school, he found his mother sitting on the doorstep, crying hysterically. All of the family's furniture was piled up on the curb. They'd been evicted! Realizing what had happened, BaeBae tried to be tough, but he was devastated inside. What emotions do you think BaeBae is experiencing? How could you help him deal with those emotions?

Situation #2
Jade lives in a low-cost housing development and excels in her school. But she's constantly teased, picked on, and called names because she does so well and behaves so properly. She's fed up and wants to flunk a class or go do something terrible, just so the other kids will get off her case. What emotions do you think Jade is experiencing? How could you help her deal with those emotions?

STEP 2

Use the following game to create camaraderie among kids of different ages. Form teams of equal numbers of junior highers and high schoolers. Set up one limbo stick per team—low enough to the ground to make it impossible to pass under it without help. The members of each team have to work together to get each person under the stick (limbo style) without letting that person fall to the floor or touch the floor with his or her arms or hands. The first team to get everyone under properly wins. Lead into a discussion about helping each other—especially when there is great need. Include the last question from Step 2.

STEP 3

When you form three teams to work on Repro Resource 7, you might want to assign Situation 1 to a group that is composed only of high schoolers. They may be more comfortable than junior highers about discussing a dating problem. The other two situations will apply as much to junior highers as to high schoolers, so assign them any way you want. If you know a high schooler or a college student who has benefited from counseling, ask him or her to share a few words with your group about the experience. This would be a great lead-in to the information on Repro Resource 8.

STEP 2

After your sixth graders indicate their responses on "Help Needed—or Not?" (Repro Resource 6), have them form teams of four or five. Either assign each team a situation from the resource, or ask the teams to choose one. Have the members of each team discuss how they might respond to a friend in that situation, focusing not only on what they might say, but also on what they should *not* say. After a few minutes, have the teams share their ideas with the rest of the group.

STEP 4

Read aloud Psalm 139:1-5. Then, as a group, talk about how well God knows us. Ask: **When you realize that God knows everything about you—including what you're thinking—does it help you feel more comfortable with expressing yourself—including your emotions? If you're shy about showing your emotions, what can you do? How can understanding *your* emotions help you know what to do when someone else needs your help?**

DATE USED:

Approx. Time

STEP 1: *Let's Work Together* _____
- ❏ Extra Action
- ❏ Small Group
- ❏ Large Group
- ❏ Fellowship & Worship
- ❏ Extra Fun
Things needed:

STEP 2: *With a Little Help from My Friends* _____
- ❏ Extra Action
- ❏ Heard It All Before
- ❏ Mostly Girls
- ❏ Mostly Guys
- ❏ Short Meeting Time
- ❏ Urban
- ❏ Combined Junior High/High School
- ❏ Sixth Grade
Things needed:

STEP 3: *A Helping Hand* _____
- ❏ Small Group
- ❏ Little Bible Background
- ❏ Mostly Guys
- ❏ Extra Fun
- ❏ Media
- ❏ Short Meeting Time
- ❏ Urban
- ❏ Combined Junior High/High School
Things needed:

STEP 4: *Three Strands* _____
- ❏ Large Group
- ❏ Heard It All Before
- ❏ Little Bible Background
- ❏ Fellowship & Worship
- ❏ Mostly Girls
- ❏ Media
- ❏ Sixth Grade
Things needed:

NOTES

Unit Three: Just Look at You!

Looks Can Be Deceiving

by Darrell Pearson

I had waited all year for this moment. The yearbook at my three-thousand-student junior and senior high school had just been released, and my picture was in it. Not just any picture, either. Earlier in the year, the yearbook staff had pulled me out of my eighth-grade science class and spent an hour shooting pictures of the homecoming queen and me together. Imagine! They had shots of the two of us standing face-to-face looking into each other's eyes (actually, I was looking *up* at her eyes), and standing back-to-back; they had faraway shots, close-ups, the whole gamut of poses—with just me and a twelfth-grade female.

I was ready for this picture—until I flipped open the book and saw what the yearbook staff had been after. There we were, all right—a full-page spread of the two of us. But the picture was *not* what I expected. *She* was standing with her back to the camera, and *I* was at the bottom of a long flight of stairs staring up at her. I realized in that instant how I really looked to the rest of the world: I was a short, nerdy, badly dressed, haircut-by-Dad kid with black glasses all over my face. I was devastated.

That moment still defines my junior high experience. How I thought I looked was critically important to the way my world was shaped and how I lived. That poor kid in the picture knew that when God passed out the looks, he got passed over.

I can't rid myself of the memory, because it was just too strong in shaping my junior high—and following—years. When I look at junior high kids struggling with the way God put them together, I remember too clearly how it felt, because it felt terrible.

Aren't most kids this way? Don't most junior high students struggle with their appearance more than any other single area? And don't they hear from adults all the time that things will change when they get older (when their body starts to "*really* develop") or that they're actually OK right now?

We've been selling kids short. Just like the photo defined me as a person, so junior highers everywhere define themselves by how they perceive they look to others. And with the media and society constantly giving them impossible comparisons, they can't help feeling awful about the way they're made, questioning the validity of a God who seems so cruel. I think there are a few things we can do to help.

Making Light of a Heavy Issue

Adults do tend to pacify kids' concerns about their appearance with too-easy answers like "Don't worry, you'll grow soon enough" or "You really are beautiful because God made you that way." Statements like these often trivialize a very important issue, even if the statements are true. There's a big dilemma here for kids: *Why did God make me look like this?* It's a good question that deserves a serious response and not just a cute phrase. Why does God make any of us the way we are? Why do we have to go through puberty at all?

The fact that you're planning to use this book is a good start. Most junior high leaders tend to pick one night periodically to talk about the subject, read Psalm 139, and move on to *dating* the next week. This topic needs some careful study. Your kids deserve some time from you in which you try to answer this major question of their lives. Quoting *"God looks on the heart"* is nice, but kids know that humans still look at the outside first—and humans are who they understand best.

Since one of the best views most kids have of God is the view they have of you, God's representative, then it stands to reason that your approach to them and how you accept the way they're made means an awful lot. Do they see in you someone who truly accepts the way they look and treats them the same as others? Can you look them in the eye and communicate God's love through your actions? You just might be the most tangible expression of Jesus they can understand. While you search for answers to the big question, teach them the truth about God by acting toward them as He would. They can feel better about themselves when they have some idea that God, and at least one adult on earth, feels OK about them right now.

Talking to Adults about the Way They're Made

How comfortable are you with the way you look? We tend to think that kids in mid-puberty are the big strugglers, but it's also true that most people wrestle with their appearance their whole lives. Most adults I know still feel funny about the way they're made, wondering why they weren't better-looking, better-shaped, or better-designed for some greater purpose in this world. Do you feel OK about the way you're made?

One of the great tests to determine if an adult is a good candidate for junior high leadership is to see how he or she feels about the way he or she looks. Adults who are still striving for their own acceptance with others may not make the best leaders. An adult who refuses to be involved in a skit that makes fun of himself or herself is not much different than the junior high student who is watching. Vain volunteers don't fit junior high ministry well. You've got to be able to put vanity aside to communicate to kids.

Jerry was one of the best junior high teachers we ever had in our church. When I first met Jerry, I was worried about how he would relate to the kids. He was overweight, and I was afraid the students would make fun of him and not respect him. One Sunday I heard the ninth graders in his class laughing about that week's lesson. I discovered that Jerry had a proposition going with his students. Every week they began class with a weigh-in. If Jerry had lost weight, the class members contributed double to their mission project. If he had gained, he contributed. Here was a guy who was comfortable enough with himself to let the kids see who he really was.

I learned another important lesson from Jerry's activity that works with junior high students: Kids love adults who can laugh at themselves and not take themselves too seriously. If kids can see that you too have shortcomings—and can live with them—they may realize that they can do the same. In my case, my kids love teasing me about the fact that I'm short. They may feel better about themselves if they know that I feel good about myself even though I'm shorter than most ninth graders. Pick something about yourself (approaching baldness, a bad habit, etc.) and make it an issue. Your kids will love you for it.

Face-to-Face

Some young people who are struggling with the way they're made may need intervention. Eating disorders, for example, demand taking the initiative to confront kids with the significance of their problem. Less serious situations require a simpler approach. Often kids don't have the support and teaching at home to learn how to take care of themselves. With a little help, they can learn to make the most of what they have. More than once I've watched leaders take kids under their wing and teach them the basics of good hygiene. Confrontation can be an appropriate approach. Look for the small but important issues that kids need to deal with. Sometimes a "minor" problem is the root of kids' self-esteem crises.

When I was in the tenth grade, my black horn-rimmed glasses broke and were replaced with gold wire rims that I was proud of. *My entire personality changed.* For the first time that I could remember, I was not embarrassed because of my face. To this day, I refuse to wear contacts, because my glasses rescued me years ago and I'll never forget them for it. (Oh, how that yearbook photo might have looked!) When you go face-to-face with your kids, is there something very straightforward that you could do to help them cope with the reality of how they look? It might not take much, just a thoughtful change suggestion from a caring adult.

To junior highers, the way they're made is defined primarily by their looks. Help them accept the reality of what they see, teach them about God through your actions, and help them take what God has given them and make the most of it. In doing so, you may help your kids take great strides in working through their confusion and frustration about the way they're made.

Darrell Pearson is cofounder of 10 TO 20, an organization headquartered in Colorado Springs that creates high-involvement youth events for teenagers, including Next Exit, *a junior high program that tours the U.S. and Canada each year.*

The images on these two pages are designed to help you promote this course within your church and community. Feel free to photocopy anything here and adapt it to fit your publicity needs. The stuff on this page could be used as a flier that you send or hand out to kids—or as a bulletin insert. The stuff on the next page could be used to add visual interest to newsletters, calendars, bulletin boards, or other promotions. Be creative and have fun!

What Do You See When You Look in the Mirror?

Are you as smart as you'd like to be?
Would you be happier if you had a better-looking body?
Do you ever wish you had a more outgoing personality?
Join the club! For the next few weeks, we'll be talking about the way you're made. We'll also focus on some of the physical and emotional changes you're experiencing (or will be experiencing soon).
Join us for a new course called *Just Look at You!*

Who:

When:

Where:

Questions? Call:

Unit Three: Just Look at You!

I've Gotta Be Me...
Whether I Like It or Not

March 1
2006

THE MIRACULOUS
SELF-ESTEEM
ENHANCER!!

SEE
YOURSELF
THROUGH
GOD'S
EYES!

YOUR GOALS FOR THIS SESSION:

Choose one or more

☐ To help kids see that God can provide a positive self-image when they can't manufacture it themselves.

☐ To help kids understand that the development of a positive self-image is a process—not an instantaneous change of opinion.

☐ To help kids take steps of faith to be sure that God is at work in their lives and to see themselves more as God sees them—as valuable and worthwhile individuals.

☐ Other:_____
_____

Your Bible Base:

Judges 6
2 Corinthians 5:17

Men of Steel and Caped Crusaders

(Needed: Copies of Repro Resource 1, pencils)

Begin the session with a discussion of superheroes. Many junior high students read a lot of comic books, so some of your group members may know about a lot of different characters. Others may be limited to Superman and Batman, but that's OK. Ask: **Who is your favorite superhero? Why? When was the last time you could have used a superhero to come to your rescue?**

If no one brings it up, mention that one common characteristic of most superheroes is a secret identity. To other people, most superheroes seem like normal, average people—or even below-average people. Few people ever suspect that beneath the humble and unimpressive exterior of Clark Kent lies the man of steel—Superman! No one who knows Diana Prince would believe she is actually Wonder Woman, or that Bruce Wayne is Batman or Peter Parker is Spiderman.

Say: **There seems to be quite a number of normal and not necessarily impressive people here today. Which of us do you think might actually be hiding a secret identity as a superhero? Why?** Let group members respond. **Who do you think would be *least* likely to be a superhero?**

After some creative speculation, hand out copies of "Your Secret Identity" (Repro Resource 1) and pencils. Let each group member create his or her own secret identity. Kids will also describe how they think others see them. Pay special attention to these self-descriptions. You might discover some specific self-image concerns to keep in mind as you lead this session and this series.

When group members finish, collect their drawings and descriptions, read one at a time, and see if the others can guess who wrote what.

Handwritten note:
SWORD DRILLS
B) Matt 10:30,31
   Luke 15:10
   Psalm 139:13-14
A) Prov 31:30
   Romans 9:20,21
   1 Sam 16:7
   (Exodus 4:10,11)

Self-Inventory

(Needed: Paper, pencils)

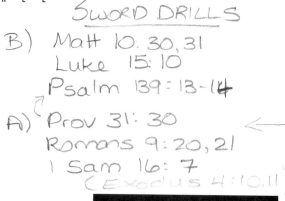

Distribute paper and pencils. Ask group members to make two columns on the paper. In the first column they should write personal characteristics they feel are assets—things they like about themselves. In the second column they should write things they don't particularly like about themselves. You might want to have everyone consider a number of categories (physical traits, feelings and emotional characteristics, academic ability, spiritual qualities, etc.). Some of these things are likely to be personal, so don't put pressure on people to share aloud. But if volunteers are willing to mention an item or two from their lists, let them do so.

OPTIONS: LARGE GROUP, LITTLE BIBLE BACKGROUND, MOSTLY GUYS, MEDIA, SIXTH GRADE

Then ask: **Which column had more entries: the list of things you liked about yourself, or the column of things you'd like to change or eliminate?**

In what specific category did you desire the most changes?

Did you make any surprising discoveries about yourself during this self-inventory?

Many junior highers will probably focus on their physical characteristics. As their bodies begin to change, much attention is given to how they look—compared to how their peers look. Physical traits frequently become sources of painful jokes or comments. Session 2 will deal more specifically with body image, but the issue needs to be recognized here as you begin to discuss self-image in general.

Say: **I'm going to ask some questions and I want you to rate your response to each one on a scale of one to 10, with one being the least. Show your response to each question by holding up the appropriate number of fingers.** Ask the following questions, waiting for a group response after each one.

- **How much do you like who you are?**
- **How much do you care what other people think about you?**
- **How much effort do you put into trying to look good to other people?**
- **How important would you say image—a person's "look"—is to most people your age?**

Memory verse
Psalm 139: 13, 14
2 Cor 5:16(a), 17

Allow volunteers to make more specific comments, but don't pressure anyone to talk who doesn't want to. Then explain that you're going to take a look at someone who would probably have rated himself very low on the ten-point scale, yet who became a "mighty warrior" for God.

Before you do, however, have group members look up and memorize 2 Corinthians 5:17: "Therefore, if anyone is in Christ, he is a new creation; the old has gone, the new has come!" Explain that no matter how bad we think things are, or how disappointed we are with the way we were created, the promise remains of being changed into something new, better, and more satisfying. The story of Gideon symbolizes this change.

Read "You Are Special"

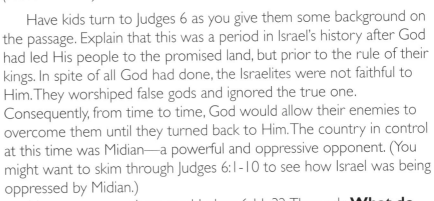

STEP 3

Not a Likely Candidate for Studs

(Needed: Bibles)

OPTIONS

EXTRA **ACTION**

HEARD IT ALL BEFORE

FELLOWSHIP & **WORSHIP**

EXTRA **FUN**

SHORT MEETING **TIME**

Have kids turn to Judges 6 as you give them some background on the passage. Explain that this was a period in Israel's history after God had led His people to the promised land, but prior to the rule of their kings. In spite of all God had done, the Israelites were not faithful to Him. They worshiped false gods and ignored the true one. Consequently, from time to time, God would allow their enemies to overcome them until they turned back to Him. The country in control at this time was Midian—a powerful and oppressive opponent. (You might want to skim through Judges 6:1-10 to see how Israel was being oppressed by Midian.)

Have group members read Judges 6:11-32. Then ask: **What do you think Gideon's self-inventory would have included if he had listed the things he liked and didn't like about himself—before his encounter with the angel?** Let kids respond, filling out two columns for Gideon as they previously did for themselves. Based on this passage, they should come up with several shortcomings, including fear, low social status, spiritual doubt, lack of confidence, and so forth. They will probably be hard-pressed to find anything positive to say about Gideon. The one thing he did have going for him was that he was eventually willing to do something risky that God asked him to do. He was very reluctant to do so, but he finally overcame his reluctance and his low self-appraisal to risk obedience. As it turned out, it was the beginning of a life-changing process for Gideon.

STEP 4

I've Got Those Hiding-in-My-Winepress Blues

(Needed: Bibles, paper, pencils, chalkboard and chalk or newsprint and marker)

Discuss the facts of Gideon's story, and allow group members to ask questions. When everyone seems to understand the events of the story, ask: **What are some of the things we could learn about self-image from this story about Gideon?** Among other things, group members should come up with these observations:

OPTIONS

LARGE GROUP

LITTLE BIBLE BACKGROUND

MOSTLY GIRLS

URBAN

JR. HIGH HIGH SCHOOL COMBINED

- God sees who you can be—with His help—rather than who you are now (vs. 12).
- Even though we may face unpleasant circumstances, that doesn't mean God is no longer in control (vs. 13).
- God is not limited by man-made social structures (vss. 15-16).
- We may desire signs from God, but God desires faithful action on our part (vss. 17, 25, 26).
- Obedience to God results in increased confidence, power, and self-image (vss. 30-32).

As group members comment, list their observations on the board. Then go one step further and ask group members to come up with one or two personal *applications* based on the things they thought were significant from this account of Gideon. Their applications should be specific rather than general. It's one thing to say, "The next time something bad happens to me, I'll trust God." It will be much more effective to make sure group members create applications such as "The next time I'm confronted by Bronco, the school bully, I will say a silent prayer and ask God to give me wisdom and courage." When everyone finishes, let any willing volunteers share their applications. Encourage group members to support each other's proposed applications with regular prayer.

Gideon: The Sequel

(Needed: Copies of Repro Resource 2, pencils)

O P T I O N S

Ask: **Do you think Gideon immediately became a new and better person as soon as he obeyed God and tore down the altars to Baal and Asherah? Why?** Let group members debate this for a while. While Gideon's obedience very likely boosted his faith in God and his self-confidence, it is unlikely that his entire personality changed in an instant. Explain that the development of important things such as faith, courage, and self-image usually requires a significant period of time. This was true in Gideon's case, as group members will see if they continue reading the Book of Judges.

To provide one more glimpse of what happened to Gideon after his nighttime tangle with Israel's false gods and his confrontation with the townspeople, have someone read aloud Judges 6:36-40.

Then ask: **After God's previous sign to Gideon** (6:21), **why do you think Gideon asked for additional ones?** (Perhaps Gideon's self-image was still low. God had kept him safe even after he tore down the altars to Baal and Asherah, but Gideon realized that it would be quite a different challenge to lead his nation against the Midianites.)

Jesus reminds us not to "put the Lord your God to the test" (Matthew 4:7). **Why do you think Gideon was allowed to test God?** (Jesus was being tempted to do something foolish just to manipulate God into intervening. Gideon wasn't trying to show off or get attention. He appeared to be genuinely concerned that God would indeed be present as he [Gideon] faced the Midianites. Sometimes it is a delicate balance to give God an opportunity to show that He is active in our lives without expecting Him to "put on a show" just because we ask Him to.)

Do you know of people today who do anything similar to "putting out a fleece" to clarify whether or not God is leading them in a certain direction? Let kids respond in general terms about what "other people" do. They will have an opportunity to consider their own responses on the repro resource.

Hand out copies of "Fleece Circus" (Repro Resource 2) and pencils. Ask group members to think of a step of faith they might be willing to take in the near future—a way to allow God the opportunity to give them some clear direction. As you do, be aware that cults and other religious groups sometimes use similar "get results from God" methods to try to mislead young people. Remind your group that God is not a vending machine, and that He may choose not to respond as we expect or hope for. We don't "control" God in any way, yet He knows what we need before we ask Him (Matt. 6:8), and He is the source of every good gift (Jas. 1:16-17). And sometimes the reason God doesn't work in our lives is that we don't ask Him to (Matt. 7:7-8). When kids finish, provide an opportunity for them to share some of the ideas they came up with.

To close the session, summarize the facts of Gideon's story that apply to self-image. Say: **Gideon went on to become the "mighty warrior" that God knew he could be. As Repro Resource 2 suggests, you might want to read Judges 7 to see what he and God were able to do together. If Gideon had waited until his friends or family treated him with the respect he deserved, he never would have accomplished anything for God—nor would he have ever known exactly what he was capable of doing. But since he overcame his reluctance and allowed God to use him in a major way, Gideon's life changed for the better.**

Positive change didn't happen immediately. For Gideon, as for most of us, developing a positive self-image was a process. Anyone can have "proud moments" here and there where image levels are high and confidence is up. But Gideon learned that, with God in control, his entire life could be lived with the assurance that he was a valuable and important person—even though he had started out as a coward, even though he and his family were "nobodies," and even though the problems he faced seemed too big for anyone to handle.

Gideon allowed God to show what He could do. When we face periods of despair, rejection, or low self-esteem, we need to do the same. If Gideon could be perceived by God as worthwhile and important, *anyone* can.

YOUR SECRET IDENTITY

From all outer appearances, Clark Kent was nothing but a mild-mannered reporter—clumsy, wimpy, shy, and helpless. Little did the citizens of Metropolis know that Clark Kent was actually the secret identity of Superman— the Man of Steel! For that matter, who knows who *you* might be beneath that cute but slightly imperfect exterior?

Here's your chance to create a superhero alter ego for yourself. First, describe yourself as you think you appear to the rest of the world most of the time. Then describe the secret identity you would create for yourself (strengths, special abilities, and at least one weakness that makes you vulnerable). Finally, decide what would be your mission as a superhero. Would you fight for truth, justice, and the American way? Or would your goal perhaps be something more self-centered?

When people look at me, they don't see all of my hidden strengths. From all outer appearances I seem to be . . .

But little does the rest of the world know that during times of need, I become . . .

Name:

Special super-abilities:

Weakness(es):

My mission as a superhero is . . .

NOTES

Fleece Circus

When Gideon asked, God did some pretty amazing things for him. The wet-fleece-on-dry-ground and dry-fleece-on-wet-ground demonstrations were truly miraculous. After witnessing such things, Gideon couldn't deny that God was active in his life.

When's the last time you looked for God to take an active role in *your* life? Maybe it's been years since you've been up early enough to check for dew. Besides, where are you going to find a sheepskin? But that won't keep God from revealing Himself to you in other ways. So you need to figure out a way to look for His involvement that will be especially meaningful to you. It took a lot of faith for Gideon to lay the fleece on the ground and make his request of God—twice. But his faith was rewarded. Sometime you should read Judges 7 to see what Gideon was then able to do with God's help! But first think about *you*.

1. What is one specific area of life in which you could really use some direction?

2. Have you asked for God's help in this matter yet? If so, in what way(s)?

3. What do you think God *might* want you to do?

4. What specific things can you do to give God an opportunity to communicate more clearly with you in some way?

5. If you try these things, what's the worst that could happen? What's the best that could happen?

ONE THING TO KEEP IN MIND: Occasionally, as in Gideon's case, God responds in an incredibly power-ful and obvious way. More often, however, He speaks in a "gentle whisper" (I Kings 19:12, 13). You may need to listen very closely, but His leading will be clear and helpful—regardless of the method He uses to communicate.

STEP 1

Rather than simply discussing superheroes, let your group members actually create some. Have group members form teams. Provide an assortment of supplies and/or old clothing items for each team. Instruct each team to select one person to be the superhero. The team should create a "history" of the superhero (where he or she came from, how the hero[ine] acquired super powers, etc.) and design an appropriate costume. When the teams finish, let each one introduce and explain its superhero. (You might want to have a camera ready to take a superhero "group picture.") Move from this activity to Repro Resource 1, where each person will have the opportunity to become a superhero.

STEP 3

Conduct a "self-esteem relay" after doing the self-inventory for Gideon. As group members list things that Gideon was lacking (confidence, courage, social status, faith, etc.), write these things on individual sticky notes. Then stick the notes to a variety of objects at one end of the room. (For example, "confidence" could be stuck to folded chairs, "courage" to hymnals, "social status" to volleyballs, etc.) Have group members form teams. Try to have an identical set of items for each team, and try to choose items that will be somewhat awkward to handle. Have teams line up in single file, facing the labeled items. At your signal, the first person in line should pick up one of the items and pass it *over his or her head* to the person behind him or her. The next person should pass the item *between his or her legs* to the next person. The "over and under" relay should continue until the last person receives the item. After that person disposes of the item (either over his or her head or between his or her legs), he or she should run to the front of the line and grab another item to pass backward. The winner is the first team to transfer "confidence," "courage," and all of the other qualities from one end of the room to the other.

STEP 1

Rather than using Repro Resource 1 after the superhero discussion, begin the session by letting each person assume the identity of a popular superhero (Batman, Superman, Wonder Woman, etc.). Have group members imagine that they are starting a Superheroes Club. Instruct the members to work together to write a "mission statement," create some common goals, determine officers, and so forth. During the discussion, the various strengths of the individuals will probably be considered. Afterward, point out that the church—and small groups—should operate in much the same way, with everyone contributing his or her unique and specific strengths for the good of the whole. Also point out that, as in the traditional superhero stories, with power comes responsibility. As you begin the discussion of Gideon, it should be easy to see that the more God boosted Gideon's self-esteem, the more He expected of Gideon.

STEP 5

After group members complete Repro Resource 2 and set individual goals, brainstorm some group goals. Instruct kids to think of things they would like to see take place in the group or things they would like the group to accomplish. Encourage them to "think big," and not settle for easily reachable goals. Small groups may be able to relate to Gideon's feelings of being outnumbered, oppressed, and insecure. They may feel isolated when they get out into the "real" world—and may even feel inferior in comparison to other churches that have flashier programs and larger numbers of people. The point of this session is that God can use anyone who is willing to serve. Try to build a level of confidence that God can definitely use your group—individually and collectively—as "mighty warriors" for Him. Kids should set goals that anticipate His involvement in their lives. After several goals have been suggested, choose one as a group and develop some strategies for reaching it.

STEP 2

Sometimes certain kids seem to get lost in a large group. If they aren't outspoken or aggressive, they may be ignored by other group members. There's no better time to make sure everyone gets recognized than while studying the life of Gideon. Have kids form groups of five or six. Ask group members to think of what each person in the group does better than anyone else. One at a time, they should focus on an individual while the other group members make suggestions as to what he or she does best. Suggest that they be as specific as possible. If the category is "Group's Best Athlete," then only one person can be recognized. But many people can be recognized if, instead of "athlete," they specify "baseball player," "tennis player," "golfer," "hackey-sacker," etc. Group members can also use categories such as Best Smile, Best Eyes, Best Attitude, etc.

STEP 4

Gideon was chosen as a "mighty warrior" for God even though he was convinced that his clan was the weakest in his tribe and that he was the least in his family. Use these same criteria to determine the mightiest warriors (potentially) in your group. Have everyone pair up. Say: **In your pairs, whoever is older, sit down.** Those still standing should find another partner. Then say: **Whoever is taller, sit down.** Continue with the following:

• **Whoever has the better grade point average, sit down.**
• **Whoever is stronger, sit down.**
• **Whoever is carrying more money, sit down.**

When you finish, you should have one of the most unlikely people from your group left as a "mighty warrior." Yet as odd as it may seem that this person might be chosen as a leader, that's exactly the position Gideon found himself in. Of the many people God could have chosen who were bigger, stronger, and more confident, Gideon was the person God had in mind.

STEP 3

When you're dealing with kids who think they've heard it all before, one thing you can do is take a different approach to the material covered. In this case, kids may know the *facts* about Gideon's being chosen to lead Israel. If so, challenge them to listen to the story again, this time trying to determine the *feelings* Gideon must have experienced as all of this was happening to him. From time to time in the narrative, stop and ask: **What three words would you use to describe how Gideon was feeling at this point?** In many cases, this will take some "between the lines" analysis of what is happening. Yet only when group members begin to put themselves in Gideon's shoes will they be able to truly know the story. Facts are of little use without genuine understanding and feeling.

STEP 5

When you get to the story of the fleece (Judg. 6:36-40), don't read the account from the Bible. Ask group members not to look up the story. If they think they know this story as well as they need to, explain that you want to test them. Tell them that you will paraphrase the story and they should correct any parts that you intentionally or unintentionally don't get quite right. Make changes in the story as you see fit, and see if group members catch them all. Or try a different strategy: Tell the story exactly according to the biblical account and see if group members will try to second-guess you. If you are very specific with the details, they are likely to think you're changing something. They may discover that they don't know the details quite as well as they think.

STEP 2

At the end of this step, the 2 Corinthians 5:17 verse is presented briefly before moving on to the next step. But if your group doesn't have much Bible background, you'll probably need to spend some time explaining the verse. Point out that this is a key verse in understanding that anyone who puts his or her trust in God can make a significant change for the better. Emphasize the word *anyone* in the verse, and point out that the verse is present tense rather than future tense. We don't have to wait for God to make wonderful changes in our lives. Those of us who have already received Jesus' forgiveness of sins and His salvation are already new creations. Sure, we're still changing for the better and may have a long way to go, but God has already begun His amazing transformation from the helpless people we were to the mighty warriors we can be as we yield to Him and receive His power.

STEP 4

When you begin to deal with the actual story of Gideon, several of the people and places will probably sound strange and intimidating for people new to Scripture. Gideon himself may be a new name to learn, much less *Midianites, Amalekites,* altars to *Baal,* and *Asherah poles.* So after you set the scene for the biblical story, try to update it as if it were taking place today. Instead of being invaded by the Midianites, have your kids suppose the U.S. were being invaded by cruel and heartless Canadians (or vice versa if you live in Canada). Replace Baal and Asherah with Buddha, Thor, Zeus, or Siva (if your kids have seen *Indiana Jones and the Temple of Doom*). When people are new to Scripture, it's sometimes hard to get past all the strange names to figure out what's going on. Try to set the scene as clearly as possible for your young people.

STEP 3

As a fellowship-building exercise, spend some time on each individual, bestowing affirmation on him or her as a "mighty warrior." You might want to raise each warrior to the shoulders of others in the group. Or have group members stand in a circle and, one at a time, let each person stand inside the circle. As he or she does, the others should offer cheers and applause, as well as relevant positive comments about the person. ("Hail, she who provides the group with excellent chocolate chip cookies for our continued nourishment!" "Huzzah for he who brings many new people to the group!") Try to build the camaraderie of the group through this exercise. Junior highers need as much affirmation as they can get, and your group is one of their best outlets to receive it.

STEP 5

Just as Gideon started out cowering in a winepress and ended up leading his nation, your group members can make a similar transition (symbolically). Begin with all of your group members in the basement of the church or huddled in a remote corner. Say a prayer to thank God for where they are now, for how far He has already brought them in life, and for uniting them in this group. Then go outside onto the church lawn or to some other public place. Say another prayer, this time asking Him to provide courage and boldness and to lead them wherever He wants them to go from this point on—into their schools, families, neighborhoods, and so forth. Thank Him in advance for His support as He gives them strength to become mighty warriors for Him.

STEP 1

Point out that most comic-book super-heroes are men. Ask: **Why do you suppose that is?** (The superheroes are created by men; they possess traits that society has often labeled as "male"; etc.) **Did that make it difficult for you to fill out your secret identity? Do you think the superheroes' qualities are ones that only men have? What are some "superhero" qualities you see in women?** Ask your girls to talk about any "superheroes" they know in real life.

STEP 4

When girls in junior high are faced with a question on self-image, their primary response—typically—is to focus only on the physical. Take a little extra time here to talk about the fact that a person's self-image is made up of many parts—talents, abilities, unique likes and dislikes, etc. Have your girls brainstorm a list of as many different things as they can think of (that aren't physical characteristics) that make up a person's self-image. After your list is finished, say: **There's a lot more to like about yourself than just how you look.** This activity will help lay the groundwork for Session 2.

STEP 2

After the self-inventory, but before you announce the topic of the session, say: **I'm looking for someone to represent this group in a contest with hundreds of other church groups. I need a guy who is strong and mighty, so we're going to have a contest to help me determine who I should choose.** Randomly pair up your guys and have them arm wrestle. Then have each person find another partner, and have a second round. Keep going with various opponents as time permits. Ask everyone to keep track of his win-loss record. Also make a big deal about walking around the room and evaluating the potential of each person as the contests are taking place. Then announce your choice—someone who is seemingly less-qualified than other contestants. When other guys object, point out that sometimes one of the least likely people you would expect may well turn out to be the best possible person for a job. Then move into your study of Gideon to demonstrate your point.

STEP 5

Discuss the difference between doing *manly* things and *macho* things. Ask:
• **Do you think there's a difference between being manly and being macho? If so, what is it?**
• **Which do you think is easier: to act like a man or to act macho?**
• **Do you think Gideon felt macho as he was tearing down the altars to Baal and Asherah? Explain.**
• **How can you do manly things without developing the macho attitude that so many other guys seem to want or expect?**

Have your guys reexamine the goals they set for themselves. Make sure they leave room for God to act in their lives. Point out that it's easy to set goals that we know we can accomplish in our own strength. However, goals should depend on faith and obedience to God, not a macho attitude toward one's own abilities.

STEP 1

Rather than simply talking about super-heroes, bring a stack of comic books so group members can do some "serious" research. Have them all skim a comic book and determine:

• **What would have happened if the superhero hadn't done his or her job?**
• **Was his or her job easy? If not, what difficulties did he or she face?**
• **What lesson(s) can you learn from your character?**

Later point out that in the church it is important for each of us to use our "powers" (our spiritual gifts) for the benefit of everyone else. If we don't, not only do we miss the opportunity to be a "hero," but other people may suffer unnecessarily.

STEP 3

As soon as you read and briefly discuss the biblical account of Gideon, have group members form teams. Instruct each team to do a skit titled "Gideon in Junior High." Your group members should be creative in imagining what Gideon would be like in today's school system. For example, rather than Midianites, he might encounter bullies or gang members. Instead of hiding in a wine-press, perhaps he would be skulking beneath the bleachers or holding his breath inside his locker. But don't give too many suggestions. Let kids come up with their own ideas. By "modernizing" the story, group members should better envision the emotions and stress of the Bible story when they might not otherwise do so.

STEP 2

Before you introduce the subject of the session, Gideon, have group members each think of one of their favorite movies that deals with an unlikely hero who comes from behind and overcomes all obstacles to eventually come out a winner. Give kids some time to think. It shouldn't take long because the theme is a very common one in movies. (Entire series have been based on Rocky Balboa, the Karate Kid, Indiana Jones, Luke Skywalker, and other similar characters. Many other movies deal with teenage romances that finally work out in spite of many near misses.) When everyone has a movie in mind, let each person give clues until the others guess what it is. The clues may be pantomimes of classic scenes, key lines of dialogue from the movie, etc. You may want to encourage kids to have a "backup movie" in mind in case someone else beats them to the one they plan to present.

STEP 5

If you have a creative group, you might want to skip Repro Resource 2 and have group members write a song that would serve the same purpose of committing to putting their faith in God in future situations. (One suggestion would be to use the tune to "Gilligan's Island" but substitute the line "Just like Gideon's life" for "Here on Gilligan's Isle." Or if your kids have other ideas, turn them loose.)

If songwriting isn't something that comes naturally to your group members, you might want to play a song for them instead. After they complete Repro Resource 2 and you summarize the session, close by playing the song "Hero" by Steve Taylor (from his album *Meltdown*, © 1983 Birdwing Music/Cherry Lane Music Publishing Co., Inc./C.A. Music/ASCAP). The song expresses a young boy's desire to be a hero like his comic book heroes, but then he sees the corruption of heroes as he grows up. The one hero he eventually finds worth imitating is Jesus.

STEP 1

Rather than having kids brainstorm their favorite superheroes, simply show pictures of five or six different superheroes and see if your kids can identify them. Along with obvious superheroes like Superman and Batman, show pictures of less-known crime fighters like the Flash and Wolverine. Award a prize to the first person to correctly identify each superhero. Then lead in to a discussion of the possible "secret identities" of your group members.

STEP 3

If you don't have time to read through the story of Gideon (and the background information on the oppression of Israel by the Midianites), briefly summarize the biblical account for your group members. As you do, be sure to emphasize Gideon's humble, perhaps even "unimpressive" (by human standards), credentials. Then as a group, brainstorm other "unimpressive" people who were used mightily by God. Among the people your kids might list are Moses, David, the disciples, and the apostle Paul. Lead in to a discussion on whether God still uses "unimpressive" people today.

STEP 1

If your kids aren't into comic books, try using a different kind of superhero for your opening discussion. Have your group members list as many athletes as they can think of that they consider to be superstars. After you've got a list compiled, vote as a group on which athlete is the "superstar of superstars." Use him or her as your comparison during your discussion. Ask: **Do you think you could beat _____ in a game of one-on-one basketball? What about in a round of miniature golf? A footrace? A spelling bee? A math quiz?** Continue listing potential competitions until everyone in the group has identified a contest in which he or she could outdo the "superstar of superstars." Then make the point that everyone has at least one skill at which he or she excels. Lead in to a discussion on the areas that kids like about themselves.

STEP 4

Spice up your study of Judges 6 by helping your kids identify with Gideon, who was experiencing "the blues." Have kids form small groups. Explain that each group is a songwriting team for one of the all-time great blues singers (perhaps B. B. King, Bessie Smith, or Gertrude "Ma" Rainey). Instruct each group to come up with a song that deals with maintaining a positive self-image in spite of the "blues" and suffering that come with urban living. For example, an opening line might go something like this: "Jesus, I'm lost—oh, oh, so lost; but I know I'll be fine if I look to the cross." After a few minutes, have each group perform its song.

STEP 1

The attraction to comic books usually peaks during junior high. If you have several high schoolers in your group, you may want to expand the discussion of heroes so that it isn't limited to comic book superheroes. High schoolers frequently look to real life for heroes, so you can make the same comparisons to Gideon by having group members discuss the "normal" people in life who become heroes. Some may personally know people they consider heroes. Others may find heroes in the worlds of sports (Dave Dravecky, Michael Jordan), history (John Glenn, John F. Kennedy), current events (President of the U.S.A.), religion (Billy Graham, Martin Luther, Charles Wesley), etc. Many of these people were unlikely candidates for "hero" status, yet they devoted themselves to a cause and stuck to it. You can then point out that God was not only Gideon's "cause," but his source of confidence and power as well. Without God's help and Gideon's faith and obedience, Gideon would never have been a hero and we would never have heard of him.

STEP 4

If you have a mixed group of junior highers and high schoolers, you have a good opportunity to help one group teach the other. When you get to this step, in which you are looking for lessons about self-image, many of your high schoolers may be willing to share what they thought about themselves two, three, or four years ago—and how that perception has changed since then. After going through their growth spurts, filling out, and getting through much of the discomfort and confusion of puberty, many kids start liking themselves a lot better. Encourage willing volunteers of high school age to share various ways they think they have improved since junior high. Junior highers may get more encouragement from their fellow students than from an adult telling them, "Don't worry. Everything will turn out OK."

STEP 2

Simplify the self-assessment exercise for your sixth graders. Instead of having them make lists on their own, have them respond to a list of statements by standing if they agree or sitting if they disagree. You can start by rephrasing the questions provided in this step as agree/disagree statements:

- **I like myself.**
- **I care a lot about what people think about me.**
- **I put a lot of effort into trying to look good to other people.**

Add other statements for group response. Don't question or make comments as you go along, or group members are likely to begin to respond as they think you expect them to (or as everyone else does). Just encourage them to be completely honest and then note their responses. Later you can raise questions or make comments.

STEP 5

Repro Resource 2 may be a bit challenging for many sixth graders. It would probably be more beneficial to do a similar activity as a group. Rather than ask kids to set *personal* goals for seeing God work in their lives, think of one or two *group* goals for which you would all like to witness God's involvement. Then think of some specific ways to determine how you can know for sure whether or not God is actively involved in your concerns. Since you're doing this as a group, be sure to follow up on it at regular intervals. Many group members will probably forget about the exercise or be only moderately involved. But a few may take it very seriously and want to see some specific results as time passes. If they don't see any significant consequences of their faith as a group, they will probably be reluctant to trust God as individuals. Be sure to come to closure at some future date.

DATE USED:

Approx. Time

STEP 1: *Men of Steel and Caped Crusaders* _____
- ❏ Extra Action
- ❏ Small Group
- ❏ Mostly Girls
- ❏ Extra Fun
- ❏ Short Meeting Time
- ❏ Urban
- ❏ Combined Junior High/High School
Things needed:

STEP 2: *Self-Inventory* _____
- ❏ Large Group
- ❏ Little Bible Background
- ❏ Mostly Guys
- ❏ Media
- ❏ Sixth Grade
Things needed:

STEP 3: *Not a Likely Candidate for Studs* _____
- ❏ Extra Action
- ❏ Heard It All Before
- ❏ Fellowship & Worship
- ❏ Extra Fun
- ❏ Short Meeting Time
Things needed:

STEP 4: *I've Got Those Hiding-in-My-Winepress Blues* _____
- ❏ Large Group
- ❏ Little Bible Background
- ❏ Mostly Girls
- ❏ Urban
- ❏ Combined Junior High/High School
Things needed:

STEP 5: *Gideon: The Sequel* _____
- ❏ Small Group
- ❏ Heard It All Before
- ❏ Fellowship & Worship
- ❏ Mostly Guys
- ❏ Media
- ❏ Sixth Grade
Things needed:

SESSION 2

Image Isn't Everything!

YOUR GOALS FOR THIS SESSION:

Choose one or more

☐ To help kids recognize that self-image involves a lot more than just body image.

☐ To help kids understand that no problem—image or otherwise—is too difficult for God.

☐ To help kids begin to shift their thinking from caring only about outer appearance to include an emphasis on inner character as well.

☐ Other:_____
_____

Your Bible Base:

I Samuel 16:1-13;
 17:1-11, 32-54
2 Corinthians 4:6-12

The Bod Squad

(Needed: Copies of Repro Resource 3, pencils)

O P T I O N S

To open the session, hand out copies of "Some Body to Admire" (Repro Resource 3) and pencils. Have group members list the 10 people (five men and five women) they think have the best bodies. As the kids make their lists, pay attention to see if this is a difficult exercise for them. Most will probably think of two or three people right away, yet might have trouble coming up with a top ten list. If so, this could indicate that young people are tending to compare themselves (and others) to one particular standard—the highest possible one. On the other hand, if group members have trouble limiting their list to 10, perhaps they are better at seeing positive traits in a variety of people.

This exercise should also give you some clues as to what group members consider to be the "ideal" body. One person might focus heavily on professional models while another lists a lot of sports figures or actors. Take some informal polls to see which figures are most frequently listed so group members can see what criteria the others are using to evaluate a "good" body.

Then ask: **Do you think people with good bodies are generally better liked than those who are skinny or overweight? If so, how do you think it makes the skinny and overweight people feel? How do you think it makes the ones with good bodies feel to think they are being evaluated solely on physical aspects?**

Do you think a lot of people would like you better if you had a better body?

• To what extent does another person's body influence how you feel about the person?

• What are some things you do to make your body look better? (Exercise, diet, use cosmetics, wear nice clothes, get a suntan, etc.)

STEP 2

The Incompetent Genie

(Needed: Copies of Repro Resource 4, pencils)

Hand out copies of "Make Some Wishes" (Repro Resource 4), which asks group members to list everything they would like to change about themselves. These changes can include physical alterations, personality characteristics, or anything else.

When everyone is finished, say: **Guess what? The genie who granted your wishes was just an apprentice, and he didn't really know what he was doing. As everyone should know, a genie can only grant three wishes; so you'll need to cross off all but three of the desired changes you listed.**

Let group members take some time to pare down their lists. When they finish, ask some volunteers to read their top three desired changes. Don't comment for a while, but pay attention to see how many are physical changes compared to those that refer to inner character improvements. Most young people usually tend to focus on external characteristics. The rest of this session will try to persuade them to work on internal character qualities as well.

STEP 3

Short People Got No Reason... to Lose

(Needed: Bibles, paper, pencils, chalkboard and chalk or newsprint and marker, basketball [optional])

Conduct a roleplay. Select one of the larger, more athletic (or domineering) group members to represent Shaquille O'Neal. The rest of the kids should roleplay themselves at a local outdoor basketball court. "Shaq" should walk up to the group, perhaps dribbling a basketball, and

OPTIONS

challenge anyone to a game of one-on-one. He should also explain that the first person to score 20 points will win everything the other person has—money, possessions, and all. If the other group members don't want to play, "Shaq" should try to press them for reasons why.

It isn't likely that any junior high student would ever take on one of the greatest basketball players who ever lived. And anyone who might even *think* about doing so would likely decline if the penalty for losing was so high.

After the roleplay, ask if any of the group members can think of a Bible story that is similar to the scene they just acted out. When someone mentions David and Goliath, have group members turn in their Bibles to I Samuel. As they do, explain that as youngsters we are told the story of David and Goliath and think it's really exciting. But as we get older, we may tend to think of it as simply a "good story." If we do, we miss out on a lot of personal applications we should observe from the account.

Divide into two groups in order to focus more clearly on the topic of body image. The first group should read and report on I Samuel 16:1-13, in which David is chosen and anointed as Israel's second king. The second group should read and report on the David and Goliath story in I Samuel 17:1-11, 32-54. As both groups read and discuss their passages, ask them to consider these questions (which you may want to write on the board):

• **What character(s) seemed to put the most emphasis on body image?**

• **What problems resulted from evaluating other people based purely on their external appearance?**

• **If a person with self-image problems were to read this story, what encouragement might he or she feel?**

• **What other things do you think we should learn from the story?**

After a few minutes, have each group share its findings and answer the assigned questions.

The members of Group I (I Samuel 16:1-13) should describe the events of David's being chosen king. Samuel was confused as to why God would pass over several outstanding physical candidates until finally arriving at Jesse's youngest son—handsome, yes, but not as physically impressive as several of his older brothers. Yet God knew the hearts of Jesse's sons as well as their outward characteristics, and He designated David as king. It is not likely that David would have been made king in a democratic election, but God knew what was best and Samuel obeyed. Many group members should be encouraged that inner character is more important to God than outward "appearance or . . . height" (vs. 7). Not everyone is a prime *physical* specimen, but everyone has the opportunity to develop the inner qualities that God desires and rewards.

The members of Group 2 (I Samuel 17:1-11, 32-54) should arrive at many of the same conclusions. With the exception of David, every single person in the combined armies of the Israelites and Philistines was considering only outward body image each day as Goliath roared his taunts. Goliath was over nine feet tall. David was "only a boy" (vs. 42). If height were the only criterion for going up against Goliath, then the responsibility should have been King Saul's because he was "a head taller" than any of the other Israelites (I Samuel 9:2). But it is obvious from this story that height and body image have little to do with courage or character. David knew that faith and godly action would more than compensate for any physical inequalities.

Built Like a . . . Jar of Clay?

(Needed: Bibles)

Certainly it is natural to try to improve one's body to whatever extent possible. But challenge your group members throughout these discussions to at least *begin* to consider that physical attributes should not be the source of low self-image. (This might become clearer if they focus more on other people than on themselves. Few of them would say that being in a wheelchair should necessarily limit a person's ability to succeed in life or be liked by others. Yet when they look at *themselves* in the mirror, they may think that a too-big nose or a too-small chest will make them unlikable.)

To help them develop some different perspectives, have group members think of analogies for the human body by completing the sentence "A body is like a _____ because _____." Give an example or two to get them started, such as "A body is like an envelope because the contents are what's important." Or "A body is like a fingerprint because no two are exactly alike." Have each group member think of at least one analogy. Then have everyone turn to and read 2 Corinthians 4:6-12.

Ask: **What was Paul's analogy for the human body?** (He referred to our bodies as "jars of clay.")

Why do you think Paul used this analogy? (Clay jars were commonplace, cheap, easily broken, and not necessarily meant to last a long time. Paul was trying to remind his readers that human bodies are only temporary.)

OPTIONS

EXTRA ACTION

HEARD IT ALL BEFORE

EXTRA FUN

What is the "treasure" he was talking about? (The message and effects of our salvation or perhaps Christ Himself.)

How much emphasis do you think Paul placed on his body image? (He practiced certain physical disciplines [I Cor. 9:27], yet it is obvious that his attitude toward his human body was far secondary to his relationship with Jesus Christ and other people.)

Name That Giant

(Needed: Paper, pencils)

Summarize some of the important points of this session: **We seem to place a whole lot of importance on how our bodies look. It's natural and good to want to look our best, but we shouldn't let body image rule how we feel about ourselves. For one thing, your bodies are in transition at this point of your life. They are changing proportions and may turn out a lot better than you would ever expect. The zits will clear up someday. You'll fill out in a lot of your underdeveloped places and lose baby fat in other spots. So you shouldn't be too critical of yourself. In addition, our bodies are just suitcases, anyway. It's what's inside that counts. We need to focus a lot more attention on developing our inner character than fretting about our height, the color of our eyes, the style of our hair, the size of our toes, or anything else.**

However, if we're honest, most of us will admit that we occasionally do struggle to like ourselves. And for some of us, that inner struggle is like, well, like David standing in the shadow of Goliath. The difference is that David was ready for the battle. He was very clear as to what his objective was, and he was packing five stones and a slingshot to take care of the problem.

Hand out paper and pencils. Continue: **Try to think of the one biggest image problem you regularly face and write it down on this sheet of paper. That problem should be your "Goliath." Then, underneath, list five things you can do to eliminate the problem—or at least considerably reduce its influence on you.**

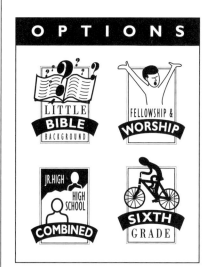

OPTIONS

LITTLE BIBLE BACKGROUND

FELLOWSHIP & WORSHIP

JR. HIGH / HIGH SCHOOL COMBINED

SIXTH GRADE

When kids finish, help them think of what they've written in terms of a David-and-Goliath type of battle. We don't ask for image problems, but when they come we need to deal with them. So the next time we are harassed by a huge self-image issue, we should not be afraid to confront it. It may loom above and around us as Goliath overshadowed David. But we, like David, need to remember that God is on our side. He doesn't want us to be intimidated by something He can eliminate for us.

Encourage your kids to keep their list of proposed ideas nearby. Goliath oppressed the entire Israelite army twice a day for 40 days (I Sam. 17:16). He was a major image problem for them. No doubt some of your group members have image problems that have hounded them for even longer. It's time for them to pick up a rock (figuratively) and take the initiative in getting rid of the problem. Assure them that it certainly won't hurt to at least try the ideas they've listed on their papers.

It took faith for David to hurl that stone at a warrior almost twice his height and armed to the teeth. But that's what faith is all about. The power and the position of the stone was just right, and the giant fell. With time, faith, and determination, the body image problems facing your young people can fall as well.

Some Body to Admire

You don't think anyone notices, but we do. We see you casting sideways glances at certain people walking down the beach. We see you paging through the latest issue of *Studs and Supermodels* magazine, pausing just long enough to admire certain photos. When your favorite actor or actress comes on TV, we see the envious look in your eyes when he or she reveals a firm tummy, a powerful bicep, or those gleaming white teeth.

And since we've been watching you as you've been watching them, you may as well come clean. We want you to list the ten people—five men and five women—you think have the best bodies. They may be young or old, famous or just next-door neighbors. But they should be the ones that you would nominate for the First Annual Best Body Award. Your top choice should be #1, and then go on down the list.

Men	**Women**
1.	1.
2.	2.
3.	3.
4.	4.
5.	5.

NOTES

Make Some Wishes

There it is. Right in the middle of the garage sale. Nobody else seems to give it a second glance as they buy baby clothes, odd-looking hubcaps, and discarded Bee Gees albums. So you grab it—the most awesome-looking lava lamp you've ever seen. From the looks of it, this thing must have been one of the first ones ever manufactured.

You take it home, plug it in, and start to rub off some of the dust. To your surprise, out pops a genie. At least you think it's a genie. The guy is wearing a tie-dyed T-shirt and wide-flared bell-bottom jeans, and he's humming a Grateful Dead tune. Then he says, "Like, wow, man. That's been some trip for the past thirty years, locked inside that lamp. So, my brother (or sister), you can make all the wishes you want, and I'll make 'em be happenin'. But, like, I'm just an apprentice genie, you dig? All I know how to do is change you in *physical* ways—your body, your personality, stuff like that. But I'm good. You tell me what you want done, man, and everything will be groovy."

Let's assume you believe the guy. If you could change anything about yourself that you wanted to, and as much as you wanted to, what would you change? List everything you can think of below. (Remember, you can change both outer characteristics and inner traits.)

NOTES

STEP 3

After completing the roleplay that opens this step, but before announcing the topic of study, conduct some David-and-Goliath-style target shooting. Set up a target (perhaps yourself) at one end of the room. Designate a line from which group members will shoot. The choice of "weapons" can vary according to your group's interest. Some of the easiest to find are rubber bands or drinking straws from which you can shoot small paper wads. Group members may compete individually or as teams, but this should be an elimination contest. Everyone takes one shot to begin with, from near the target. Those who miss it must sit down. Those who hit it get to shoot again, from farther away. Those who keep hitting keep moving back as those who miss are eliminated. The person who hits from the farthest distance is the winner. Afterward, ask: **Did this person win because he (or she) has more faith than anyone else here? Does he (or she) have the most courage?** Later in the step, when you get to the David and Goliath story, point out the difference between your winner's "victory" and David's victory.

STEP 4

To emphasize the concept of treasure in clay jars, bring a number of inexpensive jars (if possible, use fragile pottery). Place something nonbreakable (such as a baseball or a large stone) in each jar. Divide into teams and let each team be responsible for one of the jars. Then see how much abuse the jars can take before cracking or breaking. For instance, you might have the teams try to design contraptions that would allow the jars to be dropped from a considerable height (say, from the top of a ladder over asphalt) without breaking. Or you might try a type of "jousting" contest by rolling two jars against each other until one breaks. The other jar would then be declared the winner. Point out that while the jars may be destroyed in the process, the things they contain remain unharmed.

STEP 1

An ongoing problem with small groups is group members' reluctance to get too personal with discussions or applications. So in the discussion at the end of this step (and throughout the session), don't attempt to elicit responses that require potentially embarrassing information about group members. Rephrase questions so that the emphasis is on *other people* instead. For instance, rather than asking the question as written ("Do you think lots of people would like you better if you had a better body?"), you might ask instead, **What percentage of people your age would you say wish they had a better body? What percentage tends to judge others primarily on outward physical characteristics?** You can get the same answers from your young people, but without making them feel uncomfortable or self-conscious.

STEP 3

Use the David-and-Goliath story to initiate some applications that are especially relevant to small groups. After Group 2 reports on the facts of the story and makes appropriate comments regarding body image, ask: **What can we, as a small group, learn from David, a small person—at least, in regard to Goliath?** If body image is a problem for your young people, it would not be unusual to discover that they also have a somewhat negative "small group mentality." Try to show from the Bible story that size has little to do with potential accomplishments. It was, in fact, a large group mentality that paralyzed the other Israelites. Your group, even though it may be small, can accomplish significant things for God if group members change their way of thinking and develop the faith that David displayed.

STEP 2

Prior to the session, enlist the help of one of your larger and more intimidating group members. As group members are working on Repro Resource 4, have your volunteer begin to annoy many of the younger and smaller members. For example, he might roam around the room, looking over their shoulders and making fun of their answers. If anyone objects, he might act as if he's looking for a fight. (You could leave the room for a while to prevent anyone from turning to you for help.) See how your younger members respond to his aggression. After a while, explain that the incident was "staged." Have kids discuss their physical and emotional responses to being challenged by someone larger than themselves. Use their comments when you get to the David-and-Goliath story to make the account more personal and relevant.

STEP 3

The instructions to "divide into two groups" won't work in a large group. One solution would be to divide into small groups and let half of the groups study the first passage as the other half studies the second. But another option is to conduct impromptu plays as the passages are read. You should serve as narrator, reading the biblical account. As various characters are introduced in the text, designate someone in the room to represent the role. (These people need not speak or do anything other than make appropriate facial expressions or gestures.) The first Bible story will require people to represent Samuel, Jesse, Eliab, Abinadab, Shammah, and David. The second story has individual characters as well, but the rest of the group can be divided into Israelite and Philistine camps and encouraged to cheer at appropriate places. Don't let the stories get bogged down or confusing as you try to designate people. Be aware that no women are mentioned in these accounts, so you might want to have some of your girls represent male roles rather than allow them to feel left out.

HEARD IT ALL BEFORE

STEP 3

Ask: **How many of you think you're pretty familiar with the stories of David's being anointed king and his fight with Goliath?** If group members think they know a lot about the story, give them a quiz drawn from I Samuel 16–17. For example, you might ask:

• **How many people "auditioned" to replace Saul as king?** (David's seven brothers [I Sam. 16:10] and then David, for a total of eight.)

• **How many of David's brothers can you name?** (Eliab, Abinadab, and Shammah are named [I Sam. 16:6-9; I Sam. 17:13].)

• **Goliath was a Philistine from where?** (Gath [I Sam. 17:4].)

• **How tall was Goliath?** (Over nine feet [I Sam. 17:4].)

• **How many times did Goliath challenge the Israelites to a fight?** (Twice a day for 40 days [I Sam. 17:16].)

Before the quiz, announce that anyone who gets even half of the answers right will win a prize. Afterward, explain that while it isn't necessary to know each detail of every Bible story, it is a problem if we ever assume that we know enough to stop searching for new discoveries in the Bible.

STEP 4

How many times have your kids *heard* that "it's what's on the inside that counts"? But how many times have they *seen* it demonstrated? Hold up a raw egg. Explain that it's a fairly average-looking egg—nothing special about it. Then spend a few minutes "sprucing up" the egg. Use some brightly colored markers to decorate it. When you're finished, say: **Now what we have is a brightly colored, attractive, useless egg. How is this egg like our bodies?** (What's on the outside matters very little—no matter how good it looks. The useful part is what's on the inside.) To drive your point home memorably, crack open the egg into a glass and ask a volunteer to drink the yolk.

LITTLE BIBLE BACKGROUND

STEP 3

For a group without much Bible background, this session offers a good opportunity to learn how to make the Bible come alive. Skip the story of David being anointed king (I Sam. 16) and spend all of your time on the David-and-Goliath story. This is a story that everyone is likely to know, regardless of the person's level of Bible knowledge. Work together as a group as you help kids see that this is more than a good story. Help them discover that the Bible is *reality*. Have them read through the text to absorb the facts of the story. But as they do, also ask them to imagine the sights, smells, sounds, and emotions of the story as well. After working as a group and seeing that Bible study doesn't necessarily have to be dull, boring, or difficult, encourage group members to continue the practice individually. (You might want to have some other good stories listed and ready for kids to take home and explore on their own.)

STEP 5

Some young people fail to develop an interest or discipline for Bible study because they cannot see the relevance of what happened "way back then" to their lives today. So spend a lot of time brainstorming and discussing personal applications for the David-and-Goliath story. This is an excellent account for helping apathetic or unknowledgeable people learn to interact with Scripture and come away with something meaningful. Allow group members to struggle a bit (but not *too* much) as they try to think of how this centuries-old story can be relevant today. Encourage their efforts and make this as enjoyable an experience as possible.

FELLOWSHIP & WORSHIP

STEP 1

A common problem for junior highers is the tendency to make snap judgments about other people based on physical appearance. Of course, adults do the same thing, but junior highers are particularly susceptible to this tendency. You might want to stop at the end of Step 1, before you get into the Bible story, and provide a time for personal confession of past offenses. Distribute pencils and paper. Have kids write "I need to confess . . ." and then list as many things as they can think of that they've done to damage another person's body image. When everyone is finished, collect the papers and read what group members have written. (Don't use names, and paraphrase what the kids have written so that no individual can be associated with any specific confession. Explain that the *group* should take responsibility for *all* of the confessions.) Then spend some time in prayer, asking God's forgiveness for previous sinful actions and attitudes. Also ask for His wisdom in becoming able to see and appreciate a person's entire personality rather than simply his or her body.

STEP 5

Have group members brainstorm a list of "daily affirmations" to help them develop a better understanding of body image. At the top of the board, write "Things I need to do each day to have a better body image." Suggestions might include:

• Thank God for making me the way I am.

• Appreciate the variety God provides—especially in regard to people.

• Encourage at least three people with a sincere compliment.

• Find things I like about myself when I look in the mirror, instead of seeing only faults.

Distribute paper and pencils. Have group members write down the suggestions as they are named. Encourage kids to post their lists in a prominent place at home where they will see them frequently. (Mirrors might be an excellent place.)

STEP 2

Although some guys suffer from anorexia nervosa and other eating disorders, these problems occur most often in girls. Ask your group members if they know of anyone who wanted to change her body so badly that she was willing to starve herself. (It's likely that most of your girls know of someone like this.) Ask: **What do you think God would like to say to her? How do you think He feels about her body? What are some positive things about herself that she should focus on rather than her body?** If you know of someone in your group who struggles with this issue, be sensitive to what she is going through. You may wish to talk with her before the meeting to see if she would be willing to talk to the group about her struggles. This could be an opportunity for real growth and encouragement for the entire group.

STEP 3

If you have a group of girls who aren't particularly interested in basketball, substitute a woman's name from the "perfect body" lists (on Repro Resource 3) for Shaquille O'Neal. Create a scenario in which this woman challenges your group members to a beauty contest. Choose a group member who is very interested in appearance, beauty, makeup, clothes, etc. (This person shouldn't be difficult to find in a group of junior high girls!) The stakes can be the same as the Shaquille O'Neal scenario: Winner takes all. After the roleplay, ask your girls if they can think of a Bible story in which an underdog took on someone who appeared to be a guaranteed winner. Direct the group to the story of David and Goliath in I Samuel 16–17.

STEP I

Many junior high guys are going through a transition in which they find themselves no longer repulsed by girls. They may not have much guidance as they go through this transition. Consequently, they learn what little they know in school locker rooms. They may learn to see girls as physical objects—bodies and little else. If many of the women listed on Repro Resource 3 are sexy actresses or leggy supermodels, perhaps your group members are far enough along in their transition that you need to deal with the lust issue. Of course, it's natural for junior high guys to be curious and observant. But that curiosity makes it all the more imperative for them to learn to see beyond the body image of female peers and appreciate their personalities and other characteristics. Challenge them to get beyond the "Hubba hubba" mentality of so many other guys their age. Give them an opportunity to ask direct questions and get direct answers about their feelings. This will be an ongoing struggle for many of them, and the sooner they begin to deal with it, the better off they will be.

STEP 3

After the groups report on the Bible stories, ask: **Are you more like David or Goliath as you tend to deal with problems and conflict? Why?** Many guys are like Goliath. They want to be seen as tough, mean, and someone not to be tangled with. They want to handle their problems with their own strength. Few are like David, who didn't care how he looked or sounded, yet refused to be limited by age or size. Explain that many problems in life can be settled without conflict, with reason and perhaps compromise. But others need to be confronted head-on, regardless of the consequences. When faced with unavoidable conflicts, it is always best to depend on God's strength and not our own. This may not be the usual male response, but it will always be the correct one.

STEP I

Follow Repro Resource 3 with a "best body" contest among your group members. But instead of a traditional contest, select some different kinds of categories. For example, select one or two people as judges to evaluate the other group members. But the category might be Best Big Toe. (If possible, group members should stand behind a screen or blanket so that judges aren't influenced by who the people are.) Other categories might include Best Elbow, Best Ear, Best Lips, and so forth. (Many of these body parts can be projected through a hole cut in a piece of paper to help the judges focus.) This exercise should provide some laughs. Try to emphasize that people don't need to have perfect bodies to have fun or appreciate each other.

STEP 4

Use eggs to symbolize "jars of clay." One option is to have each group member hold an egg throughout the session as he or she plays games, fills out the Repro Resources, works through the Bible study, and so forth. Or, at this point in the session, you may want to go outside and have an egg toss, in which pairs of kids face each other and throw an egg back and forth, taking a step backward after each successful catch. It shouldn't take long to see that even though an eggshell is strong enough to protect its contents if left alone, outside stresses can cause damage to it. Use this exercise to point out that we shouldn't put too much emphasis on our "shells" because they are going to fail us some day. What's more important is the treasure we contain. It should be our inner, God-given strengths that attract us to each other—not our bodies.

STEP 1

Rather than doing Repro Resource 3 as written, bring an assortment of magazines and let group members tear out pictures of models. Tape all of the pictures to a wall. Point out that a significant percentage of the population is bald. Another large percentage is overweight. Many are disabled in some way. Many are over 40.

Ask: **Do you think advertising accurately reflects the population when they choose their models? Why?** (No. Obviously advertisers want to make their products seem as attractive as possible, so they use unusually attractive people in connection with them.)

Explain: **What they do makes sense. Yet we shouldn't be led to believe that it's normal to have a flawless body. If we compare ourselves to professional models, we are rarely going to be satisfied. While we may choose to set high goals for ourselves, we should never berate ourselves for not living up to a standard that only a tiny percentage of people can achieve.**

STEP 3

Most children's Bible video series have an episode about David and Goliath. Rent one of them and watch it in your group.

Then ask: **Why do you think this story is so popular with little kids? Do you remember the first time you heard this story? If so, what did you think of it? What are some drawbacks of being very familiar with a Bible story? Before today, when was the last time you read and studied the story of David and Goliath? What do you think are the "adult" lessons to be gained from this story?** Use the children's video to demonstrate the importance of transferring childlike belief, wonder, and excitement to our teenage and adult lives as we grow up.

STEP 2

Rather than having kids complete Repro Resource 4, ask them to think of their past semester at school. (For instance, if a person is in his or her first semester as an eighth grader, he or she should think back to his or her second semester as a seventh grader.) Ask: **If you could change one thing about that last semester, what would it be?** Get responses from several group members. You may find that kids would like to change things like the way they treated a friend, a decision to take a certain class, or their study habits. You probably won't find many kids wishing they hadn't worn a particular shirt or outfit. Point out that in retrospect, *external* appearances mean very little in the "big picture" of life.

STEP 3

Rather than having kids perform the scenario described in the session, use a few video clips (which you've screened beforehand) from the movie *Hoosiers* to demonstrate your point. Show the scene in which the members of the Hickory High basketball team arrive at the site of the championship game and are awed by the size of the arena. Then show the scene in which the Hickory High players first see their bigger, more talented opponents. Finally, show the scene at the end of the championship game in which Hickory High pulls off the upset. Use these clips to lead in to a discussion of David and Goliath.

STEP 1

For the opening activity, you might consider replacing the "bod squad" with the "God squad." Read aloud I Samuel 16:17. Explain that what really counts in a person is what's inside. Point out that although physical attributes are desirable in today's society, people who concentrate on their *inner* characteristics will be more pleasing to God. Then, rather than having kids list the top 10 "bodies to admire," have them list the top five Bible characters they would like to emulate.

STEP 3

Use an object lesson to make the point that people tend to concentrate on outward appearance. Bring a small bucketful of dirt. Mix in a little water, and create two "mudballs." As you're forming one of the mudballs, place a quarter in the middle of it—but make sure your kids don't see you do this. Don't put anything in the second mudball. When you're finished, ask: **Which mudball looks better—or more "valuable"—to you?** Encourage most of your kids to respond; press them for explanations as to why they chose the one they did. Then break open the "valuable" mudball to reveal the quarter inside. Use this activity to lead in to a discussion of I Samuel 16:1-13.

STEP 2

After completing Repro Resource 4, explain to your kids that it is still very early in life for them to be making wishes about changes in their physical appearance. It is better to wait for a few years to see how their bodies are going to turn out. To demonstrate this point, have group members bring in pictures of themselves that are about five years old. Give the kids a chance to mingle about, looking at each other's pictures. Then, after a few minutes, vote as a group on who has changed the most since his or her picture was taken. If applicable, you may want to point out that the high schoolers have changed more in the past five years than the junior highers. Younger members should take comfort in seeing what they have to look forward to, while the high schoolers can see how much they've changed. Explain that none of them is "stuck with" the way he or she looks now. All of them are continuing to grow and change, and should look forward to the changes yet to come.

STEP 5

In some combined groups, high schoolers feel out of place and perhaps superior to the younger kids. They expect preferential treatment, or perhaps use their age and size to boss the others around. In other groups, however, high schoolers take on a mentoring role for their younger peers. They discover the joy of serving and teaching. To help high schoolers see their potential, use Goliath as an example. They've already seen the drawbacks of having a bossy, superior attitude. So have them create a skit (working together or in smaller groups) showing Goliath as a caring, concerned mentor for people who were not as big or strong as himself. In what situations would he be helpful? How might his story have turned out differently? What could we learn from a kinder, gentler giant of a role model? After kids perform their skits, challenge your older students to work on developing more of a caring, nurturing role in regard to other group members.

STEP 2

At the beginning of the junior high years, body image may not yet be a concern for everyone. Some sixth graders may not have given the matter much thought at all, so we need to be sure not to *initiate* fear and insecurity for such kids. Rather than having your group of sixth graders complete Repro Resource 4, it might be much better to ask: **If you could be anyone in the world, who would you want to be? Why?** You will still be able to determine what changes your group members are looking for, but in a less direct context. Encourage them that any answer other than "me" may need to be reconsidered. Help them feel good about themselves as they approach puberty with its many changes.

STEP 5

Rather than end the session with the summary as written (which assumes most of the group members are already in the throes of puberty), let your sixth graders ask any questions they might have about what to expect during the next several years in terms of body changes. To avoid potential discomfort, have them write down the questions and hand them in to you. Then you can mix them up and read them at random, discussing each one. Try to alleviate any anxiety or potential fear your young people might have. It's never too soon to start affirming young people in regard to body image.

DATE USED:

Approx. Time

STEP 1: *The Bod Squad* _____
❏ Small Group
❏ Fellowship & Worship
❏ Mostly Guys
❏ Extra Fun
❏ Media
❏ Urban
Things needed:

STEP 2: *The Incompetent Genie* _____
❏ Large Group
❏ Mostly Girls
❏ Short Meeting Time
❏ Combined Junior High/High School
❏ Sixth Grade
Things needed:

STEP 3: *Short People Got No Reason...to Lose* _____
❏ Extra Action
❏ Small Group
❏ Large Group
❏ Heard It All Before
❏ Little Bible Background
❏ Mostly Girls
❏ Mostly Guys
❏ Media
❏ Short Meeting Time
❏ Urban
Things needed:

STEP 4: *Built Like a ... Jar of Clay?* _____
❏ Extra Action
❏ Heard It All Before
❏ Extra Fun
Things needed:

STEP 5: *Name That Giant* _____
❏ Little Bible Background
❏ Fellowship & Worship
❏ Combined Junior High/High School
❏ Sixth Grade
Things needed:

SESSION 3

Comprehensive Coverage

March 8th

YOUR GOALS FOR THIS SESSION:

Choose one or more

☐ To help kids recognize that good health involves much more than good diet habits and occasional exercise.

☐ To show kids a biblical example of how to respond to temptations to do things that might damage their health.

☐ To help kids set goals in several specific areas of their lives that will contribute to ongoing good health in the future.

☐ Other:_____

_____

Your Bible Base:

Daniel 1
Luke 2:52

1. Charades
2. Snack
3. Alphabet Game

STEP 1

Magazine Scavenger Hunt

(Needed: Newspapers, magazines)

OPTIONS

EXTRA ACTION

MOSTLY GIRLS

EXTRA FUN

JR.HIGH HIGH SCHOOL COMBINED

Have group members form teams for a health scavenger hunt. Provide a large assortment of old newspapers and magazines, and have team members go through them in search of as many references to health as they can find. References can come from articles (about AIDS, cancer, congressional bills, etc.), advertisements, obituaries, want ads, personal ads, or any other section. In addition to overt references, encourage group members to look for subtle or subliminal messages as well. For example, a recent milk campaign ("It does a body good") is an obvious association of a product with a healthy benefit. But less obvious would be a candy bar ad that shows thin and happy people enjoying the product and suggests that the dairy and nut contents fulfill nutritional standards for two food groups. Both ads refer to health benefits, though the second one is much more subtle than the first. But both should be accepted, whether or not you agree with the claims of the ad. (You should act as judge if one group questions the validity of another group's choice.)

Your group may be surprised at how many references they discover. Health is a major topic of interest today. It should be easy to see from the many businesses built around the desire for good health (insurance companies, food and drink, sports stores, health clubs, and so forth) that many people take their health quite seriously.

What Is Health?

(Needed: Paper, pencils)

Point out that people may have quite different meanings when they speak of "health." Distribute pencils and paper. Ask group members to write a definition—in 25 words or less—of the word *health*. After a few minutes, ask a couple of volunteers to read what they've written. Then compare their definitions with this one from *Webster's Ninth New Collegiate Dictionary:* "the condition of being sound in body, mind, or spirit; esp: freedom from physical disease or pain."

Explain that while we may tend to focus almost exclusively on the physical aspects of health, there are other important elements. Someone who is truly healthy must have more than a good-looking body that works right. A sound mind is needed to be considered healthy, as is emotional stability. It's easy to evaluate health only by what we see in the mirror, but we also need to include thoughts, emotions, attitudes, and other aspects of personality as we consider our state of health.

Ask: **What are some of the things you do to try to stay healthy?** (Diet; exercise; take vitamins; wear seat belts; avoid harmful, addictive practices; etc.)

Do you do anything intentionally that you know isn't healthy? (Eat too much junk food; take needless risks; have an occasional cigarette; etc.) **If so, why?**

Do you think having a healthy body should be a goal even if the time and energy it takes cuts into time you could use developing your mind and character? Explain. (Perhaps some of your group members know people who are very proud of their bodies, yet shallow and self-centered.)

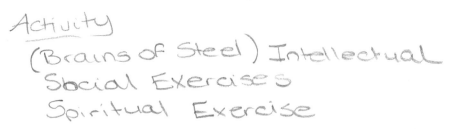

Activity
(Brains of Steel) Intellectual
Social Exercises
Spiritual Exercise

STEP 3

Sword drill
(6) B) Luke 2: 52

A
✓ Then

Health Report Card

(Needed: Copies of Repro Resource 5, pencils)

Hand out copies of "Making the Grade?" (Repro Resource 5) and pencils. As you do, explain: **We frequently look at the life of Jesus as a model for how we should live. However, we know very little about Jesus' teenage years. We get a glimpse of Him in the temple at age 12, where He amazes the religious leaders with His wisdom and maturity** (Luke 2:41-51). **The next thing we know about Him, He's 30. But we have one verse that tells us how He grew up. That verse is on the handout sheet, and it provides some guidelines by which we can evaluate our levels of health.**

Give group members some time to complete their sheets. Then ask: **Did anyone get straight A's?**

In which area did you rate the highest?

In what area were you weakest?

Before this activity, had you ever thought that all of these categories should be considered as you try to develop into a healthy adult?

OPTIONS

EXTRA ACTION

LITTLE BIBLE BACKGROUND

MOSTLY GIRLS

MEDIA

SHORT MEETING TIME

(2) A) 1 Timothy 4:8 (spiritual > physical)

(3) B) Romans 12:2 (mind)

(4) A) 1 Cor 6:19 (temple/body)

(5) B) Prov 18:24

(6) A) James 1:5 (intellect)

Daniel Is Traveling Tonight on the Plain

(Needed: Bibles)

OPTIONS

Have kids form four groups. Instruct all groups to read Daniel 1. Then have each group look for references to a different aspect of health in the passage. Group 1 should look for references to intellectual health. (How did Daniel "grow in wisdom"?) Group 2 should look for things Daniel did to ensure physical health ("stature"). Group 3 should look for instances of healthy social interaction ("favor with men"). And Group 4 should record things related to Daniel's spiritual health ("favor with God").

When everyone is finished, a representative from each group should report on his or her group's discoveries.

The members of Group 1 should discover that Daniel was a young man "showing aptitude for every kind of learning, well informed, quick to understand" (vs. 4). They should also see that Daniel wasn't only "book smart"; he also had common sense. When it seemed that he was in a no-win situation of being forced to do something against his standards, he thought up a creative alternative that neither made him uncomfortable nor insulted his host. And because Daniel took the initiative in developing his mind to the extent that he was able and in applying what he knew, "God gave [him] knowledge and understanding of all kinds of literature and learning. And Daniel could understand visions and dreams of all kinds" (vs. 17). When Daniel and his friends committed themselves to mental health and received God's help along the way, they were ten times better than King Nebuchadnezzar's wise men "in every matter of wisdom and understanding" (vs. 20).

The members of Group 2 should see that Daniel was chosen to go to Babylon because he was a prime physical specimen: "young . . . without any physical defect, handsome" (vs. 4). Some might tend to think that Daniel's physical traits were all God's doing and not his own, yet it's easy to see that when he got to Babylon Daniel helped ensure his own continued health. He declined the rich food and wine of the king, perhaps because they had been offered to idols or included "unclean" animals that he could not eat in good conscience. Even so, he could have asked for any kind of special menu, but instead he requested vegetables and water for a 10-day trial period. That was long enough for the Babylonian overseer to observe that Daniel and his friends looked healthier than all of the others who ate and drank the king's rich foods. Daniel's emphasis on physical health was rewarded.

The members of Group 3 should explain that in spite of Daniel's bold stands for physical and intellectual health, he was no social recluse. When dragged away from his home by a foreign enemy, Daniel had a number of options. He could have fought, pouted, rebelled, thrown a tantrum, or taken a number of actions. But he seemed to have a genuine respect for the person put in charge of him. Daniel didn't want to get the guy in trouble with his boss, the king. In this chapter, and throughout the Book of Daniel, we see that Daniel was in no way intimidated by kings or others who may have influenced his future. But neither was he defiant or arrogant toward them. Daniel's commitment to God allowed him the freedom to be himself wherever he was—at home with his friends or in captivity serving a foreign king.

The members of Group 4 should focus on the ways that God was at work in Daniel's life. It was Daniel's devotion to God that allowed him to take a stand in refusing the initial offer of food and wine by the servant of Nebuchadnezzar. Certainly God was the source of Daniel's strengths, yet it was up to Daniel to take bold stands when the time called for it. (Daniel 6 describes his night in the lions' den.) And God rewarded Daniel's healthy spiritual commitment with additional insight that was unavailable to other people.

Ask: **Which of these aspects of health do you think is most important: intellectual, physical, social, or spiritual?** (The tendency may be to say spiritual, which isn't necessarily wrong. Yet true spiritual health should be reflected in social interaction, increased wisdom, and the desire to take care of ourselves. In truth, all of these aspects are closely interrelated.)

If you were forced to give up one aspect of health, which would you forfeit? Why? (When faced with the possibility of becoming a social leper, losing IQ points, or missing out on a relationship with God, physical health may not seem so terribly important—even if that's where many people tend to place the most emphasis.)

Which of these aspects of health do you most need to work on? Why?

Healthy Choices

(Needed: Copies of Repro Resource 6, pencils)

Hand out copies of "Get on the Scales" (Repro Resource 6), which deals with the issue of health on a more personal and specific level. Some of the items listed on the sheet (such as smoking, drinking, drug use, and sexual activity) are not things that some of your group members will want to discuss openly. Don't be too specific as you deal with these things, but give the group as a whole the opportunity to share goals they have set for each category. Also provide time for group members to ask any questions they have that haven't yet been dealt with.

To close, summarize: **When we consider the issue of health, we may only tend to take into consideration the physical aspect. But as we have seen, there are also mental, social, and spiritual aspects. As young people, both Daniel and Jesus devoted time to the development of all these aspects. If we try to limit our attention to only one or two of these considerations, we will suffer in all of them.**

It's easy to tell that certain activities, such as drug use and premarital sexual activity, are certainly unhealthy. But it's less obvious to tell that certain other activities are unhealthy. Suppose someone is so caught up in physical development that he or she spends every spare minute at the gym or out running. This person doesn't study enough, so grades drop. No time is spent with other people, so friends and family relationships deteriorate. And church attendance and quiet times only interfere with exercise, so no relationship with God is developed. Would you say this person is healthy? Wait for response.

You've set personal goals for each of the aspects of health. I hope you will take them seriously in the weeks and months to come. The decisions you make at this stage of your life can affect your health for your entire lifetime. They should not be made thoughtlessly.

Conclude with a prayer, asking for God's wisdom in helping group members make good and healthy decisions in the future.

Making the Grade?

"And Jesus grew in wisdom and stature, and in favor with God and men" (Luke 2:52).

The little we know about Jesus' teenage years is summed up in this verse. But if you look again, the verse says quite a lot. It suggests that Jesus was concerned with intellectual health (wisdom), physical health (stature), spiritual health (favor with God), and social health (favor with men).

How about you? If you had to grade yourself in each of these areas, how would you do? Below is your report card. Put some thought into each section, consider the guidelines we've provided, and then give yourself a letter grade for each aspect of health.

	GRADE
INTELLECTUAL HEALTH Are you excited about all you can learn at school? Are good grades (as good as possible) important to you? Even when you're not in school, do you enjoy learning? Do you have hobbies and interests that make you a better person? Do you like to learn new things even when you don't have to?	
PHYSICAL HEALTH Do you take the initiative in making sure you don't become a couch potato? Do you try to get athletic games started, or do others have to plead with you to get involved? Do you try to eat right, or are your four food groups chocolate, sugar, cola, and pizza? Do you regularly take part in activities that might damage your health now or later?	
SPIRITUAL HEALTH Do you feel exhilarated about your spiritual development, much like an athlete feels after a good run? Do you "work out" spiritually, or are you involved in prayer and Bible study only when you *have* to be? If faith were muscles, what kind of shape would you be in? Do you regularly seek God's will for your life, or do you make Him come looking for you?	
SOCIAL HEALTH Do you love your neighbor as you love yourself? Do the joys and problems of other people really matter to you, or are you content as long as you're all right? Do you have a small, tight, exclusive circle of friends, or are you friendly with everyone who wants to be your friend? Do you work at maintaining strong relationships with parents, teachers, and others?	

NOTES

GET ON THE SCALES

One way to monitor health is to step on the scales at regular intervals to see whether or not your weight is where it should be. But here are some different scales for you to consider. In each case, place an X on the line to indicate how "heavily" involved you are in that category. (Non-involvement is at the extreme left, and total involvement is at the extreme right.) Then, for each category, set one goal to help you stay more to the left of the scale rather than drifting toward the right.

DRINKING

Never touch alcohol ——————————————————— Get drunk regularly
GOAL:

SMOKING

Cigarettes? Yuck! ——————————————————— A pack a day
GOAL:

JUNK FOOD

No fats, no salt, no sweets ——————————————— Junk food junkie
GOAL:

DRUGS

I'm just high on life. ——————————————————— I experiment quite a bit.
GOAL:

STRESS

I never worry about anything. ——————————————— I have ulcers.
GOAL:

SPIRITUAL HEALTH

Growing stronger every day ——————————————— Waiting till I get older
GOAL:

SEXUAL ACTIVITY

I'm saving myself for marriage.———————————————— I'll take what I can get.
GOAL:

MENTAL HEALTH

I love to learn. ———————————————————————— I hate to learn.
GOAL:

SOCIAL HEALTH

Always expanding ————————————————————— Leave me alone!
my circle of friends
GOAL:

LEISURE

I take plenty of ——————————————————————— Who has time for fun?
time for myself.
GOAL:

NOTES

STEP 1

Begin the session with a marathon aerobics class. Designate one person as the leader. The rest of the group will follow along. Periodically change leaders (without stopping the action, if possible) and let each new leader do whatever kinds of exercises he or she chooses. One person might do standard jumping jacks or toe touches. Someone else might do Marine push-ups. This should be a lighthearted event, and not something that would make out-of-shape group members feel uncomfortable. The goal is to set a pace so frenetic that *everyone* will quickly be huffing and puffing. Then move into the magazine scavenger hunt as kids catch their breath.

STEP 3

In the middle of your discussion on good health, have a marshmallow stuff contest. Everyone can compete if you wish, though this is a pretty funny (and disgusting) competition to watch, and it usually works best when you use only three or four volunteers. One at a time, each competitor should put a marshmallow in his or her mouth and say, "My name is _____." No one is allowed to swallow his or her marshmallow. For Round 2, insert another marshmallow in each contestant's mouth and have the person state his or her name again. Continue adding one marshmallow at a time until contestants become unable to speak and all but one person is eliminated. (At that point, have some wastebaskets ready.) Afterward, discuss how this game, as exaggerated as it is, may symbolize our poor eating habits. We sometimes know we're eating too much or eating the wrong kinds of things, but we continue until we almost make ourselves sick. For some people, the health report card on Repro Resource 5 might be a mere exercise to pass the time. But if group members give it a little thought, it can challenge and inspire them to discipline themselves a little better in all areas of health.

STEP 2

In a small group, discussing one's personal health and habits may make young people uncomfortable. If only one or two of the group members are overweight or out of shape, the questions in this step may cause them embarrassment. Rather than conduct the discussion, perhaps you can spend this time planning a pro-health activity for your group. Small groups usually suffer when trying to play large-scale games like softball or football. But there are other options available to them that aren't available to large groups. Your group members can play tennis or handball (perhaps even on the same court at the same time). Your group could rent a gym for a night. Your group can get together to walk or go bike riding without a lot of scheduling difficulties. See what your group members like to do and try to plan a special activity outside the usual group time.

STEP 4

Dividing into four groups to study Daniel 1 may not be the best approach for a small group. But a similar activity that will work just as well or better is to assign each person (or pair) one of the aspects of health (intellectual, physical, social, and spiritual) to keep in mind during the Bible study. You can then begin to read the chapter aloud and have group members stop you whenever you get to a portion of Scripture that relates to their designated areas. That way you work together as a single group, but each individual will have a different responsibility. This approach will also show how the various aspects of health are often related to each other.

STEP 2

With a large group, you should have a lot of anecdotes to draw from to help you demonstrate the importance of good health. The problem is getting kids to open up. One method that usually works is to have everyone write down a "true confession" that is not known by most of the other people present. This true confession should be an action or perhaps a meal from the person's past that may not have been a very healthy choice. Perhaps one person tested Uncle Jack's chewing tobacco at age four. Someone else may have parachuted out of a barn loft holding a sheet. Other people may have stories about fireworks, chemistry sets, sledding terrors, or other near-miss incidents having to do with health and safety. Have the ones who can't think of anything better complete this sentence: "The strangest thing I have ever eaten in my life is _____." Have group members form teams of five or six. One member of each team will collect the team's "confession slips," shuffle them, and read them one at a time. The rest of the team members will then try to guess who did what.

STEP 5

If you don't want to limit your emphasis on health to this one session, you might consider a fun type of "homework" assignment. Ask group members to each solicit five or 10 "healthy" recipes from parents, friends, or fellow church members. Ask them to look for salads, appetizers, entrées, desserts, drinks, or anything else. Then find some volunteers to keyboard the recipes and put them together into your own cookbook. It will be easy enough to photocopy the cookbooks and give a copy to each contributor, but you may be able to find someone willing to desktop publish the book and make it look a bit more professional. Either way, encourage group members to use the recipes as part of their overall health regimen in the future.

STEP 2

Rather than merely discussing good safety habits, make the exercise more challenging. Have everyone think of a number of actions (gestures) that might be healthy under certain circumstances. For instance, someone might pantomime buckling a seat belt, replacing the batteries in a smoke alarm, double-checking a parachute before jumping out of a plane, being handed a lit cigarette and crushing it out, shaking head no (in response to extra dessert or a can of beer), or whatever. The more obscure the action, the better. Let each person perform the action as the others try to guess what it is.

STEP 5

Before group members set personal goals on Repro Resource 6, spend some time having kids name everyone they know of who has a health problem (family members, kids at school, neighborhood people, etc.). Even if they don't know the people personally, most junior highers know of someone who has cancer, diabetes, a physical disability, or some other health problem. Subtly help group members see that health is a very real issue for some people. Those who are healthy sometimes take it for granted and don't give it much thought. But as the kids set goals, they need to think in realistic terms rather than theoretical ones. You can also challenge them to use their good health to help anyone else who might need it. [NOTE: Be sure to remember in your closing prayer the people your group members name.]

STEP 3

Your group members may need some help in seeing the significance of Jesus as a model of total health. To give them a better perspective, evaluate some people who may excel in one of the four areas to see how they rate in the others. For example, every TV season seems to provide another batch of actors who are excellent specimens when it comes to physical health and good looks, yet seem to lack any degree of common sense or intelligence. Other people are intelligent and witty, yet would never be mistaken for models of strength and health. You might want to let group members come up with a list of names, and then rate each person using a 10-point scale in each of the four categories (intellectual, physical, social, and spiritual). A perfect score would be 40. See how well your other celebrities rate.

STEP 4

Rather than breaking into groups to cover the story of Daniel, you may prefer to have kids work together. First, review the reason that God's people were taken into captivity in the first place. You may also discuss some of the practices of a devoted Jewish person, which will help explain why Daniel was reluctant to eat the rich foods and wines offered him. Then go through the story together and let group members ask questions as they arise. While your group members may know about Daniel in the lions' den, they may never have heard this story (which precedes the lion's den adventure by several years). Point out that God helped Daniel to have excellent health (1:15), but first Daniel had to *choose* to try to be healthy (1:8). Ask: **How might this principle work in much the same way today?** (People who choose not to get drunk are far less likely to develop liver disease or drive their cars off the side of the road. People who rarely exercise and frequently indulge in fattening foods should not blame God if they suddenly decide to pray to lose weight and it doesn't happen immediately.)

STEP 4

Junior high is a time when many young people begin to feel tremendous peer pressure for the first time. As you discuss the story of Daniel, take a few minutes to point out how important it is to sometimes take a minority stance. When we choose to go along with the crowd, we discover the crowd is frequently wrong. Only by holding firm to the things we know to be true will we be able to rise *above* the crowd. Point out how Daniel was rewarded for his faith—not just when he got to heaven, but also as soon as 10 days after his decision (1:15). Ask your group members to commit to following God—no matter what happens—and to also commit to supporting each other. Just as Daniel had the support of Shadrach, Meshach, and Abednego, your group members should feel that they can lean on each other during times when they feel alone.

If you have time, you might have group members perform skits demonstrating how Christians can support each other. Each scenario should feature one Christian who is facing ridicule or rejection for not going along with the crowd, and another Christian who supports the first Christian in his or her minority stance.

STEP 5

So far in this session the discussion of health has been pretty general. But it can become as specific as you want to make it. In closing, have your group members say a sentence prayer that praises God for specific things that contribute to health: lungs that absorb oxygen from the air; taste buds that make eating more enjoyable than it might be; hands with opposable thumbs; the senses of hearing, seeing, touch, and smell; a heavy sweat after a hard workout; and so forth. Encourage people to contribute to the prayer as many times as they wish. Challenge them to think of as many specific items of health and fitness as they can, and to thank God for each and every one.

STEP 1

If your girls seem to concentrate on references from the cosmetic or beauty industries, take a few minutes to talk with them about the difference between being healthy and "looking good." Ask: **Can someone be healthy and not look good? Can someone look good and not be healthy?** Emphasize that just because a person looks beautiful on the outside doesn't mean she takes good care of her body. You may want to talk about some models who have admitted to going on unhealthy diets just to maintain a certain look.

STEP 3

Girls in junior high are typically much more emotional—and more willing to talk about their emotions—than guys are. Have your girls add "Emotional Health" to Repro Resource 5. Discuss as a group what it means to be emotionally healthy, to be able to talk about our feelings with others. Ask: **What feeling do you have the most trouble expressing? What feeling is easiest for you to express? Is it always easy to know what you're feeling? Why or why not?** Point out that Jesus was very honest about His feelings. There are many passages in the Bible that reveal Jesus' emotions—from sadness to anger to joy. Help your girls understand that it's natural to feel many different emotions.

STEP 2

When you get to the discussion question concerning involvement in things that may not necessarily be healthy, most junior high guys will have stories to tell if prodded a little. Set aside a few minutes for volunteers to tell "Tales of Reckless Abandon." Some of them have probably taken ridiculous dares. Some may have been goofing off, which resulted in an accident that could have been much more serious than it turned out to be. Some may just seem to lack any sense of potential limitations. Once you get the stories going, many of your guys will probably join in. After a while, begin to discuss the attitude of some young people that "Nothing will happen to me." The myth of immortality has led to far too many serious or fatal accidents as young people get involved with drugs, guns, heavy drinking, and other unhealthy practices. Try to have a true story or two of your own to end with, detailing a tragedy of someone you know that could have been avoided if a young person had used some discretion instead of acting foolishly.

STEP 5

The guys in your group probably vary greatly in their levels of activity in the four areas of health. So as you wrap up the session, encourage your group members to form "accountability pairs" (or groups) to spur each other out of potential lethargy. Perhaps those who live near each other can work out a time when they could jog together, shoot baskets, or play tennis. Or they might plan to go see a movie, work on a chemistry project together, or perhaps talk about some of the spiritual struggles they're having. Even a once-a-week meeting will be constructive. It's easy to discuss health. It's not even hard to set goals. But until group members actually begin to do something to change their current habits, they won't get any healthier.

STEP 1

As a variation of (or an addition to) the magazine scavenger hunt, have kids form groups. Give each group a different kind of junk food, such as candy bars, chips, hot fudge, and so forth. Ask each group to create a TV ad that will promote the benefits of using the product. Their claims might stretch the truth until it breaks, but group members should try to be as convincing as possible. After a while, have each group present its ad for the other groups. Conclude by challenging kids to recognize actual ads that use the same technique to sell products to gullible buyers.

STEP 2

You can have a little extra fun in creating definitions for health by doing them as a group. Have group members sit in a circle. Explain that you will go from one person to the next, and each person should contribute a single word. No one will have any idea what the definition will turn out to be because each person has to go with what has already been said. Try this a few times, and kids will quickly get better at it. Some other questions you could ask to be answered by the same means include the following:

• **What kinds of exercise are best for good health?**

• **What is the most important thing to remember about good hygiene?**

• **What do you think is _____'s** (choose someone from the group) **secret to always looking so good?**

STEP 3

After discussing the various aspects of health, watch portions of a number of exercise videos. (Try to find a good mix of serious ones and ridiculous ones.) Then have group members form three groups. Explain: **There seems to be no shortage of videos to demonstrate physical health. But now it's up to you to develop something in the other three areas.** One group should create some exercises to develop intellectual health (*Brains of Steel?*). Another group should design some socially healthy exercises (*Shoppin' with the Oldies?*). And the third group should think of some spiritual workout activities (*Walking in the Spirit?*). When the groups finish, let them demonstrate some of their recommended exercises.

STEP 5

Theoretically, school should stimulate your group members' *intellectual* health. And ideally, your youth group or Sunday school class should stimulate their *spiritual* and *social* health. So as you wrap up this session, focus on *physical* health. Prior to the meeting, pick up a selection of health and fitness magazines. Let group members leaf through them as they consider personal goals for physical health. You might also want to subscribe to one of them on behalf of your group. Your group members have busy schedules and are likely to forget what is said in this session by this time next week. But if you have a magazine coming in once a month to pass around and discuss, the things you teach about health will be remembered and emphasized.

STEP 2

Having kids write a definition of *health* and then list the things they do that are and aren't healthy may take up a lot of meeting time. Instead, simply hold up various items and ask kids to determine whether each item is healthy or not. Among the items you might use are fresh fruits and vegetables, a Twinkie, a cigarette, a can of diet pop, cheese, a comic book, a Bible, a jump rope, and a TV remote control. Lead in to a discussion on the importance of *all-around* health.

STEP 3

Rather than having kids fill out Repro Resource 5, simply have them call out ways in which a person could improve in each area. So when you say, **Intellectual,** group members should call out practical suggestions a person could use to improve his or her intellectual health. Among the responses they might give are "Go to summer school," "Get a tutor," and "Read more in your spare time." Write group members' suggestions on the board. Then lead in to the Bible study.

STEP 2

With all of the serious problems associated with living in the city, it's likely that your urban kids face more health risks than other kids do. Have your group members form teams of three or four. Instruct each team to come up with a list of health risks that may pose more of a threat to city kids than to other kids. Teams' lists may include things like AIDS, drug dependency, alcoholism, injuries due to street violence, poor nutrition, lack of proper exercise, etc. After a few minutes, have each team share its list. As the teams share, create a master list on the board. Afterward, discuss as a group how to educate people regarding urban health risks.

STEP 4

You might want to paraphrase the story of the diet "contest" in Daniel 1 to make it more applicable to today's kids. For instance, you might say that Daniel and his friends ate three square meals a day (with the proper food groups represented), beginning with breakfast. On the other hand, the king's men skipped breakfast and spent the rest of the day snacking on candy bars, doughnuts, chips, and pop. Or you might paraphrase in terms of exercise. For instance, you might say that Daniel and his friends got proper exercise, either by working out, playing sports, or performing regular physical labor. The kings' men, however, either partied all of the time or spent their time lying around watching TV. Use this paraphrase to lead in to a discussion on physical health.

STEP 1

Instead of the magazine scavenger hunt, you might want to have a debate between your high schoolers and junior highers. (If the idea of a debate seems too academic, make it a courtroom trial in which you are the judge.) The issue should be to determine which group is less healthy: junior highers or high schoolers. But instead of hurling accusations at each other, have the junior highers try to prove that they are less healthy than high schoolers, while the older kids try to prove that *they* are less healthy. This will force each group to admit to the many unhealthy habits they (or people their age) participate in. Give each group a few minutes to come up with its best arguments, and then moderate the debate/trial. You may be surprised to discover how brutally honest some group members will be just to win an argument. Use group members' specific examples to personalize the points you want to make.

STEP 2

In addition to the discussion questions, add a series of agree/disagree statements. Designate one side of the room as "Totally Agree," and the opposite side as "Totally Disagree." After each statement, kids will move to a spot that indicates their level of agreement. Explain that you want to see whether there are any trends according to age. Use the following statements:

• **The older you get, the more you need to watch what you eat.**
• **The older you get, the more you need to exercise regularly.**
• **Everybody makes too big a deal about health.**
• **I don't worry about my health.**
• **When you start dating, you take a lot better care of yourself.**

There may be little, if any, difference between the attitudes of your junior highers and high schoolers. But these statements are likely to generate some discussion in certain areas in which the older kids will pass along some good advice to the younger ones.

STEP 2

Instead of having your sixth graders try to write definitions of health, it might be a lot easier to have them complete this sentence: **Other than dying, the worst thing that could happen to someone's health is . . .** This is something of a backdoor approach to the topic, yet it is an issue many young people tend to think about. Let them describe their fears and concerns. Some may be things they (or friends and family members) have experienced personally. Others may be things they speculate about. Afterward, explain that while we cannot avoid suffering and tragedy in life, we can keep such things to a minimum by developing good health habits and taking better care of ourselves.

STEP 4

For sixth graders, you might want to create a modern parallel to introduce the story of Daniel. For example, you might say: **Suppose our country were suddenly invaded by Tahiti. They conquer us and decide to take back the very sharpest young people they can find to be brought up in their culture. This is the group that has been chosen. The bad news is that you are carried away from your homes and families, and are given different names.** (Feel free to create a few Tahitian names for some of your members.) **The good news is that you are given all the privileges of royalty. The finest food and drink available are yours. You report only to the leader of the country—no other people tell you what to do. How would you feel?**

After group members express some of the pros and cons, introduce the story of Daniel and his dilemma. Throughout the story you can compare his actions with those expressed by your group members.

DATE USED:

Approx. Time

STEP 1: *Magazine Scavenger Hunt* _____
❑ Extra Action
❑ Mostly Girls
❑ Extra Fun
❑ Combined Junior High/High School
Things needed:

STEP 2: *What Is Health?* _____
❑ Small Group
❑ Large Group
❑ Heard It All Before
❑ Mostly Guys
❑ Extra Fun
❑ Short Meeting Time
❑ Urban
❑ Combined Junior High/High School
❑ Sixth Grade
Things needed:

STEP 3: *Health Report Card* _____
❑ Extra Action
❑ Little Bible Background
❑ Mostly Girls
❑ Media
❑ Short Meeting Time
Things needed:

STEP 4: *Daniel Is Traveling Tonight on the Plain* _____
❑ Small Group
❑ Little Bible Background
❑ Fellowship & Worship
❑ Urban
❑ Sixth Grade
Things needed:

STEP 5: *Healthy Choices* _____
❑ Large Group
❑ Heard It All Before
❑ Fellowship & Worship
❑ Mostly Guys
❑ Media
Things needed:

A Body to Die For?

☐ To help kids recognize that an intense desire for a better body might be motivated by something other than good health.

☐ To help kids understand that even having a perfect body is no guarantee of happiness or success.

☐ To have kids identify some of the more common "body abusers" and commit to avoiding them in the future.

☐ Other:_____
_____

Your Bible Base:

Judges 14—16
1 Corinthians 6:19-20

Too Bad to Be True

(Needed: List of scenarios for group members to respond to)

Begin the session by creating some scenarios that would involve strange behavior on the parts of selected group members. For example, suppose Dena is the one person in your group who would never get in trouble. You might say: **Imagine that Dena were to get picked up for public drunkenness and disorderly conduct. What do you think could possibly be the reason?** Other situations could include unlikely kids putting a hand through a wall in rage, getting caught stealing money from a teacher, lying about their age and enlisting in the military, joining a gang, quitting school, and so forth.

Point out that it may seem strange to think of your "model" group members in such predicaments, yet similar stories are not uncommon. Newspapers and TV news shows frequently report on young people who shock their friends and family members by unexpectedly stealing, running away, committing murder, getting involved in strange cults or abnormal sexual behavior, and so forth. Interviews with neighbors almost always include a comment like "He [or she] seemed like such a quiet, normal person."

Try to help your group members begin to see that some things a person does may make sense to the person, yet appear completely irrational to observers. Any number of underlying causes (stress, fear, depression, physical problems, etc.) can create significantly erratic behavior. Through your scenarios, group members will probably be able to speculate what might cause such strange behavior—when it relates to someone else. Yet they may have "eccentric" behavior of their own without realizing it.

Explain: **Sometimes people develop "tunnel vision," which means they lose the big picture of life and see only one narrow segment. For example, when someone focuses only on his or her body to the exclusion of everything else, it's almost impossible to be satisfied. No matter what kind of shape they're in, they think, I can improve. I should be a couple of pounds thinner or a bit more pumped up. But that kind of thinking leads people to do some pretty strange things as they are obsessed with improving their bodies. Their actions may make perfect sense to them, but other people may think they are just plain weird.**

Risky Trade-offs

(Needed: Copies of Repro Resource 7, pencils)

Have your kids think of the large number of people their age who want to look better than they do now. Then hand out copies of "Paved with Good Inventions" (Repro Resource 7) and pencils. Ask your group members to invent a product that would be in tremendous demand among such people. Give your kids enough time to be creative. Products may be imitations or adaptations of actual things they have seen, or completely original ideas. The feasibility of the product doesn't matter. Its claims can be ludicrous and unbelievable. The point is primarily to encourage your group members to identify the feelings and needs of many of their peers.

When everyone is finished, let each person explain what he or she has designed. You may even want to vote for the best idea(s) and award prizes.

Then ask: **Which of these products would you buy if you had the opportunity?**

What needs and desires of your age group did you identify that helped you create your product?

What are some actual products kids your age buy that deal with those same needs? Let kids list as many products as they can think of. They may name cosmetics, toiletries, name-brand clothes, foods, exercise equipment, diet aids, braces, contact lenses, and so forth.

Explain that while some products are truly beneficial, others exist only because companies know they can prey on the insecurities of young people. No one would argue that buying toothpaste and dental floss are preferable to letting their teeth rot out. Yet we need to beware of claims of "miracle diets," pills, steroids, and other harmful (and potentially fatal) products.

STEP 3

What's It Worth?

(Needed: List of "What if" questions)

Ask some questions to see to what extent your group members would be willing to change the way they look. Create some "What if" situations that you think would get the attention of your kids. The following few questions are provided to get you started. After each question, take a poll to see how many people would act on the opportunity and how many would refuse.

1. What if you saved the life of a plastic surgeon and he offered you a free operation of your choice: Would you take him up on it? If so, what kind of operation would you have done? Statistics tell us that unprecedented numbers of young people are having costly and unnecessary cosmetic surgery just to look a little bit better.

2. Suppose a pill existed that with one dose would give you a perfect body—just exactly what you want to look like. Would you want one?

- **What if one percent of the people who took it died? Would you still take it?**
- **What if 10 percent of the pill takers died? How about 30 percent?**
- **What if the financial cost were so great that you had to work 20 hours every week all the way through junior high and high school to pay for it?**
- **What if only one pill existed, and your best friend wanted it? What if a physically handicapped person wanted it?**

3. What if a pill existed that changed your perspective of yourself so that you became perfectly happy with the body you have: Would you want it? Why or why not?

4. What if you had the power to change other people's bodies into exactly what they wanted them to be: Would you use your power?

- **Would you grant every request? Explain.**
- **If a severely thin girl asked you to make her even thinner, would you?**
- **Would you feel any responsibility for making unwise changes, even though you were asked to make those changes?**

5. What if you had a perfect body? Do you think you would be completely content? Why or why not?

STEP 4

What Good Is a Good Body?

(Needed: Bibles, paper, pencils)

OPTIONS

SMALL GROUP

LITTLE BIBLE BACKGROUND

MOSTLY GIRLS

After group members have had some time to consider the last question in Step 3, explain that a near-perfect body is no guarantee of a happy life. To illustrate this point, have them study the life of Samson.

Divide into three groups. Distribute paper and pencils to each group. Group 1 should read and report on Judges 14. Group 2 should cover Judges 15. Group 3 should study Judges 16. As the kids are getting into groups, set the scene for them (from Judges 13). Explain that the nation of Israel had been disobedient to God, so He had allowed them to be subdued by the powerful Philistines for 40 years.

But God had promised Samson's parents that He would work through Samson to deliver the Israelites from the Philistines. Samson was to be "set apart to God." The one stipulation God made was that Samson never get his hair cut. (See Num. 6:1-21 for additional information on this type of Nazirite vow.)

Group members should focus on Samson's amazing God-given strength. But in addition, they should list any other of his character traits they discover in their reading. One person from each group should report on the content of the group's assigned chapter—or perhaps creative groups will want to act out the stories they discuss.

Group 1 should discover that Samson appeared to be fearless. He was attacked by a lion, but God's Spirit empowered him to kill it with his bare hands. Later his strength was used to overpower 30 men simply to pay off a lost bet. In addition to his strength, Samson is seen as some-what stubborn or self-centered as he went against his parents' wishes in choosing a bride. He also seemed very sure of himself as he created a riddle he didn't think anyone could solve. And when he was tricked by his wife and her people, he is seen as "burning with anger" (vs. 19).

Group 2 should describe even better stories about Samson's strength. First, he seemed to have no problem catching three hundred foxes, tying their tails together in pairs, attaching torches, and burning down the fields, vineyards, and olive groves of the Philistines. Next, he slaughtered many men for killing his Philistine bride and her father. And finally, after being tied up in new ropes, he easily broke them. Then he picked up the jawbone of a donkey and proceeded to kill a thousand Philistines. Yet despite his physical strength, Samson seems emotionally insecure. He is seen as wanting to "get even" (vs. 3), seeking "revenge" (vs. 7), vicious (vs. 8), and complaining (vs. 18).

Group 3 should describe Samson's ability to rip apart the gate to a Philistine city and carry off the doors, posts, bar, and all. (The estimated distance he carried the gate is 38 miles—uphill!) He also demonstrated strength in his many escapes from the traps set by the Philistines: being tied with fresh thongs, with new ropes that had never been used, and so forth. He also single-handedly pushed down the supporting beams of a Philistine temple. But this chapter also shows his most prominent weaknesses. He slept with prostitutes (vs. 1) and he couldn't resist the continual pleading of a woman (vss. 15-17). He forfeited everything God gave him to do the things *he* wanted to. At last, blinded and humbled, he asked for (and was given) one more opportunity to use his miraculous strength to defeat Israel's enemies. As the temple crashed down, Samson killed more Philistines than ever before.

After all the groups report, say: **We can't assume that because Samson was strong he was also necessarily good-looking. But let's suppose for a moment that he was. After all, his muscles and long hair probably combined the look of an athlete and a rock star. Yet even with what was perhaps the most perfect body on record, do you think he was happy? Do you think he was content? If you had a perfect body, do you think you could avoid the mistakes Samson made? If so, explain.**

Oh, C'mon! What's the Worst That Could Happen?

(Needed: Bibles, copies of Repro Resource 8, pencils)

Explain that since a perfect body is no guarantee of happiness, contentment, or success, we should be careful not to go too far in trying to improve our bodies. Some people cross the line of good taste or good sense and begin to do things or use products that abuse the body.

Hand out copies of "Deadly Shortcuts" (Repro Resource 8) and pencils. On the repro resource, group members will be alerted to the dangers involved in the shortcuts promised by various "body abusers." They will then be asked to create some long-term goals that would accomplish the same results in a safe and beneficial way, without harming themselves physically or otherwise.

Remind group members of what you've already discussed: **If someone has a tendency to abuse his or her body in an attempt to look better or feel better about himself or herself, more than likely there is a deeper, more serious motivation. And when people don't deal with the real issue(s), no amount of dieting, pills, or anything else will compensate for it.**

What might be some of the underlying reasons that would cause people to take steroids? Try dangerous diet pills? Become anorexic or bulimic? (The underlying reasons for many different body abusers may be the same: a powerful lack of self-esteem and a desperate desire to better oneself physically to get attention and affirmation.)

What would you say to a friend who was seriously involved with any of these body abusers? Let kids respond, but then alert them to the fact that many times the problem is beyond the point where a friend's concern or advice will make any difference. These are issues that are likely to need extended counseling or professional therapy. Sometimes the best thing a young person can do to help a friend is connect him or her with an adult willing to deal with the issue over an extended period of time.

Who are some adults you could recommend to a friend you know who has a problem with one of the body abusers on your list? Be sure to provide several names of people to contact—preferably written down, with their phone numbers.

What do you think is the most dangerous of the body abusers that were listed? Kids may have different opinions, but they should come to see that any of these things can become deadly.

What's the worst that can happen when people get involved with these kinds of body abusers? (People die from these things—not always, but too frequently. And even those who recover must usually go through a long and painful transition back to health. In addition, all the time they spent in the grip of their body abusers is lost.)

To emphasize the dangers of various body abusers, use some personal stories of people you know (if possible). Let kids know that these are very real problems—not theoretical issues. If you don't know of anyone who has undergone struggles in these areas, you may want to use stories of celebrities who have. The following stories are of two people who died from different body abusers, their shortened lives a reminder of what can happen if we don't deal with the emotional and physical problems that plague us.

OPTIONS

SMALL GROUP

LARGE GROUP

HEARD IT ALL BEFORE

FELLOWSHIP & WORSHIP

MOSTLY GUYS

MEDIA

SHORT MEETING TIME

URBAN

JR. HIGH / HIGH SCHOOL COMBINED

SIXTH GRADE

Karen Carpenter was drummer and lead singer of the Carpenters, a duo that was very popular in the 1970s. They won Grammies for Best New Group in 1970 and Best Vocal Duo in 1970 and 1971. They sold more than 60 million records and were awarded numerous gold singles and albums. But Karen was a victim of anorexia nervosa. In her pursuit to be thinner and thinner, her health declined as her weight kept going down. She died in 1983 at age 32.

Lyle Alzado had a reputation for being one of the toughest men in professional football for 15 seasons. He played for the Denver Broncos, Cleveland Browns, and Los Angeles Raiders. But in his early forties he was diagnosed with a rare brain cancer. At that point he admitted that he thought (as did some of his doctors) that his condition may have been the result of his heavy use of anabolic steroids since 1967. (At that time he was a 195-pound college freshman. He "bulked up" to 300 pounds by his senior year.) Even after he retired from football in 1985, he couldn't stop taking steroids. After discovering his brain cancer and dropping 60 pounds in a few months, he said, "I was so muscular. I was a giant. Now I'm sick. And I'm scared." At another point he said, "I lied to [my wife]. I lied to everyone. . . . Maybe the message God wants me to give people is that they should stop using steroids." He died in 1992, in his mid-forties.

Point out that these are only two examples of the thousands of people who die as a result of body abusers each year. Emphasize the abbreviated life spans of those who choose to get involved with such deadly shortcuts, and challenge your group members to stick to the long-term goals they've set as they mature.

Remind your group members that Christians have another good reason to avoid any substances or practices that would abuse the body. Have everyone look up and read I Corinthians 6:19-20. Discuss what it means for a Christian's body to be a "temple of the Holy Spirit" and to be "bought at a price." Then close the session with prayer, asking God to protect your group members from body abusers as they continue to grow. Also pray for anyone they may know who is struggling with image problems to the point of getting involved with such things.

NOTES

PAVED WITH GOOD INVENTIONS

You can be an inventor. Yes, that's right. You *can* be an inventor. All you have to do is complete this simple exercise. First, think of all the young people in the world who aren't satisfied with themselves. They think they're too fat. Too short. Too zit-covered. Not muscular enough. Not pretty. Not handsome. Wrong-colored eyes. Wrong-colored hair. Wrong type of hair. Not enough hair. Too much hair. Hair in all the wrong places. Well, you get the idea.

Before you begin, envision the emotions of these people. Feel what they're feeling. Then invent a product that you think you could really sell to them. Your product should promise them something they desperately want. (All you have to do is come up with the idea. Someone else will figure out how to make it do what you want it to do—so be as wild and creative as you can be.)

Who knows? If you do well with this, maybe we'll see you down at the patent office soon.

NAME OF PRODUCT:

FUNCTION AND SPECIAL FEATURES OF PRODUCT:

ILLUSTRATION:

DEADLY ShOrTCuTs

Most "body abusers" are things that people use to accomplish personal goals. The goals themselves aren't usually bad. It's natural to want to lose weight or be stronger. But problems arise when people become willing to take dangerous shortcuts to accomplish their goals.

Below is a list of common body abusers and the goals of many people who are involved in them. After each one, come up with a better, safer goal that will accomplish the same results. In most cases, the goals you create should be long-range plans rather than potentially harmful shortcuts.

BODY ABUSER: Anorexia (loss of appetite and inability to eat)
GOAL: To be thinner
DANGER OF THE SHORTCUT: The eating disorder, *anorexia nervosa,* primarily affects adolescent girls and young women. Symptoms include intense fear of becoming fat, distorted body image, excessive dieting, and abnormal thinness due to lack of nutrition.
BETTER GOAL FOR BECOMING THINNER:

BODY ABUSER: Bulimia (abnormally intense appetite or unnatural constant hunger)
GOAL: To enjoy food without gaining weight
DANGER OF THE SHORTCUT: The eating disorder, *bulimia nervosa*, is a repeated disturbance in eating behavior mostly affecting young women of normal weight. It is characterized by frequent episodes of grossly excessive food intake followed by self-induced vomiting to avoid weight gain.
BETTER GOAL FOR ENJOYING FOOD WITHOUT GAINING WEIGHT OR PURGING:

BODY ABUSER: Diet aids
GOAL: To reduce or control body weight by suppressing appetite or reducing stomach space
DANGER OF THE SHORTCUT: Many of these aids, such as amphetamines, can be dangerous or addictive—especially to young people whose bodies are still growing. Others have been proven to be medically ineffective.
BETTER GOAL FOR REDUCING OR CONTROLLING BODY WEIGHT:

BODY ABUSER: Anabolic steroids
GOAL: To gain body strength
DANGER OF THE SHORTCUT: Excessive use can lead to infertility, liver dysfunction, severe personality changes, increased risk of heart disease, and other severe problems.
BETTER GOAL FOR GAINING BODY STRENGTH:

STEP 1

Bring in a tire pump and a half-inflated rubber ball. Call volunteers to the front of the room one at a time. Describe to each volunteer a scenario that involves physical appearance. Then have the person inflate or deflate the ball to indicate how he or she would like to look in that scenario. (Deflating the ball might indicate that the person wants to lose weight; inflating the ball might indicate that he or she wants to "bulk up.") Here are some scenarios you might want to use:

• **You're going to the beach tomorrow for the first time this summer—in your new swimsuit.**

• **In the school parking lot, a couple of older guys start pushing you around and threatening you.**

• **You just bought a pair of jeans to wear on a date Friday night.**

• **You're going to a family reunion to see aunts, uncles, and cousins you haven't seen since you were eight.**

STEP 2

You can add a bit more action to Repro Resource 7 by having group members build replicas of their products or ideas rather than simply drawing them. Provide an assortment of Tinkertoys, Legos, modeling clay, or any other building materials you can find. Let your "inventors" create a "mock-up" of their products to hold up as they "pitch" the benefits of each item. The three-dimensional replicas will also be more effective as you vote on which ones group members would use if the products were actually available on the market.

STEP 4

Make the Bible study less structured as you look at the life of Samson. Focus primarily on Judges 16. Summarize the events of his life prior to that point. Then try to encourage a discussion rather than a simple retelling of facts. Ask: **Why do you think so many people want to have bodies like Samson's? Do you think someone could be as strong as Samson and avoid all the problems he had? Why or why not?** In a small group you have the opportunity to let everyone express opinions, and you should encourage group members to do so. The questions and comments that arise will be far more personalized and helpful than those designed to communicate basic truths to a large group.

STEP 5

It may be that none of the "body abuser" activities you discuss are serious problems for the members of your small group. It is unwise to make assumptions about young people you don't know well. But if you are reasonably sure that no one is involved with such things, spend some time at the end of the session determining how your group might help people who *do* struggle with these serious involvements. Can your group members become a support group for such people? Brainstorm a number of ways they can help people they know. Then set some goals for how to implement the ideas they come up with.

STEP 1

Rather than trying to single out a few people to use in the scenarios, you can accomplish much the same purpose by staging a fake argument. Prearrange this with one or two volunteers before the meeting. Then, as you begin the meeting, have one of your volunteers become gradually more vocal and belligerent. Perhaps his or her emotional outbursts can be directed at you. If, for example, he or she starts talking to someone and disturbing the rest of the group, you could politely ask him or her to be quiet. Then he or she could start talking back to you. Or if you choose two volunteers, an argument between the two of them could escalate. Either way, the volunteer(s) should wind up storming out of the room. While the other group members are still stunned, ask: **What do you think might have caused him** (or **her**) **to act like that?** Let group members respond. Then ask your now-grinning volunteer(s) to return. Discuss the emotions your group members felt during and following the argument. Explain that even though people may have good reasons for doing what they do, their actions can have significant (if unintentional) results for others.

STEP 5

A large group is likely to have a certain number of people involved with one or more "body abusers." If you suspect this to be true in your group, you might want to ask volunteers to do further investigation into the dangers of such things. (Perhaps they can use their research for school term papers as well.) The lives and deaths of people such as Karen Carpenter and Lyle Alzado (as well as more recent examples) will likely be of more interest than simply investigating the problem areas. Ask people who are willing to do some additional research to report back to the group. (It may be that the people who take more interest in these problems are the ones who struggle with them.)

STEP 3

The concept of body abusers may not immediately capture the attention of a group of kids who grew up hearing "This is your brain on drugs" and "Just say no." They may assume your message will be just as trivial. So introduce the topic by dealing purely from the abuse aspect. Ask: **What images come to your mind when I say the following words: Child abuse?** (Wait for response.) **Spouse abuse? Verbal abuse? Sexual abuse?**

It is likely that the images brought to mind by such terms will be strongly negative. Then explain that while we may feel intense emotions for victims of such abuses as well as toward their abusers, we may not feel strongly when we tend to abuse our own bodies in various ways. Yet we need to see the tremendous amounts of potential pain and destruction involved when we choose to get involved with various body abusers. We should be just as vehemently opposed to such things as we would be to someone's abusing a spouse or child.

STEP 5

This would be a good session to consider bringing in a speaker. If you know of someone who is well-informed on a number of the various body abusers listed on Repro Resource 8, see if he or she would be willing to speak to your group. Such a person would be especially good if your group is hard to penetrate. A Christian doctor, for example, may have seen a lot of anorexia, bulimia, steroid abuse, effects of drug use and drinking, and so forth. He or she could tell true stories, hold the interest of your group, and make the problems seem much more real. In addition, he or she can look for warning signs of any of these things among your group members.

STEP 3

You may discover as you discuss the opinion questions that some of your group members seem to have little, if any, kind of ethical basis for making decisions. If you find this to be a potential problem in your group, take time immediately following the questions to provide a Christian perspective for some of the things you've been discussing. You want your young people to express honest opinions, but in some cases you can't assume they all have a biblical perspective of right and wrong. It might be helpful for you to be ready with appropriate Bible references, explanations, and other insights that will help people new to the Bible discover that sometimes there is a moral absolute that they can hold to while making hard decisions.

STEP 4

If your group is hearing the Samson story for the first time, don't overdose them on it by covering all three chapters in separate groups. Instead, gather group members around and give them all the facts they need in a storytelling format. Begin with "Once upon a time . . ." and move on to the rather tragic ending to Samson's life. While the events of Samson's life may not seem very thrilling to you, they probably did the *first* time you heard the story. And since this might be the first time your group members are hearing them, try to make sure all the excitement and adventure come through as you tell the story. Keep the focus on Samson's one-of-a-kind strength—the kind of strength that many of your members would envy. Then make it clear that having a near-perfect body did not ensure success or happiness for Samson. As you move into the personal applications in Step 5, group members should be more responsive after putting themselves in Samson's place for a while.

STEP 3

After going through the questions in this step, ask: **Would you say most young people you know are content most of the time? Why or why not? Would you say you are content? What thing(s) would you need to be more content?** Then have someone look up and read Philippians 4:11-13. Ask: **What is "the secret of being content"?** Let kids arrive at the conclusion that Paul had learned to be content because he knew that as long as he was doing what he knew Jesus wanted him to do, nothing else mattered. He could eat or go hungry. He could be rich or poor. He could live or die. And, in the context of this session, it would be safe to assume that he could be content with either an athletic and good-looking body or one that was quite average. Challenge your group members to be more thankful and offer praise to God for the many gifts they have already received from Him rather than be discontented with any of their physical features.

STEP 5

As you conclude the session, be sensitive to the possibility that one or more of your members may have a serious, yet undiscovered problem with some kind of body abuser. Offer assurance that God is greater than any problem your group members can ever have. (See Rom. 8:35-39.) Yet when dealing with problems as severe as the ones described in this session, we shouldn't give the impression that all kids need to do is say a prayer and expect the problems to disappear. These are areas that may require a lengthy, ongoing struggle before victims can find complete healing. Be supportive of group members and remind them that no matter how we feel, we can count on God. We *do* need to be patient and persevering in the meantime, however. Ask group members to remember the needs and weaknesses of one another in the weeks to come.

STEP 2

As your girls brainstorm actual products that kids their age buy, list the products on the board. Afterward, go through the list as a group; identify each product as "Necessary"; "Nice to have, but not essential"; or "Harmful." Talk about some of the risks involved in using some of the "harmful" products (such as diet pills). Ask: **How can you tell if a product is something that will be truly beneficial or something that could be potentially harmful?**

STEP 4

Ask your girls to name a female who they think has a "perfect" body. Then ask them what they think makes a woman beautiful. Most will probably name physical characteristics. Have them turn to Proverbs 31:10-31. As a group, list the qualities God thinks makes a woman beautiful. Then distribute paper and pencils. Instruct group members to make two columns on the sheet, one labeled "Physical Beauty" and the other labeled "Inner Beauty." Under each column, have the girls write the activities they perform (fixing their hair, putting on makeup, reading the Bible, etc.) that contribute to that particular category and how much time per day they spend doing that particular thing. When they've completed their lists, challenge them to think about the time they spend on their physical appearance versus what they spend developing inner beauty. Be sure to comment that God isn't saying we need to neglect our appearance, but rather that He wants us to keep our priorities in order.

STEP 2

Rather than doing Repro Resource 7, have your guys work on devising exclusively masculine products—things that would build muscles and/or make them stronger. After each person presents his invention, ask the group: **Is this something you would be interested in? Explain.** Afterward, as a group, come up with reasons why some guys are so much more determined to look a certain way than others are. With enough prodding, group members may come to the realization that perhaps it is insecurity that motivates many bodybuilders. Only by becoming noticeably muscular and receiving attention from others do they feel a sense of self-esteem. (This isn't true of everyone, of course, but it may be a common feeling.) Explain later that the problem with this attitude is that steroids seem much more attractive when all that matters is a bigger and better body.

STEP 5

Because anorexia and bulimia are almost exclusively problems for girls, spend your time dealing with steroids, alcohol, and sex. Ask: **Do steroids, alcohol, and sex really abuse the body, or are they just bad habits? Explain. Why do some guys take steroids even when they know the risks? Do you think most guys who drink do it because they enjoy the taste of alcohol? Explain. Do you think most guys who have sex do it purely because of the physical sensation they experience? Explain.**

If your guys are honest, they will admit that many of these activities are done primarily for the reputation they will earn the person. Some of the behaviors may be harmful—even life threatening. But if they are considered cool or macho things to do, many guys will be willing to participate. Challenge your group members to be strong enough to stand in the minority in such instances, not only because of the faith they profess, but for their own health.

STEP 1

If you have access to an amusement park or similar place that features feats of skill and strength, try to spend some time there prior to the meeting. If not, set up some games of your own. Individuals could compete in weight lifting, sumo wrestling, or some similar type of activity. Or teams can compete in games such as tug-of-war. As group members compete, listen for their comments toward each other. Do the winners gloat in their victories and put down the losers? Do the weaker kids seem frustrated or apathetic? Do the games cease to be fun for some people as they become intent only on winning? Record any relevant comments and use them at appropriate places throughout the session.

STEP 3

As you get ready to move into the Bible study, spend a few minutes playing a drawing game using Pictionary rules. Use a list of words that will be discussed during the Bible study (Step 4) and application (Step 5), such as *anorexia, bulimia, steroids, foxes, temple, prostitute, strength, jawbone,* and so forth. Group members should divide into teams, with drawing responsibilities being rotated and shared equally. A volunteer from each team should look at the assigned word, return to his or her team members, and await your signal to begin. As one person draws, all of the others guess what the word is supposed to be. No letters or numbers may be used—only pictures. The first team to guess the word is the winner of that round.

STEP 3

Pick up a few bodybuilding magazines prior to the meeting. At the beginning of Step 3, show group members some selected pictures from the magazines and let them express how they feel about attempting to sculpt the body to such an extent. Then read quotes from some of the articles about what is required to be a successful bodybuilder. See to what extent group members agree or disagree. Finally, read some of the ads and what they promise. Do any advertised products (pills, powders, diet supplements, etc.) sound as if they might be somewhat dangerous or at least risky? Use the various parts of the magazines to prompt group member opinions and response. Then move into the discussion questions in Step 3.

STEP 5

Try to collect a group of songs, paintings, movie clips, and so forth, from artists who died as a result of some kind of body abuser. Play short segments from the songs and show the clips as you ask group members to imagine what these people might have done if they hadn't died prematurely. Many group members are likely to know some of the bigger names (Jimi Hendrix, Marilyn Monroe, Elvis Presley, Janis Joplin, Judy Garland, John Belushi, and so forth). You may know of others as well. Try to collect a significant body of material to show. Remind group members that many of these people might well be alive today if they hadn't abused their bodies. Challenge them to learn from others' mistakes and not make the same mistakes themselves.

STEP 2

Before the session, prepare several index cards. On half of the cards, write legitimate examples of ways to improve one's physical appearance. (For instance, taking a shower and brushing your hair are legitimate examples of improving one's physical appearance.) On the other half of the cards, write examples of "going overboard" to improve one's physical appearance. (For instance, getting up at 4:00 a.m. to start "primping" is an example of going overboard to improve one's physical appearance.) Put all of the cards in a container. Have kids come to the front of the room one at a time, draw a card, read it, and then determine whether it's a "legitimate" example or an example of "going overboard." Use this activity instead of Repro Resource 7.

STEP 5

Rather than having kids work on Repro Resource 8, simply read aloud some of the descriptions of the "body abusers" listed on the sheet. Then, as a group, brainstorm a list of "warning signs" that might indicate a person is involved with one of these body abusers. After you've listed several warning signs, encourage kids to look for these signs in their friends and family members—as well as in themselves. Then wrap up the session by reading I Corinthians 6:19-20.

STEP 2

Announce that there's a new experimental cologne/perfume called "Metropolitan Magnetique" available on the street. It creates an irresistible psychomagnetic charge that causes members of the opposite sex to see the person wearing it as the sexiest person in the world. With this cologne/perfume, there is no need to dress up, take showers, pop pimples, or work out. However, the cologne/perfume has a side effect: one out of every 10 people who use it will look hideously ugly for two weeks. Hold up an actual bottle of cologne or perfume. Say: **I have some Metropolitan Magnetique right here. How many of you are willing to risk the side effect to try it?** Get a show of hands. Ask a couple of kids to explain their responses. Afterward, emphasize that we need to be leery of "quick fixes" when it comes to physical appearance. The problem may not be with how we *look*, but how we *feel* about ourselves.

STEP 5

Add the following "body abuser shortcuts" to Repro Resource 8:

• *Body Abuser:* Using improper chemicals to sear or burn hair

Goal: To have the latest hairstyle

Danger of the Shortcut: Permanent scalp damage, poisoning, even death can result from using hair chemicals improperly.

• *Body Abuser:* Continuing to play sports after being diagnosed as having a serious medical condition

Goal: To continue competing or perhaps to be a jock (or jockette)

Danger of the Shortcut: Several people have died (including basketball players Hank Gathers and Reggie Lewis) from continuing strenuous exercise despite their medical conditions.

STEP 3

With a wide range of ages in your group, you may get a variety of responses to the questions in Step 3. See if you can identify phases in which the dangers of body abusers are most prevalent.

Ask: **Would you be willing to lose an hour of sleep every night if you could lose weight? Would you be willing to drop your grade average by a letter grade if you could have a more muscular body? Would you cut the time you spend with friends and family in half if you could somehow make your body change the way you wanted it to?**

In each case, some people may be willing to make the required sacrifice, while others aren't. Point out that choosing to use (or avoid) body abusers is essentially the same decision. Can you detect a difference between junior high and high school attitudes? In some cases, high school students may feel more pressure to look "right" than junior highers. In other instances, older students may have already gone through a "phase" and seen the dangers involved in not accepting themselves for the way they are.

STEP 5

The concept of sexual activity as a body abuser is not heavily emphasized in the session. But if you have several high schoolers in your group, you might want to spend more time having them consider the risks of premarital sex. Explain that I Corinthians 6:19-20 explicitly refers to sex. Then show how the underlying needs and desires that lead to the problems of anorexia, bulimia, steroid use, and drug abuse can also lead to sexual promiscuity. Remind group members that in today's society, sex is no longer simply a moral issue. Even those who might not choose to abstain because of religious beliefs would be wise to do so because of the increasing possibility of contracting the HIV virus or some other sexually transmitted disease.

STEP I

It may be that some sixth graders have not yet experienced many self-image problems and will not understand all the commotion about body abusers. So rather than opening the session with a number of scenarios of unusual group member behavior, you might want to read the story of "The Princess and the Pea" by Hans Christian Andersen. The fairy tale describes a prince's discovery of a true princess who was so sensitive that she could not sleep comfortably because of a pea placed in her bed—even though 20 mattresses and 20 featherbeds were placed on top of the pea. Then explain that as ludicrous as it might seem to think that someone could be so sensitive, that is a good illustration of how strongly some people feel about the way they look. When they become so easily hurt by comments (or even by self-perception), they turn to whatever they think will help.

STEP 5

While sixth graders are still at the initial stages of potential self-image problems, try to make applications that are as personal and effective as possible. Ask: **What comments have you received this week that affected the way you felt about yourself?** See if most of their responses are positive or negative. Also explain that simply because someone makes a comment doesn't mean the comment is necessarily true. Then ask: **What comments have you made that affected how other people felt?** Point out that sometimes their comments that are intended as jokes or harmless statements may have much more impact than they intended. Begin now to help your sixth graders deflect insensitive comments—and to carefully monitor the comments they make to others.

PLANNING CHECKLIST

DATE USED:

Approx. Time

STEP I: *Too Bad to Be True* _____
- ❏ Extra Action
- ❏ Large Group
- ❏ Extra Fun
- ❏ Sixth Grade

Things needed:

STEP 2: *Risky Trade-offs* _____
- ❏ Extra Action
- ❏ Mostly Girls
- ❏ Mostly Guys
- ❏ Short Meeting Time
- ❏ Urban

Things needed:

STEP 3: *What's It Worth?* _____
- ❏ Heard It All Before
- ❏ Little Bible Background
- ❏ Fellowship & Worship
- ❏ Extra Fun
- ❏ Media
- ❏ Combined Junior High/High School

Things needed:

STEP 4: *What Good Is a Good Body?* _____
- ❏ Small Group
- ❏ Little Bible Background
- ❏ Mostly Girls

Things needed:

STEP 5: *Oh, C'mon! What's the Worst That Could Happen?* _____
- ❏ Small Group
- ❏ Large Group
- ❏ Heard It All Before
- ❏ Fellowship & Worship
- ❏ Mostly Guys
- ❏ Media
- ❏ Short Meeting Time
- ❏ Urban
- ❏ Combined Junior High/High School
- ❏ Sixth Grade

Things needed:

March 15th

Cruisin' through Puberty

YOUR GOALS FOR THIS SESSION:
Choose one or more

☐ To assure kids that the changes that take place in their bodies during puberty are natural and normal, and happen to everyone.

☐ To challenge kids to mature spiritually during this period as they mature physically.

☐ To make kids feel more comfortable during their own puberty, and in doing so, to have them commit to not being so insensitive to each other during this time.

☐ Other:_____
_____

Your Bible Base:

1 Samuel 1; 3
Ephesians 5:1-4

Transformation Mimes

(Needed: Charade ideas written on individual slips of paper)

When group members arrive, have some slips of paper ready on which you've written a number of situations the kids should act out. One at a time, ask a volunteer to draw a slip and act out what is written there. Volunteers may not speak or make any sounds. They must simply try to convey the action described.

Don't announce the common theme to all of the mime activities, but each one should have something to do with major transformations. For example, you might have volunteers act out

- a tadpole becoming a frog
- a caterpillar becoming a butterfly
- a frog becoming a handsome prince
- a baby being born
- a chick inside an egg, pecking its way out
- a snake shedding its skin
- Dr. Jekyll becoming Mr. Hyde
- Clark Kent becoming Superman

Afterward, ask: **What did all of these charades have in common?**

Which of these changes do you think would be hardest? Which would be easiest?

How do you think you would feel if you had to shed your skin every year? How about growing and losing antlers? How about swimming upstream to your birthplace to spawn?

Do you think human beings have it easy compared to other members of the animal kingdom? Why or why not? See if anyone brings up the subject of puberty. If not, introduce the subject at this point, defining it as "a transformation from childhood to adulthood."

On a scale of 1 to 10—with 10 being the most— how difficult would you say puberty is? Why?

STEP 2

Presto Change-O

(Candy and a "loaded" squirt gun [optional])

OPTIONS

EXTRA ACTION

HEARD IT ALL BEFORE

MOSTLY GIRLS

MEDIA

SHORT MEETING TIME

URBAN

Before you get too deep into a discussion of puberty, set up a roleplay. Have your kids suppose that an alien visitor to our planet has suddenly joined them. He explains that on his planet, pods drop from trees and hatch full-grown adults. He's very confused as to how things work on earth. He has many questions concerning the stages of human life, especially how a baby becomes an adult, and he has come to your group for answers.

If you think one of your group members can ask the right questions and keep the discussion going, let him or her play the role of the visitor. If not, you might want to do so. Individuals shouldn't be singled out for answers. It should be a group response, with many people contributing ideas, facts, and opinions. No doubt most of your group members have covered the *facts* of puberty in school or at home. But sometimes no one deals with the strange and awkward *feelings* that arise during this time of life. The visitor should press a bit to see how group members really feel—whether they are going through puberty at this time or merely anticipating it. [As an option, you might provide the visitor with a bag of candy and a filled squirt gun. If he hears something he believes, he may reward the person with a piece of candy. If not, he can zap the person with his (sp)ray gun.]

Some aspects of puberty may be too sensitive for junior highers to discuss openly with each other (or with a strange visitor from another planet). Encourage openness, but don't let the discussion get uncomfortable for anyone. Things that aren't covered in this conversation are likely to be dealt with on the repro resources that follow.

Puberty Checklist

(Needed: Copies of Repro Resource 9, copies of Repro Resource 10, pencils)

Hand out copies of "What's Going On? (The Male Version)" (Repro Resource 9) and pencils to the guys in your group. Hand out copies of "What's Going On? (The Female Version)" (Repro Resource 10) and pencils to the girls. These sheets list the signs of puberty. Their purpose is simply to describe the more common changes that take place during puberty and reduce any potential confusion for group members. The sheets are for group members' information and self-assessment only. The content may not be something they are anxious to discuss, though you probably should provide an opportunity for them to ask questions.

Follow up with some assurances for group members:

- **Puberty, as strange and awkward as it may seem, is something that everyone goes through.**
- **This transition from childhood into adulthood is temporary. The zits will clear up, the rapid growth spurts will taper off, and coordination will return.**
- **If it seems that no one but you is going through these changes, don't worry. You are not a freak. Everyone else will catch up.**
- **If it seems everyone but you is growing breasts or a mustache—hopefully not both—don't worry. You'll catch up. Within a year or so, everyone will be pretty much even again.**
- **It helps a lot to find someone you can talk to about what you're going through. If your parents aren't likely candidates, find a person you trust who has been through it.** You might want to make yourself available, and suggest someone of the opposite gender as well.

Also point out that one of the best antidotes to "puberty blues" is the advice offered in previous sessions: Don't put all of your focus on your physical body. Anyone—adult or young person—who goes to the mirror in search of physical imperfections is going to find some. Imperfection is part of being human. Learning to live with our flaws is part of maturity. So rather than becoming depressed or otherwise affected by the downside of puberty, we can turn our attention elsewhere. If our bodies aren't doing what we want them to do, at least we can work on other aspects of maturity. And one of the most important things we can do is try to develop spiritually.

O P T I O N S

EXTRA ACTION

LARGE GROUP

FELLOWSHIP & WORSHIP

MOSTLY GUYS

EXTRA FUN

URBAN

JR. HIGH / HIGH SCHOOL COMBINED

SIXTH GRADE

STEP 4

Voices in the Night

(Needed: Bibles)

The Bible records several accounts of young people who stood for God and made a major difference in the world around them—David, Joseph, Daniel, Ruth, Esther, Mary, Timothy, and so forth. But perhaps one of the youngest people to be devoted to God was the boy Samuel. Have your group members see what they can discover about his early life. Form two groups. The first group should read and report on I Samuel 1. The second group should read and report on I Samuel 3.

In addition to simply reporting on what they read, ask your two groups to look for anything they can find about the relationship between age and maturity. For example: **What is the appropriate age to get serious about serving God? At what age should kids begin to express their personal opinions to adults? At what age should kids expect adults to take their opinions seriously?** Also ask them to make a list of principles that young people might want to keep in mind as they go through puberty.

Group 1 will read and report on the birth of Samuel, which is actually Hannah's story. They should discover that Samuel was a literal answer to his mother's prayer. Hannah (who, in the tradition of that culture, may have been quite young herself when she got married) was emotionally distraught. In a time and place where having kids was essentially a woman's only source of recognition, Hannah was unable to conceive. She was still loved by her husband, but his other wife antagonized her at every opportunity. Consequently, Hannah's self-image reached an all-time low. Yet she knew what to do in such a situation—she turned to God.

Her faith was rewarded. God gave her a baby boy. It must have been hard for Hannah to honor her promise to give young Samuel to God—to take her only child to the temple and then walk away. (Due to the inability to store milk, it was customary for mothers at this time to nurse children for three years or so. Yet even after being weaned, Samuel would still have been very young.) But Hannah fulfilled her promise to dedicate him to God. Samuel went on to become a faithful servant of God, and Hannah had five more children (I Sam. 2:21).

O P T I O N S

SMALL GROUP

HEARD IT ALL BEFORE

LITTLE BIBLE BACKGROUND

FELLOWSHIP & WORSHIP

JR. HIGH HIGH SCHOOL COMBINED

SIXTH GRADE

Memory verse
I Tim 4:12

Principles from I Samuel I to keep in mind while going through puberty might include the following:

- Other people tend to try to irritate you if you are different in any way (vs. 6).
- Regular involvement with the church is always a good idea—especially when you're confused or depressed (vss. 7, 10-11).
- Authority figures may not fully understand what you are feeling and experiencing (vss. 12-14).
- Some problems can't be solved immediately, but will work out, given enough time (vss. 7, 20).
- We need to be very honest with God about the way we are feeling (vss. 10-11).
- God can solve problems that seem impossible to us (vss. 5-6, 20).
- When we allow God to work in our lives, it is both to our satisfaction (vs. 27) and His glory (vs. 28).

Group 2 will read and report on young Samuel's unexpected encounter with God. Samuel was trying to be obedient to the voices he heard, but he didn't realize that the source was God instead of Eli. And then, God's very first assignment was for Samuel to deliver some bad news to Eli. (Read I Sam. 2:12-36 to get a clearer understanding of the magnitude of the sins of Eli's sons—and the prophecy against them.) By this time, Eli must have been like a father to Samuel, and it certainly would have been very difficult to go to an older, respected, loved person with a tragic message. Yet Samuel did so. And as the young boy grew, everyone could tell that he was a true prophet of God.

Principles from I Samuel 3 to keep in mind while going through puberty might include the following:

- Complete physical maturity is not a requirement for spiritual maturity. God can use young (or old) people who are willing to serve Him (vs. 1).
- We need to listen closely and realize when God is trying to tell us something (vss. 4-10).
- Sometimes young people may have their lives together better than adults do (vss. 11-14).
- Honesty (with ourselves and with others) is important even if the truth may be painful (vss. 15-18).
- Spiritual maturity, at any age, is recognized by others and should be respected (vss. 19-21).

After the groups have reported, emphasize once again that even before and during puberty, on the way to physical maturity, it is wise to begin to try to develop spiritual maturity. We can't do anything about the growth rate of our bodies. But we can set the pace for maturing spiritually. Of course, significant growth cannot take place overnight—either physical or spiritual. Yet the adolescent years provide a wide-open opportunity to focus on spiritual maturity. For one thing, it is comforting to stay in close touch with God while experiencing the physical strains of puberty. And for another, spiritual disciplines begun during the young teen years will serve young people well throughout their lives. The sooner we get serious about spiritual maturity, the better off we will be.

"Sticks" and "Bones" and Other No-No Nicknames

(Needed: Paper, pencils)

Going through puberty is hard enough for adolescents with positive, loving families and supportive friends. But all too often, parents and/or friends make the experience seem even worse. The entire process of puberty is a physical change from childhood into adulthood. But frequently parents don't realize how important it is to build up kids emotionally to make them feel wanted and needed during this transition. Young people need to be assured that they are valuable and worthwhile—as children, as awkward and confused adolescents going through puberty, and as young adults in their own right.

And while parents are sometimes insensitive to the emotionally vulnerable state of adolescents, the adolescents' peers are even more so. It might seem that someone going through puberty would have some empathy for others experiencing the same thing. Yet too often the way young people try to feel better about themselves is by putting others down.

Say: **Perhaps nowhere are the signs of puberty more evident than in the locker room. Unfortunately, that's where the comments and conversation tend to be the crudest. We need to be careful what we say to each other as we are going through puberty. Sometimes the names people are called and the comments they hear stick with them throughout their lifetimes, even though they outgrow being a "pizza face," a "fatso," or a "stick." They start to believe what they hear, and what they hear isn't all that nice—or correct.** (If you've gone through Session 4, explain that one reason people turn to various "body abusers" is to quickly get in better shape in order to end the stinging comments they hear from others.)

OPTIONS

SMALL GROUP

LITTLE BIBLE BACKGROUND

MOSTLY GIRLS

MOSTLY GUYS

MEDIA

Think for a moment about the way you feel as you are going through puberty—or anticipating it. What adjectives would you use to describe the experience? (Confusing, scary, strange, worrisome, etc.)

How do you feel when other people suggest that something's wrong with you or different about you—just because you're going through a physical change? If group members are honest, many will admit to feeling insecure about many of the changes they are experiencing.

Can you think of a person you tease a lot about being different, simply because he or she is going through puberty a bit sooner or later than you are? Or if you don't actually tease the person, do you get with friends and talk about others who are different? Let group members respond.

Help your young people see that as much as they feel insecure about what they're going through, they may be guilty of making the same experience even harder for others. Then ask them to set some goals for themselves.

Ask: **First, how could this youth group meeting be improved to allow you to feel better about yourselves?** (Prohibit cruel teasing, name-calling, unflattering nicknames, and so forth.)

As much as is possible, youth group meetings should be a time in which kids get the affirmation they may not be receiving at home or from their peers. They need regular glimpses of the way things truly are—of a perspective of life that is far wider than what they can see from their limited view. Whatever ideas group members come up with, ask them to make a commitment to each other to see that those improvements are made in future meetings. (It will probably take a bit of reminding and perhaps some enforcement from the leader[s], but try to get a verbal agreement from group members at this point.)

Then ask: **Next, what are some things you can do to make sure that you're more affirming to other people when you aren't in this group? For instance, tomorrow at school, what are some things you can do to keep from making others feel uncomfortable about themselves?**

Make a list of the suggestions group members come up with. Then, by next meeting, have them typed up and copied. Challenge kids to remember their commitments to each other after they leave.

Close by having someone read aloud Ephesians 5:1-4. Emphasize verse 4, which warns about "obscenity, foolish talk or coarse joking." Such things should be replaced with "thanksgiving." In spite of the confusion and other emotional turmoil your young people may be experiencing, encourage them to give thanks to God for the changes they are going through. Before long they will be physically (and, it is hoped, spiritually) mature young men and women.

What's Going On?
THE **MALE** VERSION

Puberty. Even the word sounds weird. And the things it does to your body as it hits are even weirder. To say the least, going through puberty is a confusing time of life. And for many of us, it's pretty miserable. But it helps to know what you're facing. So go through the chart below and see what you can expect. Then put a check in the appropriate column to gauge your progress.

SIGNS OF PUBERTY IN MALES	NOT YET— I'M STILL WAITING	THIS IS JUST STARTING	I'M USED TO THIS BY NOW
Development of acne (zits)			
A period of rapid growth, which frequently causes temporary awkwardness or clumsiness			
Appearance of facial and pubic hair			
Larynx elongates, causing a change in voice			
Change in the overall shape and composition of the body			
Accelerated growth of penis and testicles, accompanied by reddening and wrinkling of skin of the scrotum			
First ejaculation of seminal fluid (semen), frequently in connection with a sexual dream (known as a "nocturnal emission" or, more commonly, a "wet dream")			

**"I praise you because I am fearfully and wonderfully made; your works are wonderful, I know that full well"
(Psalm 139:14).**

What's Going On?
THE **FEMALE** VERSION

Puberty. Even the word sounds weird. And the things it does to your body as it hits are even weirder. To say the least, going through puberty is a confusing time of life. And for many of us, it's pretty miserable. But it helps to know what you're facing. So go through the chart below and see what you can expect. Then put a check in the appropriate column to gauge your progress.

SIGNS OF PUBERTY IN FEMALES	NOT YET— I'M STILL WAITING	THIS IS JUST STARTING	I'M USED TO THIS BY NOW
Development of acne (zits)			
A period of rapid growth, which frequently causes temporary awkwardness or clumsiness			
Appearance of hair under arms, in the pubic area, and other places			
Larynx elongates, causing voice to become less childlike			
Development of a more rounded female body contour (Ovaries begin to produce estrogen, causing fat deposits to develop on the hips and thighs.)			
Nipples begin to enlarge and breast tissue starts to develop			
Redness and presence of white discharge from vagina			
Menstrual periods begin			

**"I praise you because I am fearfully and wonderfully made;
your works are wonderful, I know that full well"
(Psalm 139:14).**

EXTRA ACTION

STEP 2

As an alternative to the question-answer exercise provided, you can set up a "food feel," similar to what kids might encounter at a haunted house. Blindfold kids and have them stick their hands into bowls of various foods as you plant suggestions in their minds as to what they might be feeling. The old standbys are peeled grapes to represent eyeballs and cold cooked spaghetti for brains. But take a walk around your local market to get some other creative ideas. Afterward, make the point that sometimes things we perceive as gross and disgusting might actually be good and beneficial. The same is true about the process of puberty.

STEP 3

Since the growth of facial hair that comes with puberty will eventually lead to the need for your guys to shave, give them a head start. Pair guys with girls as equally as possible. Lather up the guys' faces with shaving cream and give the girls squirt guns. (You might want to have each guy wear some kind of protective tarp—perhaps made by cutting a couple of holes in a plastic garbage bag.) Mark off a designated distance and give a signal. The first girl to completely remove the shaving cream by squirting it off wins.

SMALL GROUP

STEP 4

While the two groups are reading and discussing their assigned chapters, you or another person (perhaps someone your group members don't know well) should try to get as close to possible (without being seen) to kids on the fringe of the group and whisper their names very quietly. Ideally, the kids should *think* they hear their names, yet not be sure. The group covering I Samuel 3 may figure out what's going on, but the other group members may not be as aware of what's happening. Afterward, discuss how disconcerting it must be to hear unidentified voices calling one's name. How many of us, especially young people, would ever guess that God might actually be speaking to us? Try to help group members get past the facts of the story to the sensations Samuel must have felt.

STEP 5

In a small group it's easy for members to get a bit apathetic about coming to youth group. When young people feel "on the spot" to answer questions or to attend simply to keep the leaders from being alone, interaction can become more difficult and strained. On the other hand, some small groups recognize the special opportunities they have for closeness that large groups do not have. One way to help your group members bond is to have some "inside" nicknames for each other that are used primarily during your meetings. So as you conclude the session, provide a few minutes for everyone to suggest positive, uplifting, cool nicknames for each other. Use the nicknames in future sessions and see if they catch on. If so, challenge group members to continue being positive toward each other in new and different ways.

LARGE GROUP

STEP I

The transformation mimes may not entertain a large group adequately—at least, not if they are done one at a time. But in a large group you can find volunteers to perform each mime and then have them perform *simultaneously*. Assign each volunteer a number. Have the volunteers stand at intervals around a large room. Give everyone else a pencil and paper. Instruct these remaining group members to walk around the room, observing the Mime-A-Rama. They should number their papers according to the number assigned each mime, and should write down what they think each person is acting out. When everyone has had an opportunity to see all of the mimes, announce the action that was being demonstrated for each one. See who guessed the most actions correctly and give him or her a rousing round of mime applause.

STEP 3

Have group members create "Cruisin' through Puberty: The Game." First, design a room-size game board, using floor tiles or sheets of paper laid on the floor. Designate a starting point and a finish line. Many squares should be blank, but others should read, "Draw a Card." Divide into teams to create the cards, which should all have something to do with puberty. (They might also use humor as it is appropriate.) Some examples might include:

• You get big zit on the night of a big date. Go back one space.

• Your chest is filling out nicely. Move ahead one space.

• You discover hair where it never was before. Faint and lose one turn.

When each team has written several cards, get some volunteers to play the game. Use a spinner from some other game and see which of your volunteers is the first to successfully cruise through puberty.

STEP 2

Rather than doing the skit as written, let some of your more self-assured group members form an "expert" panel to field questions from other group members concerning puberty. Have a medical reference book on hand to help out with answers if needed. You might suggest a few questions to get things started, such as "What causes my voice to change during puberty?" or "Why does hair begin to grow all of a sudden? Why aren't we just born hairy?" If you sense that group members are too embarrassed to ask questions from the floor, let them write down the questions. Then you can act as moderator for the panel. Afterward, move on to Repro Resources 9 and 10 for some of the answers concerning what group members can expect during puberty.

STEP 4

If the Samuel stories are "old hat" to your group members, and if your kids have a good working knowledge of other Bible stories, let some of them represent other young people in the Bible. Many are listed in the session. Add others as needed. (For example, many people may not know about Eutychus [Acts 20:9-12] or other young people described in Scripture.) Each character should explain why he or she was mentioned in the Bible and what we can learn from him or her. Try to make the same point for each person: Even though we have little control over the rate of our physical growth, we *can* choose to increase our level of spiritual growth.

STEP 4

If possible, precede the Bible study with a brief report on a recent newspaper article or reference to a child care problem in your area (perhaps an incident of child abandonment). Then, rather than split into two groups, cover I Samuel 3 together. To people unfamiliar with Bible stories, it may sound quite strange for a mother who desired a child so intensely to take him to the temple and leave him with an old priest. Encourage questions from your group members and try to make sure they understand that Hannah was certainly not abandoning Samuel. Rather, she was entrusting him to God, whom she knew would take better care of him than even she could. And if you have group members who are adopted, from single-parent homes, or from other variations of non-nuclear families, assure them that devotion to God can make up for much of what they might miss from not having a flesh-and-blood mother or father.

STEP 5

For young people without much Bible background, it is hard to absorb so many of the important verses that are covered in a typical meeting. These group members need more time to let God's truth sink in. So consider having your group members make bookmarks containing the words of Ephesians 5:1-4. Each group member may print the passage on a bookmark and then design it according to his or her own tastes. Or you could have the text preprinted (perhaps by a friend who knows calligraphy) and reduced to bookmark size. Then group members could spend more time in the coloring and design of their bookmarks. Encourage kids to stick the bookmarks in a book that they see frequently throughout the week. Explain that we all need regular reminders to imitate God, to refrain from foolish talk and coarse joking, and to offer thanks to God on a regular basis—especially as we are going through the trauma of puberty.

STEP 3

Habakkuk 3:17-18 is a much overlooked testimony to God's presence and help even during what appears to be the worst of circumstances: "Though the fig tree does not bud and there are no grapes on the vines, though the olive crop fails and the fields produce no food, though there are no sheep in the pen and no cattle in the stalls, yet I will rejoice in the Lord, I will be joyful in God my Savior." Let group members paraphrase these verses to apply to the less-than-desirable things that might be happening to them during puberty and to affirm their faith in God during this especially trying time. ("Though _____ is happening to me, I will still trust God to _____.")

STEP 4

After the Bible study, dwell on what it meant that Hannah dedicated Samuel to God. Ask: **What does it mean to be dedicated to God? What if your mothers didn't bother to bring you to church when you were three and leave you with Pastor Jones? Does that mean you can't be as "spiritual" as Samuel?** Group members should realize that they should dedicate themselves to God. Spend some time letting each person come up with three things he or she could do in order to become more fully dedicated to God. At least one of those things should be a short-term goal that can be implemented right away. Challenge group members to take action this week to begin to live a more dedicated life for God. And be sure to follow up on their progress at the next meeting.

MOSTLY GIRLS

MOSTLY GUYS

EXTRA FUN

STEP 2

Your girls may have a hard time understanding the feelings guys have as they're growing. If possible, bring a male visitor to your group who would be able and willing to share with the girls how it feels for guys to grow up. If no such person is available, ask the girls how they think guys their age feel as they experience the changes puberty brings. (Be sure to curb any discussion that starts to head in an inappropriate direction.) It may be difficult for your girls at first, especially if they're not very aware of all that guys experience; but such a discussion could help them better understand their male counterparts.

STEP 5

Locker-room talk is often more common for guys than girls, so many girls may want to say this doesn't happen. Help them see that girls their age *do* talk about such subjects. Brainstorm places where this happens (around the rest room mirror, at the cafeteria table, next to lockers, etc.). Ask: **What do you typically do when you hear girls making fun of others?** (Laugh along with them, join in wholeheartedly, stand back and just listen, leave, etc.) **What are some positive things you could do—things God would want you to do—when you hear such negative conversations?**

STEP 3

A discussion of puberty is a good time to have an all-guy or mostly guy group. You might want to separate any girls from the majority of guys and cover the Repro Resource sheets separately. You should be able to deal more in-depth with guys' questions and concerns if girls aren't around, though guys still may be reluctant to "show their ignorance" or ask questions that might cause comments or laughter from the others. So as you discuss the Repro Resource sheet, ask the guys to write down any questions they have. You can then read and discuss their questions without anyone knowing who asked them.

STEP 5

As you close by challenging group members to be more sensitive to the pains of puberty that other people might be going through, give your guys a special assignment. Since much self-image discomfort arises from comments from members of the other gender, advise your guys that they can do a lot to build up the self-esteem of their female peers. Ask everyone to compliment at least three girls during the next 24 hours. Warn them against cheap flattery. Their comments should be sincere. Also, they should not let on that they are being coerced to make such statements. Most junior high guys need practice saying things such as "You look nice today," "I like your hair," or "You have a cool laugh." But after they try it, they may find that it's not as difficult as they had imagined.

STEP I

As an alternative to the opening transformation mimes, collect a number of transformer toys that have one shape to begin with, but can be maneuvered into a completely different object. If you don't have one for each person, form teams so that each team has one of the toys. At your signal, each team should try to be the first to transform the toy from one object to the other. (Some of them are quite complicated and might take a while.) You can also use blocks or spheres that break down into pieces, having team members try to "transform" a pile of pieces into a unified whole.

STEP 3

After going through the Repro Resources and discovering the many changes to be experienced during puberty, have your group members try their hand at songwriting. Your song title should be "The Puberty Blues." Begin by providing a basic blues beat. Then form groups to write verses that fit the rhythm. Many blues songs require only couplets, such as "My voice won't stop cracking and my face is all zits/My jeans are too short and there's hair in my pits." Take turns letting groups sing the verses they write; then everyone join in with the repeated lines: "I got the blues/I got the puberty blues" (or some equivalent).

STEP 2

Ask group members to create a concept for a magazine geared to help young people understand and get through puberty. One group might brainstorm ideas for articles. Another group could come up with ideas of people to interview and questions they would ask those people. Artistic group members might rough out a cover design or illustration for the premiere issue. Work together to come up with a good title for your magazine. Let each group report back to explain or demonstrate its ideas.

STEP 5

Prior to the meeting, watch some popular videos geared to teenagers. Look for sections you can play for group members to demonstrate the insensitive language young people use toward each other. (It may take a while to find sections suitable for public play at a church youth group.) As you play a few sections, ask group members to list all of the derogatory names and comments they hear. Then ask them to add to the list based on what they have personally heard at school during the previous week. Point out that as frequently as some young people hear themselves referred to in such terms, it's difficult for them not to begin to believe at least some of it. Challenge your group members to determine *this minute* to stop contributing to the problem.

Also ask for volunteers who are willing to monitor any videos they watch during the next several weeks. Have them write down the negative names and phrases used, as well as keep a running total of how many times each name is used. It may surprise them to discover just how much negative input they hear.

STEP 1

Try a shorter opener. Before the session, collect pictures from several adults in your church showing what they looked like in seventh or eighth grade. Be sure to include a picture of yourself as well. Mount the pictures on a piece of poster board. At the bottom of the poster board, write (in no particular order) the names of the people whose pictures appear. Have a contest to see how many of the people your kids can identify from the pictures. Award a prize to the person who correctly identifies the most people. Afterward, discuss how people have changed over the years and how many of those changes began at puberty.

STEP 2

If you're *really* short on time, use the following activity instead of Steps 1 and 2. After introducing the session topic, explain that one of the biggest problems with puberty is that it takes so long. It's hard to be patient about the nonexistent changes in your body when you see the bodies of your friends changing practically every day. So give your kids an opportunity to make *instant* changes in their body. Explain that a "miracle drug" has been discovered that allows kids to rush through the puberty process *in one night*. The only problem is that the drug can only work in *one* area of physical development. Distribute paper and pencils. Instruct group members to write down the one area of physical development they'd like to speed up with this miracle drug. For guys, it might be the growth of facial hair or the development of a "manly" speaking voice. For girls, it might be the development of breasts or the elimination of zits. Assure kids that their answers will remain anonymous. After a few minutes, collect the sheets and read aloud some of the responses. Then move into Step 3 in the session.

STEP 2

The assumption that junior highers have learned the facts of puberty at home or at school is not necessarily accurate. For many urban kids, the lessons and facts of puberty tend to be learned, described, and defined by the "street grapevine" of the urban youth subculture. With this in mind, try an activity called "Puberty Grapevine." Distribute paper and pencils. Ask each group member to write everything he or she knows about male and female puberty. Emphasize that group members should *not* write their name on the sheet. After a few minutes, collect the sheets, shuffle them, and redistribute them (making sure no one receives his or her own sheet). Instruct group members to read the statements listed on their sheet. They should then put an "X" next to the ones they think are false and a check mark next to the ones they think are true. When they're finished, collect the sheets again. Go through the sheets, randomly choosing examples of statements that were marked as true, but that are actually false—and vice versa. Afterward, emphasize that young people cannot always depend on the "grapevine" for accurate information—especially regarding something as important as puberty.

STEP 3

Your kids may feel isolated as they navigate the uncharted waters of puberty. So it might be helpful to arrange to have a couple of older teenagers (a male and a female) talk with your kids about puberty. It would probably be very reassuring for your kids to hear "one of their own" talk about what puberty's like. As an added bonus, you might want to bring in some pictures of yourself (and your spouse, if you're married) as a junior higher to show what you looked like during puberty.

STEP 3

Have some fun by combining two concepts: TV public service announcements and before-and-after ads. Since your group spans a wider variety of ages (and sizes), try to pair up some of the youngest and smallest people with the larger and more mature ones. Let other group members act as narrators. The goal of group members is to convince young listeners who are "watching" that puberty, as difficult as it might appear, will have positive end results. They should contrast the "before puberty" person (the small one) with the "after puberty" one, and explain that this is what young people have to look forward to. The "before" people might speak in high and squeaky voices while the "after" ones can lower their voices as much as possible. Girl groups might show the difference between a young "tomboy" and a mature, filled-out young lady. By putting together contrasts to convince other people that puberty won't be so bad, perhaps group members will be able to convince themselves as well.

STEP 4

As you form groups for the Bible study, try to mix junior highers and high schoolers together as evenly as possible. The younger students should have little problem understanding the story and getting the facts straight, yet may not be very good at filtering out applications that should be relevant to young people today. High schoolers will probably have had more practice at doing so. Explain that just as young Samuel needed help from Eli to find out how to hear and pay attention to God, your high schoolers can have a similar influence on younger Christians today.

STEP 3

Depending on the maturity level of your sixth graders, you should exercise discretion in using the Repro Resources. If you think it's a little premature to have group members get so involved in learning about the various aspects of puberty, you can pick and choose what you want to cover with them. Rather than hand out copies of the Repro Resources, create a Puberty True-or-False Quiz to give them verbally. Make up a lot of humorous statements that are obviously false and then mix in the actual facts about puberty. You can still deal with most of the same material, but it will be a lot less threatening for younger students.

STEP 4

Rather than study the story of Samuel in groups, tell group members the story as a parody of the film *Home Alone*. As you explain what happens in *Temple Alone*, featuring young Samuel in the lead role, try to make his situation real to your group members. He is left at the temple by his mother when he is only a few years old. He is raised by an aged priest. The priest's sons are older and selfish troublemakers, and so forth. On top of everything else, he hears voices in the middle of the night. Your group members will get a lot more out of the story if they are able to associate with Samuel's potential fears and insecurities.

DATE USED:

Approx. Time

STEP 1: *Transformation Mimes* _____
❏ Large Group
❏ Extra Fun
❏ Short Meeting Time
Things needed:

STEP 2: *Presto Change-O* _____
❏ Extra Action
❏ Heard It All Before
❏ Mostly Girls
❏ Media
❏ Short Meeting Time
❏ Urban
Things needed:

STEP 3: *Puberty Checklist* _____
❏ Extra Action
❏ Large Group
❏ Fellowship & Worship
❏ Mostly Guys
❏ Extra Fun
❏ Urban
❏ Combined Junior High/High School
❏ Sixth Grade
Things needed:

STEP 4: *Voices in the Night* _____
❏ Small Group
❏ Heard It All Before
❏ Little Bible Background
❏ Fellowship & Worship
❏ Combined Junior High/High School
❏ Sixth Grade
Things needed:

STEP 5: *"Sticks" and "Bones" and Other No-No Nicknames* _____
❏ Small Group
❏ Little Bible Background
❏ Mostly Girls
❏ Mostly Guys
❏ Media
Things needed: